Adobe®
Photoshop® CS 2.0:
Photographers' Guide

David D. Busch

ISBN: 1-59200-725-2

Library of Congress Catalog Card Number: 2005923911

Printed in United States of America

05 06 07 08 09 BU 10 9 8 7 6 5 4 3 2 1

Publisher and General Manager, Thomson Course Technology PTR:
Stacy L. Hiquet

Associate Director of Marketing:
Sarah O'Donnell

Manager of Editorial Services:
Heather Talbot

Marketing Manager:
Heather Hurley

Senior Acquisitions Editor:
Kevin Harreld

Senior Editor:
Mark Garvey

Marketing Coordinator:
Jordan Casey

Project Editor:
Jenny Davidson

Technical Reviewer:
Michael D. Sullivan

Thomson Course Technology PTR Editorial Services Coordinator:
Elizabeth Furbish

Interior Layout Tech:
William Hartman

Cover Designer:
Mike Tanamachi

Indexer:
Kelly Talbot

Proofreader:
Sara Gullion

THOMSON

COURSE TECHNOLOGY
Professional ■ Trade ■ Reference

Thomson Course Technology PTR, a division of Thomson Course Technology
25 Thomson Place ■ Boston, MA 02210 ■ http://www.courseptr.com

For Cathy

Acknowledgments

Once again thanks to Andy Shafran, who realizes that a book about working with color images deserves nothing less than a full-color treatment, and knows how to publish such a book at a price that everyone can afford. It's refreshing to work for a publisher who has *actually written* best-selling books on imaging, too. Also, thanks to senior editor Kevin Harreld, for valuable advice as the book progressed, as well as project editor Jenny Davidson; technical editor Michael D. Sullivan; book/cover designer Mike Tanamachi; interior design William Hartman; proofreader Sara Gullion; and indexer Kelly Talbot.

Also thanks to my agent, Carole McClendon, who has the amazing ability to keep both publishers and authors happy.

About the Author

David D. Busch has been demystifying arcane computer and imaging technology since the early 1980s. However, he had a successful career as a professional photographer for a decade before he sat down at the keyboard of his first personal computer. Busch has worked as a newspaper photographer, done commercial studio and portrait work, shot weddings, and roved the United States and Europe as a photojournalist. His articles on photography and image editing have appeared in magazines as diverse as *Popular Photography and Imaging, Petersen's PhotoGraphic, The Rangefinder*, and *The Professional Photographer*, as well as computer magazines such as *Macworld* and *Computer Shopper*. He's currently reviewing digital cameras for CNet.

Busch has written more than 80 books since 1983, including the mega bestsellers *Digital Photography All-In-One Desk Reference for Dummies* and *The Hewlett-Packard Scanner Handbook*. Other recent books include *Mastering Digital SLR Photography, Mastering Digital Photography*, and *Mastering Digital Scanning with Slides, Film, and Transparencies*, all from Thomson Course Technology PTR.

He earned top category honors in the Computer Press Awards the first two years they were given (for *Sorry About The Explosion*, Prentice-Hall; and *Secrets of MacWrite, MacPaint and MacDraw*, Little, Brown), and later served as Master of Ceremonies for the awards.

Contents

Chapter 3
Darkroom Techniques with
Photoshop CS 2.0   67

Chapter 4
Secrets of Retouching   113

Chapter 5
Compositing in Photoshop CS   139

Chapter 6
Correcting Your Colors   185

Chapter 7
Beyond Black and White   227

Chapter 8
Using Photoshop CS's Filters   249

Chapter 9
Hardcopies Made Easy 293

Appendix
Illustrated Glossary 319

Index 343

Preface

If you're serious about photography, you should be serious about Photoshop CS 2.0 and its exciting new features, too. Whether you're a casual snapshooter, a dedicated photo buff, or a professional photographer, you have a major advantage over those who approach Adobe's flagship image editor from other backgrounds. You have everyday working experience with the kinds of imaging or darkroom techniques that Photoshop was designed to mimic, enhance, and surpass. You'll find that approaching Photoshop from a photographer's perspective can put you on the fast track to mastering all the tools Adobe puts at your disposal.

Thinking about Photoshop as an extraordinary photography tool can also work for you even if you are *not* currently a serious photographer. If you specialize in computer technology, art, or graphics, you will find that learning about the imaging techniques that form the basis for each Photoshop capability can help you, too. A deeper understanding of photography will help you use the image editor better, while improving those latent photographic skills you didn't know you had. Anyone who fine-tunes and manipulates photos will find that this book makes them a more proficient, well-rounded image worker.

If you feel there isn't enough photography in the average Photoshop book, and there isn't enough Photoshop in the average photography book, the book you're looking for is right in your hands. Whether you're a snap-shooting tyro, or an experienced photographer moving into the digital realm, you'll find the knowledge you need here.

Introduction

Photoshop and photography were made for each other. Whether you're using a digital pixel-grabber or hanging onto your beloved film camera, Adobe's revamped flagship image editor, Photoshop CS 2.0, has the tools you need to fine-tune your photos, correct errors in exposure, lighting, or color balance, and go beyond your basic picture to create triumphant prize-winning photographs from shoebox rejects.

Adobe Photoshop CS 2.0: Photographers' Guide is aimed squarely at those who want to use photography creatively to produce compelling images, and want to master all the tools available to them. The emphasis here is on both traditional and leading-edge photographic techniques, and how to reproduce or enhance them in Photoshop.

You don't need to be an ace photographer or Photoshop expert to create these eye-catching effects. All you need is this straight-forward, "all meat" book that shows you how to use Photoshop to enhance your images with the kinds of effects you admire. Did you know that using easy-to-master Photoshop tools you could do the following?

- Duplicate colorful "cross processing" darkroom effects.

- Work with Photoshop's Panorama stitching features.

- Match colors between shots taken under wildly different lighting conditions.

- Fix perspective in architectural photos even if you don't own an expensive perspective control lens.

- Add zoom lens blur effects without using a zoom lens.

- Move a storm-ravaged seashore 500 miles inland to the foothills of a mountain range.

- Excise your obnoxious ex-relative from a family reunion photo without resorting to violence.

- Change daylight scenes into moody dusk or ruddy dawn pictures.

- Make mountains out of foothills.

- Morph images to blend or distort them.

- Seamlessly extract images from their backgrounds.

This book cuts right to the heart of all of the most misunderstood, but easily applied, tools in the latest version of Photoshop, examined from a photographer's perspective. It bristles with surprisingly effective examples, simple-to-follow techniques, and tricks that serve as a jumping-off point to spark your own creativity into action.

While other Photoshop "photography" books give lip service to true photography, this book examines each topic from every photographic angle. Which effects are best achieved with a film or digital camera? Which effects are best applied in Photoshop? How can in-camera techniques and Photoshop augment and enhance each other?

Just browsing through the book can lead you to a half-dozen stunning effects you can re-create in five minutes or less, and a wealth of photographic techniques you can reproduce with Photoshop. Invest a few hours, and you'll be able to:

- Process your digital camera's RAW files with Photoshop CS 2.0's improved Camera RAW plug-in.

- Fix colors and tones, even if you don't know color correction or gamma correction from brightness-contrast controls, and think a histogram is a cold remedy. Photoshop has at least four different ways to bring off-color or dull originals to blazing life, ready for use in web pages and other applications.

- Build composites that fool the eye, or which form gateways to fantasy worlds. Blend multiple images to create a new one in which all the elements work in perfect harmony to create that photo you never could catch with your camera.

- Duplicate darkroom effects not easily accessible to darkroom-challenged digital photographers.

Why This Book?

There are dozens, if not a hundred or more books on how to use Photoshop. There are already three dozen books on digital photography, and hundreds more on conventional photography. Yet, oddly enough, only a half dozen of these combine Photoshop and photography in any meaningful way. One or two are written for professional photographers and contain little that the average picture taker can use or understand. A few more are dumbed-down, include lots of pretty pictures, but not much text on each page, and contain techniques that you'll outgrow quickly.

Others are weird hybrids that tell you more than you wanted to know about camera technology, CCD, CMOS, and CIS image sensors, how cameras work, the history of digital photography, and *less* than you wanted to know about image editing. I suspect you don't need any convincing that photography is a great idea, and you don't need detailed comparisons of Photoshop with the other image editors on the market. Instead, you want to know how photography and Photoshop can work together to give you great pictures that will astound your friends and astonish your colleagues.

I wrote this book for camera buffs, both digital and conventional, and business people who want to go beyond point-and-click snapshooting and explore the world of photography to enrich their lives or do their jobs better. If you've learned most of your camera's basic features and now wonder what you can do with them, this is your dream guide to pixel proficiency. If you fall into one of the following categories, you need this book:

- Individuals who want to get better pictures, or perhaps transform their growing interest in photography into a full-fledged hobby or artistic outlet using Photoshop as a catalyst.

- Those who want to produce more professional-looking images for their personal or business website.

- Small business owners with more advanced graphics capabilities who want to use photography and Photoshop to document or promote their business.

- Corporate workers who may or may not have photographic skills in their job descriptions, but who work regularly with graphics and need to learn how to use digital images for reports, presentations, or other applications.

- Professional Webmasters with strong skills in programming (including Java, JavaScript, HTML, Perl, and so on) but little background in photography.

- Graphic artists and others who may already be adept in image editing with Photoshop, but who want to learn more about its relationship with digital and conventional photography.

- Trainers who need a non-threatening textbook for digital photography classes.

Who Am I?

With a few exceptions, Photoshop books aren't purchased because the author is famous or is pictured in an attractive photo on the cover. You may have picked this book off the shelf because you found some of the gorgeous, meaty books from

Course Technology PTR useful in the past and were looking for more of the same. Then, like most Photoshop book buyers, you flipped through the pages looking for cool pictures or interesting techniques. If I've captured your interest enough to have you reading this far, you probably don't need my life story at this point. However, a little background might be useful to help you understand exactly where this book is coming from.

Before I was seduced by the dark side of technology, I was a professional photographer. I've made my living as a sports photographer for an Ohio newspaper and an upstate New York college; I've operated my own commercial studio and photo lab; and served as photo-posing instructor for a modeling agency. People have actually paid me to shoot their weddings and immortalize them with portraits. I even wrote several thousand articles on photography as a PR consultant for a large Rochester, N.Y. company you may have heard of. Since 1980, I've successfully combined my interests in photography and computers to an alarming degree, bringing forth a few thousand articles, eight books on scanners, and a dozen that encompass photography.

In practice, this means that, like you, I love photography for its own joys, and view technology as just another tool to help me get the images I want to produce. It also means that, like you, when I peer through the viewfinder, I sometimes forget everything I know, take a real clunker of a picture and turn to Photoshop to help me out of the hole I dug. My only real advantage is that I can usually offer quite detailed technical explanations of what I did wrong, and offer a convincing, if bogus, explanation of how I intentionally manipulated technology to correct the error.

You can learn from my mistakes, and benefit from what experience I have, so your picture taking and image editing can travel a more comfortable gain-without-pain route than I took.

How to Use This Book

I'm not going to weigh you down with sage advice about reading this book from front to back, reviewing portions until you understand what I'm trying to say, or remembering to hunt for dozens of icons lodged in the margins that point out the only portions actually worth reading. I don't care if you go through and read just the chapters that interest you, or scan only the odd-numbered pages, as long as you get busy having fun with your camera and Photoshop. Each of the chapters should stand alone so sufficiently well that you can read them in any order. A book that needs its own instruction manual to use hasn't done its job.

I've tried to make your job easier by relegating all the boring parts to the bit-bin long before this book hit the printing press. Here's a summary of what you'll need to work through this book:

- You'll need a Windows PC or Macintosh OS system with enough RAM to run Photoshop comfortably (that is, from 512 to a gazillion megabytes of RAM).

- To ease the learning process, you'll want to work with Photoshop CS 2.0. Earlier versions, especially Photoshop CS 1.0 (also known as Photoshop 8.0) can also be used with this book, because the core feature set remains largely unchanged. There are few menu migrations or spanking new palettes like those found in previous upgrades. Of course, you'll need Photoshop CS 1.0 or 2.0 for the sections dealing with newer features like the Photo Filter, Match Color, and Live Histogram capabilities. However, if you're using Photoshop 7, nearly everything applies. For Versions 6.0 and before, this book will probably provide additional incentive for upgrading.

- You'll need digital photos, probably captured with a digital camera. If you're shooting on film, you or your photolab will need to convert your pictures to pixels before you can use them with Photoshop. It doesn't matter whether you scan the pictures, receive them on a Photo CD, or originate the pictures electronically with a digital camera; Photoshop will work with them just fine.

- The Web site www.courseptr.com/downloads.asp contains working files you'll need to complete the exercises in this book. You can substitute your own photos, of course, but if you want to closely duplicate my work, you'll need to use the same photos I worked with.

Your Next Stop

While I'm not your one-stop source for toll-free technical support, I'm always glad to answer reader questions that relate to this book. Sometimes I can get you pointed in the right direction to resolve peripheral queries I can't answer. You can write to me at *photoguru@dbusch.com*. You'll also find more information at my website at *http://www.dbusch.com*. Should you discover the one or two typos I've planted in this book to test your reading comprehension, I'll erect an errata page on my website, along with kudos to readers who report anything that, on first glance, might appear to be a goof.

A final warning: I first came to national attention for a book called *Sorry About the Explosion!* This book earned the first (and only) Computer Press Association award presented to a book of computer humor. Since then, my rise from oblivion to obscurity has been truly meteoric—a big flash, followed by a fiery swan dive into the horizon. So, each of my books also includes a sprinkling of flippancy scattered among all the dry, factual stuff. You aren't required to actually be amused, and you can consider yourself duly cautioned.

Chapter Outline

This section is a brief outline of the chapters in this book. If you want to know exactly where to find a topic that interests you, consult the table of contents or index.

Chapter 1: Photoshop and Photography from 50,000 Feet

This chapter provides an overview of Photoshop's origins, secret identity, and evolution, along with an overview of the basic skills that photographers can expect to transfer directly to their Photoshop experience. These include knowledge of composition, use of lenses, selective focus, film choice, and other valuable skills that serve Photoshop users well.

Chapter 2: Camera and Lens Effects in Photoshop

Here, you'll learn how to duplicate creative traditional effects like perspective control, zoom, lens flare, motion blur, and selective focus using Photoshop's built-in tools. These techniques are great to have on hand when you just don't happen to remember to take the exact lens or other accessory you really need on a photo shoot.

Chapter 3: Darkroom Techniques with Photoshop CS 2.0

Those who remember fondly the acid-tinged, humid air of the photo darkroom will love this chapter's tips for reproducing solarization, reticulation, push-processing, cross-developing, and dodging/burning techniques with Photoshop. Best of all, you won't need to ruin expensive film experimenting!

Chapter 4: Secrets of Retouching

This chapter reveals the most valuable secret of retouching: how to avoid the need for it in the first place. However, if you must remove the dust, you'll also find information on how to enhance and repair photos using advanced retouching techniques. Best bet: learn the new Photoshop CS Healing Brush and Patch tools.

Chapter 5: Compositing in Photoshop CS

Although each chapter explains how to use the Photoshop tools needed for a task, this one delves deeply into the fine art of making selections and extracting images from their backgrounds. You'll also discover how to merge objects smoothly and match lighting, texture, colors, scale, and other factors that scream FAKE when they aren't considered.

Chapter 6: Correcting Your Colors

Color can make or break an image. This chapter offers four ways of adjusting color in terms photographers will understand immediately. If you've ever slipped a CC 10 Cyan filter into a filter pack, or stocked your camera bag with an 85B or 80A conversion filter, you'll appreciate the advice here. However, even if your color correction experience extends no further than using the white-balance control on your digital camera, this chapter has everything you need to correct your colors in Photoshop.

Chapter 7: Beyond Black and White

Photoshop includes a simple command that can magically transform a great color picture into a terrible grayscale image. You'll learn why the most common color-to-black-and-white travesties happen, and how to avoid them. Also included is a slick trick for mimicking the orthochromatic film look.

Chapter 8: Using Photoshop CS's Filters

This chapter explains how to get the most from Photoshop's built-in filters, with an emphasis on reproducing traditional camera effects, such as diffusion, cross-screen filters, and polarizers. Then, you'll get a glimpse of how Photoshop can transcend conventional photography with some amazing new capabilities.

Chapter 9: Hardcopies Made Easy

You'll find lots of useful information in this chapter that relates traditional printing of film images onto photosensitive paper with the modern digital printing alternatives. Learn about your options, calculate the maximum print size you can expect from a given digital camera resolution, and glean some tips for getting the absolute best digital prints.

Appendix A: Illustrated Glossary

This illustrated compendium of all the jargon words you'll encounter in this book (and a bunch of them you'll run across in the real world) provides a quick reference guide to photography, digital imaging, and Photoshop terminology.

1

Photoshop and Photography from 50,000 Feet

There's no rest for the leader of the pack. Although Photoshop has been the undisputed top dog among image editors for as long as most of us have been working with digital photography, Adobe's flagship pixel pusher has not been resting on its laurels. From the moment I finished work on the first edition of this book, which dealt with Photoshop 7.0, Adobe has been enhancing the program non-stop, adding features of special interest to photographers, such as enhanced manipulation of digital camera RAW files, new filters, and improved red-eye correction tools. Many improvements have been going on behind the scenes, too, where they are less obvious until you start digging. Photoshop CS 2.0 now can work with more than 2GB of RAM, which can be important for photographers who've loaded up their computers to deal with the 8- to 16-megapixel images that are becoming common among serious advanced digital cameras.

Adobe has been gradually folding the features of its stand-alone web-oriented tool, ImageReady, into Photoshop itself; the company has announced that this is the last version of Photoshop to include ImageReady functionality in a separate program. And, Photoshop is growing to meet photographers' image management needs, too. You'll find Adobe Bridge, a stand-alone program that can be used with other Adobe applications, to be the most advanced file browser you've ever used, especially when you see that it's integrated tightly with the other components of the Adobe CS (Creative Suite) software tools, such as Adobe Illustrator CS and Adobe InDesign CS.

Yet, even as Photoshop grows in features and power, the best news is that Adobe has avoided the trap Microsoft falls into, of packing in features that, at best, few people want, most people don't understand, and, at worst, lead to an endless parade of bugs and security holes. Most of the new features in Photoshop CS 2.0 are those most desired by users. And, if you happen not to be enamored of a particular feature, this new version of Photoshop lets you customize your menu system to make features you don't need invisible, color code the features you use the most so you can find them quickly, and restore your system to the default user interface with a few clicks.

This customizability can be important because there are as many different types of users of Photoshop as there are types of photography. For example, I began my career as a photographer working for newspapers; later I worked in a studio and eventually became a roving photojournalist. Like many photographers, I was seduced by the dark side of technology (computers) when I saw the many ways the desktop computer could help me do my work. I first approached Photoshop from a photographer's point of view.

Other Photoshop fanatics reach the same destination through other routes. Artists who originally may have had little or no photography experience find computers invaluable for enhancing digitized versions of their canvases, or for creating original works from scratch. Those whose job descriptions involve graphic arts and pre-press production find tools like Photoshop priceless for enhancing scans or fine-tuning color separations. Other Photoshop masters start out in the classic computer nerd mold and wallow in pixel pushing for the same reason that Tenzing Norgay first climbed Mt. Everest: because it's there, and, as a bonus, there's a little money to be made doing it.

No matter which route you used to arrive at Photoshop, when you disembarked two things probably grabbed your immediate attention. First, even a cursory examination of its feature set reveals that Photoshop can do just about *anything* you need to do with images. The second thing you doubtless noticed is that the program has about five dozen completely different tools; millions of menu entries (actually, closer to 500 menu items, including some that are duplicated, and another 100 or so menu entries for Photoshop's plug-in filters); and 10,000 different dialog boxes (that estimate is accurate, I think).

How do you *learn* all this? With Photoshopoholics Anonymous, the challenge is the same as with any 12-step program: one day at a time. Your advantage as a photographer is that you already have an understanding of much of the underlying techniques that make Photoshop what it is. You don't have to rediscover the wheel. In fact, if you're a halfway serious photographer and more than a casual Photoshop user, you're ready to shift into overdrive with this book.

This brief chapter, a view of Photoshop CS 2.0 and photography from 50,000 feet, provides an overview that's oriented, like the rest of this book, from a photographer's perspective. You'll learn why Photoshop was created expressly to meet *your* needs, and how you can use what you *already* know to make Photoshop work for you right from the start.

Images in the Digital Domain

There's so much power in Photoshop CS that if you're a photographer and don't use all the tools it has to offer, you're putting a crimp in your creativity, and seriously restricting your flexibility. For the devoted photographer, both amateur and professional, not using Photoshop is like limiting yourself to a single lens or zoom setting, using only one film, or using a digital camera exclusively in fully automatic mode. (And if you'd like to break out of *that* mold, you might want to check out my books *Mastering Digital SLR Photography* and *Mastering Digital Photography,* both from Course Technology.)

Certainly, some incredible images have been created by photographers who work under mind-boggling limitations (a few ingenious pictures taken with pinhole cameras come to mind). For example, one of the photos shown in Figure 1.1 was taken with a sophisticated digital SLR camera equipped with a $700 macro close-up lens, and using studio lighting equipment priced at another grand or two. The other photo was taken with a $200 4-megapixel point-and-shoot camera with a fixed focal-length lens (no zoom!), no optical viewfinder (just the LCD for composing the picture), and a pair of $7.00 high intensity desk lamps for illumination.

Figure 1.1 One of these photos was taken with a digital SLR camera, the other with a cheap point-and-shoot camera. Which setup would you rather use?

Can you tell which is which? And, even if you can tell the difference, won't you agree that even the cheapie photo is acceptable for many applications, such as, perhaps, display on a website? Have I discovered a way to save thousands of dollars? Or have I shown that trying to get by using the bare minimum tools is nothing more than an easy way to impose limitations on your creativity?

Unless you enjoy hobbling yourself as a creative constraint (and that's a valid exercise), I'd wager that you'll want to use all the photographic tools at your disposal, and Photoshop is one of them. To my mind, Photoshop is the most important innovation in photography since, say, the zoom lens or through-the-lens viewing, or, in the computer age, the solid-state sensor.

The best part about adding this image editor to your repertoire is that many of the skills you acquired working behind the viewfinder are directly transferable to Photoshop. If you have darkroom skills that stood you in good stead before the current transition to digital photograph, so much the better. I'll list some of these valuable skills later in this chapter.

Seasoned photographers who adopt digital imaging and Photoshop as their primary tools have a commanding advantage over those who approach Adobe's flagship image editor from the computer or traditional art realms. Terms like *lens flare*, *motion blur*, and *grain* are familiar to you. If you are a more advanced photographer, you probably understand techniques like *solarization*, or perhaps even graphic reproduction concepts like *halftones*, *mezzotints*, or *unsharp masking*. Those whose perspective is more pixel- than photography-oriented must learn these terms the hard way.

To see what I mean, examine Figure 1.2. Many photographers will recognize the traditional photographic effects used to create that image. (Bear with me for a moment if you are not steeped in photographic technical minutiae.) The "sun" image appears to have a halo caused by lens flare with the telephoto or zoom lens used to take the picture. The odd flag colors could be produced by partially exposing transparency film during development, a technique which reverses some colors to produce an effect called solarization. The rich colors were a direct result of the photographer's choice of a film stock known for vivid colors. And, of course, the flag and buildings appear compressed in space because that's what telephoto lenses do.

The advantage photographers have is that they've seen all these techniques before, and have probably used them. The ability to reproduce every one of these effects within Photoshop is a powerful additional tool. In truth, Figure 1.2 never saw a piece of film. It was taken with a digital camera using the "normal" (non-telephoto/non-wide-angle) zoom setting, cropped tightly in Photoshop to simulate a telephoto picture, and then a "sun" was added and flag colors were manipulated to create the image you see here.

Figure 1.2 Can you find all the traditional photographic techniques used to produce this picture?

Don't panic if your photographic interests don't run to camera techniques or darkroom magic. Even if your photography skills emphasize other worthy areas of expertise, such as composition or the mechanics of camera operation, you'll still find Photoshop a comfortable fit with what you already know, and a great tool for applying what you plan to learn in the future. From its earliest beginnings, Photoshop was modeled on photographic concepts. Many features incorporated into the latest version of Photoshop have their roots in photography, such as the new Lens Blur effect, seamless panorama photos with PhotoMerge, and the Photo Filter Effects plug-in that mimics standard photographic filters.

Like photography itself, Photoshop was born in a darkroom. Thomas and John Knoll, sons of an Ann Arbor, Michigan college professor, worked in their photo-enthusiast father's basement darkroom and grew to love the Apple computer he brought home for research projects.

By the mid 1980s, Thomas and John were working with imaging on a professional basis. Thomas was doing Ph.D. work in digital image processing, and John was approaching a career at Industrial Light and Magic, the motion-picture computer graphics firm in California. One big problem the brothers saw, was that the most advanced graphics-oriented consumer and business personal computer of the time—the Macintosh—couldn't manipulate full-color images properly.

They set out to fix that. The product that was to become Photoshop went through various early incarnations under different names, and a few copies of an application by that name were actually distributed by a company called BarneyScan Corporation with their slide scanner. Finally, the Knolls licensed their product to Adobe Systems, Inc., then known primarily for its PostScript and font technology, and a drawing program called Adobe Illustrator. Photoshop 1.0 was released to the world in January, 1990.

You can see the original tool palette of Photoshop 1.0 along side its Photoshop CS counterpart in Figure 1.3. Although the icons have been moved around or combined (and the latest Mac OS has added a 3D look), it's amazing how little has changed. The 24 tools in the original palette are all still in use today. Nine of the tools have been nested together under five multi-purpose icons, the Airbrush has become a checkbox on the Options toolbar, and a few, such as the Type and Brush tools, have been transmogrified so much they have little in common with their ancestors.

Figure 1.3 Photoshop's original tool palette (left) and its latest (right) share more features than you might expect.

Photoshop wasn't the first image editor for the Macintosh by any means, and actually drew a great deal on the concepts and interface popularized by Apple's own MacPaint as early as 1984. There were programs with names like PixelPaint, ImageStudio, and SuperPaint, and, notably, Silicon Beach's Digital Darkroom. But the precocious Photoshop was the first program to really grab the imagination of photographers and the publications that employed them.

Happily, reasonably priced color scanners became available (earlier color scanners could cost up to a million dollars each, making them practical only for the largest newspapers and magazines). Scanners supplied Photoshop with ample fodder for its magic, and vast numbers of publications adopted Macs and Photoshop as key tools within a very short period of time. By then, the key battles in the imaging war were over and Photoshop was all but crowned the victor.

Adobe augmented its darkroom paradigm with some other powerful advantages. The first of these was a program interface that made it possible to seamlessly incorporate add-on mini-programs called plug-ins, developed by Adobe and third-party developers. Although plug-ins first appeared in Digital Darkroom, Photoshop's already commanding lead in the image-editing market made the ability to use *Photoshop compatible plug-ins* a must-have feature for competing products of the time, such as PixelPaint and Fractal Design Painter.

The final battle was won in April 1993 when Adobe released a version of Photoshop 2.5 for Microsoft Windows 3.x. There had been earlier image editors for PC-compatibles that (barely) worked under Windows, or which used proprietary DOS-based interfaces. But once Photoshop became a cross-platform tool available to both the Macs that were dominant in the graphics and photographic industries, as well as to die-hards in the Windows realm, there was really no reason to use anything else for sophisticated image-editing tasks.

Today, the term *digital darkroom* has become a generic description. You'll find it used in websites, books, and magazine articles by pixel pushers who've never set foot in an actual darkroom. (Alas!) And, as an interesting footnote, the rights to the Digital Darkroom trademark were purchased by MicroFrontier after Silicon Beach was purchased by Aldus Corporation, which in turn, ironically, was bought out by Adobe.

Each new version of Photoshop has improved on the last, offering new capabilities. Some have been rather earth-shattering in their scope, such as Photoshop's move from "floating selections" to full-fledged layers in Photoshop 3.0. Others have had chiefly ergonomic or convenience benefits, such as the Palette Well introduced with Photoshop 7. Users screamed for a few features for a decade or more before they became a reality, such as the ability to bend text along a path, introduced in Photoshop CS. Other features were relegated to "junior" programs, such as the sophisticated red-eye correction tool found in Photoshop Elements, but which didn't make an appearance in Photoshop until CS 2.0. The improvements in Photoshop have been gradual and, over time, fairly impressive, as the program grows to meet the needs of our new digital age. For example, the ability to edit digital camera RAW files is now an integral part of Photoshop CS, which is important at a time when so many photographers are going all-digital and need the ability to manipulate their digital "negatives," work with 16-bit images, and control image noise.

Perhaps the best news is that, unlike an office suite that shall remain nameless, Photoshop has generally escaped "feature bloat," which has been described as features few need and which are added purely to justify an upgrade. You may not need all of Photoshop's features now, but, as you grow in experience and skills, you'll find that those "mystery" features may prove to be lifesavers for you farther down the road. As sophisticated as it has become, there's very little fat in Photoshop CS.

Transferring Skills

Whether you acquired your photographic skills working with film cameras, or entirely from shooting digital pictures, they can be transferred to Photoshop in a variety of ways, as befits the multifaceted nature of photography itself. Photography has always been part art, part craft, and part technology. Some of the earliest photographers were originally trained as artists, and used their cameras to produce landscapes, portraits, and other works from a classical artistic perspective.

Modest skills as an artisan were also helpful, for many of the earliest cameras were hand built by the photographers themselves. Even as mass produced cameras became available, photographers continued to craft their own custom-built devices and accessories. Today, you'll still find that some of the coolest gadgets for photography are home-brewed contraptions. (You'll find a few of them as special projects in my book *Mastering Digital Photography*, from Course Technology.)

Early photographers also had to be something of a scientist, as the first photographers experimented with various processes for coating and sensitizing plates and film, exposing images by the illumination from electrical sparks. The first-ever photograph, made by Nicéphore Niépce in the early 19th century was created on a piece of pewter coated with what was, for all intents and purposes, asphalt. As late as the mid 20th century, serious photographers were still dabbling in photographic chemistry as a way to increase the sensitivity and improve the image quality of their films through refined darkroom technology. Now that many chemical tricks can be reproduced digitally, photo alchemy has become the exception rather than the rule.

In the 21st century, acquiring the skills a photographer needs is not as difficult as in the 19th century, although a basic familiarity with computer technology has become something of a prerequisite for using microprocessor-driven digital and conventional film cameras. Digital photography has made picture taking easier in many ways, but opened new realms of expertise for photographers who choose to pursue them. But, while photography has become more automated, don't underestimate the wealth of knowledge and skills you've picked up. A great deal of that expertise is easily transferable to Photoshop. The things you already know that will stand you in good stead when you advance to computer-enhanced photo manipulation in Photoshop fall into ten broad categories. I'll run through them quickly in the next sections.

Basic Composition

Compositional skills, so necessary for lining up exactly the right shot in the camera, are just as important when you're composing images in Photoshop. Indeed, Photoshop lets you repair compositional errors that escaped your notice when you snapped the original picture. If you want your subjects in a group shot to squeeze together for a tighter composition, Photoshop lets you rearrange your subjects after the fact. The ability to recognize good composition and put it into practice with Photoshop is an invaluable skill that not all image-editing tyros possess.

Lens Selection

The choice of a particular lens or zoom setting can be an important part of the creative process. Telephoto settings compress the apparent distance between objects, whereas wide angles expand it. Faces can appear to be broader or narrower depending on lens selection. If you understand these concepts, you'll find you can apply them using Photoshop's capabilities, too.

Selective Focus

Choosing which objects in an image are in focus, and which are not, is a great creative tool. With a conventional or digital camera, you need to make the decision at the time you take the photo. To complicate things, digital cameras of the non-SLR variety (with their much smaller sensors and shorter focal length lenses) often make *everything* reasonably sharp regardless of what lens settings you use. With Photoshop, selective focus is not only easier to apply, but can be used in a much more precise, repeatable, and easily modified way. Figure 1.4 shows a close-up photo, at left, in which the background is fairly blurry but still obtrusive. The version on the right was processed in Photoshop to create an even blurrier, darker background that shows off the flower more dramatically.

Figure 1.4 Photoshop can make techniques like selective focus more precise and easier to apply.

Choosing the Right Film

Selecting the right film can be as important as choosing an appropriate lens. Some films are known for their bright, vibrant colors. Others are considered more accurate or capable of better reproducing flesh tones. Some films are sharper or have finer grain. Others are more sensitive to light and make it possible to shoot pictures in near darkness, or when very short shutter speeds are needed to freeze action. Your digital camera, too, probably provides the equivalent of film choice in the ISO (sensitivity) options, or various sharpness and color saturation settings. Photoshop can help when you choose the wrong film, or don't set your digital camera's controls exactly right. Your image editor will let you boost colors or tone them down, disguise noisy grain or emphasize it, and compensate for images exposed under less than ideal lighting.

Darkroom Techniques

There's a reason why Photoshop's predecessors had names like Digital Darkroom. The number of darkroom techniques that have been directly transferred to Photoshop is enormous. From the Dodging and Toning tools to the tremendous range of masking techniques, dozens of Photoshop capabilities have direct counterparts in the darkroom. If you've used a darkroom, you'll be right at home in Photoshop, but even if you haven't dipped your fingers into stopbath, you'll find this image editor performs its manipulations in a logical, photography-oriented way.

Retouching

When I started in photography, retouchers were true artists who worked directly on film negatives, transparencies, or prints with brush and pigment. Photoshop enables those with artistic sentiments who lack an artist's physical skills to retouch images in creatively satisfying ways. You can remove or disguise blemishes, touch up dust spots, repair scratches, and perform many tasks that were once totally within the purview of the retouching artist.

Compositing

Would you like to transplant the Great Pyramid of Egypt to downtown Paris? Or perhaps you're just interested in removing your ex-brother-in-law from a family photo. Photographic masters of the past spent hours figuring ways to combine images in the camera, or spent days sandwiching negatives or transparencies, cutting film or prints to pieces, or using other tedious tasks to build great images from multiple originals. Compositing still requires skill with Photoshop, but you can do things in a few hours that were virtually impossible to achieve only 20 years ago. The scene shown in Figure 1.5 doesn't exist in the real world, but it took me only five minutes to fake it using Photoshop, using the original photos shown in Figure 1.6.

Figure 1.5 It took only five minutes to create this composite in Photoshop.

Figure 1.6 These are the original photos used to produce the composite shown in Figure 1.5.

Color Correction

With traditional photography, color correction is achieved in several ways. You can put filters over the lens of your camera to compensate for a slight bluish or reddish tint to the available light. Other filters can correct for the wacky lighting effects provided by some fluorescent lamps. Some color correction can be done when making a print. Digital cameras can even do a bit of color correction internally, using the white balance settings. Yet Photoshop has an advantage over most traditional methods: it's fast, repeatable, and reversible. You can fiddle with your image editor's capabilities as much as you like, produce several corrected versions for comparison, or really dial up some outlandish color changes as special effects. If you don't like what you come up with, return to your original image and start over.

Photoshop CS has a Match Color feature that you can use to match color schemes from one shot to the other when consistency is important, as in commercial or fashion photography. In conventional film photography it's common to restrict a series of photos to a single "batch" of film having the same emulsion number to provide this consistency. Now you can offer this kind of color correction with digital photos or film photos taken with varying types of film, even under different lighting conditions, usually providing a great improvement over the color correction possible in-camera.

Creative Use of Black and White

Black-and-white photography, like blues music, seems to enjoy a resurgence every five or ten years. In truth, neither black-and-white imagery nor blues ever goes anywhere: It's only widespread public perception of them that changes. Monochrome photos are a great creative outlet, letting you strip down your pictures to the basics without the intrusiveness and bias of color. Photoshop is a great tool for working with black-and-white images, both those that were originally conceived and created in monochrome as well as those that were derived from color images. Indeed, Photoshop offers some powerful tools for transforming a full-color image into black and white, mimicking specialized films and filters in flexible ways. In most cases, these procedures offer much more flexibility than you'd get shooting in black-and-white mode with your digital camera, too.

Filters

Let's not get started on filters, just yet. In traditional photography, filters are handy gadgets you place in front of the camera's lens to produce a variety of effects. These can range from multiple images to split-field colorization (that is, blue on top and reddish on the bottom of an image, or vice versa) to glamour-oriented blur filters. Using third-party add-ons like those from Andromeda or Alien Skin, Photoshop can reproduce virtually any optical effect you can get with glass or gelatin filters, plus hundreds more that are impossible outside the digital realm. If you've used filters with your film camera, and perhaps purchased a set of the Cokin series, you'll love what Photoshop can do.

Next Up

Now that we've taken a look at Photoshop and photography from 50,000 feet, it's time to sky dive down to treetop level, and below, to investigate some of the techniques you can use to improve your images at the pixel level. The next chapter explores camera and lighting effects in Photoshop.

2

Camera and Lens Effects in Photoshop

With the new popularity of digital single lens reflex (SLR) cameras, the focus on lenses and their effects has increased. Everyone wants to get the compressed look found in long telephoto shots, or simulate the excitement possible by zooming a lens during exposure. But not every digital photographer is equipped with a camera that has a super-long zoom range, nor can those who've sprung for the price of a dSLR always afford to buy every lens they want to own. Lenses are very cool, but you may not have all the lens power you really want.

Of course, photography is not the only artistic endeavor in which tools can hold as much fascination as the process itself, or even the end result. Serious cabinet-makers may be just as proud of their sophisticated new hollow chisel mortiser as they are of the drop-front desk crafted with it. In the same vein, it's common to meet a photographer who feels you can never be too rich, too thin, or have too many lenses.

Fortunately, you don't actually *need* a dozen lenses, a bag full of filters, or enough light sources to illuminate the Statue of Liberty to take great pictures. Many of you probably get along very well with nothing more than the zoom lens or electronic flash built into your camera. But whether you're a photo gadget freak or a photo gadget phobe, Photoshop has some tools you'll find extremely useful. Built into your favorite image editor are capabilities that let you duplicate many camera and lighting effects.

Simulating traditional photographic techniques in Photoshop is useful for several reasons. First, even if you own every lens or piece of gear known to civilization, you may not always have your prized gadget with you when you need it. For example, I've traveled to Europe carrying just one camera body, a 35mm and a 105mm lens. More recently, I've gone on trips with a digital camera, its built-in zoom lens, and a stack of memory cards as my sole still photography equipment. It's also possible that you had a particular piece of equipment available but didn't think to use it, or were unable to put it to work in a fast-moving shooting situation.

A second reason to use Photoshop to mimic traditional photographic techniques is that you simply don't have the interest in or budget for a particular item, but, from time to time, would still like to take advantage of its capabilities. Many photographers who generally work with a single zoom lens (including the one built into their digital camera) might want a fisheye picture on occasion. Photoshop can help.

Yet another reason to use Photoshop is to apply some creative camera and lens techniques to older photos in your collection. A favorite old photo can mimic the effect you can achieve with a lens that you only dreamed about when the original was snapped.

This chapter will show you how to mimic many traditional camera and lens effects using Photoshop. In each section, I'll describe the traditional camera technique first to give you an idea of what the technique is supposed to do. Then, I'll follow with some instructions on how to duplicate, or improve on, the effect in Photoshop.

Lens Effects

Photoshop can duplicate the look of many different lenses, particularly some of those specialized optics that cost an arm and a leg, even though you probably wouldn't use them more than a few times a year. For example, for my film cameras, I happen to own two fisheye lenses (7.5mm and 16mm versions), a perspective control lens, several zoom lenses, and a massive 400mm telephoto. Other than the zooms, I don't use any of these very often. I use even fewer lens add-ons with my digital point-and-shoot cameras, relying on my favorite electronic viewfinder (EVF)-equipped camera's unadorned built-in lens 28mm to 200mm (35mm equivalent) for 95 percent of my shots.

The situation is a little different with my digital SLR, of course, as I've succumbed to the Lens Lust disease in a big way, and own four zoom lenses that cover the 35mm equivalent range from 18mm to 750mm, plus a 105mm macro close-up lens. In addition, five or six of my film camera lenses also can be used with my digital SLR.

So, my lens swapping ranges from nil (with the digital EVF camera) to as-needed with my dSLR, but I still find myself encountering shooting situations that call for a lens or focal length I don't have available. I often end up taking a straight photograph and using Photoshop to apply the special effects.

Perspective Control

Most of the pictures we take, whether consciously or unconsciously, are taken head-on. In that mode, the back of the camera is parallel to the plane of our subject, so all elements of the subject, top to bottom, and side to side, are roughly the same distance from the film or digital sensor. Your problems begin when you tilt the camera up or down to photograph, say, a tree, tall building, or monument. The most obvious solution, stepping backwards far enough to take the picture with a longer lens or zoom setting while keeping the camera level, isn't always available. You may find yourself with your back up against an adjacent building, or standing on the edge of a cliff.

Indeed, it's often necessary to use a wide-angle setting and *still* tilt the camera upwards to avoid chopping off the top of your subject. Figure 2.1 shows the relationship between the back of the camera and a monument when the camera is held perpendicular to the group. Notice that both the top and bottom of the subject are cut off.

Figure 2.1 When the back of the camera is parallel to the plane of the subject, it's sometimes impossible to include the entire subject in the photo.

Switch to wide-angle mode and tilt the camera to include the entire subject, and you get the distorted photo shown in Figure 2.2. The monument appears to be falling back, and the base appears proportionately larger than the top, because it's somewhat closer to the camera.

Figure 2.2 In wide-angle mode, tilting the camera makes the monument look like it's falling backwards.

The traditional workaround to this dilemma is one that's generally available only to those who do a great deal of architectural photography. The solution for 35mm photographers is to use something called a perspective control lens, an expensive accessory which lets you raise and lower the view of the lens (or move it from side to side; perspective control can involve wide subjects as well as tall) while keeping the camera back in the same plane as your subject. A more sophisticated (and more expensive) solution requires a professional camera called a view camera, a device that usually uses 4 × 5-inch (or sometimes larger or smaller) film, and has lens and film holders that can be adjusted to any desired combination of angles. Some perspective control can be applied in the darkroom by tilting the paper easel to compensate for image tilt (although the need to use very, very small f-stops to achieve the necessary depth-of-focus limits this technique). Those who can't afford such gadgets, or who own digital cameras without interchangeable lenses, appear to be left out in the cold.

That's where Photoshop comes in. You can make some reasonable adjustments to the perspective of an image within your image editor. Often, the manipulations are enough to fully or partially correct for perspective distortion. There are four methods you can use in Photoshop CS 2.0, and we'll look at all of them.

No-Brainer Correction with the Grid

This section explains a basic perspective correction method you can use to fix a selection in your photo, using Photoshop's Grid as an aid. The procedure assumes that your image is oriented correctly (that is, it doesn't need to be rotated). Just follow these steps using the original image medinaceli.jpg from the Course website (**www.courseptr.com/downloads**), or use an image of your own.

1. Open the file medinaceli.jpg in Photoshop. The image will look like the one shown in Figure 2.3.

Figure 2.3 This arch appears to be falling backwards, because the camera was tilted up to shoot the picture.

2. To give yourself a little working space, choose Image > Canvas Size, and change the width of the image to 1500 pixels, and the height to 2500 pixels.

3. Choose View > Fit on Screen (or press Ctrl/Command + O) to allow the enlarged image to fit comfortably on your screen.

4. Choose View > Show > Grid (or press Ctrl/Command+' (apostrophe)) to turn on display of Photoshop's grid overlay on your image, as shown in Figure 2.4.

Figure 2.4 The Grid helps line up your image as you change its perspective.

5. If your grid's squares are too large, use Edit >Preferences > Grid, Guides & Slices to define a grid layout. I chose one line every 200 pixels for this project.

6. Use the Rectangular Marquee tool to select only the image of the arch, not the blank space you created around it.

7. Choose Image > Transform > Perspective to activate Photoshop's Distortion feature.

8. Drag the corner selection handles until the lines of the arch are lined up with the grid.

9. Crop the image to arrive at the final version, shown at right in Figure 2.5.

Using Guides for Alignment

The first method let you use your eyeballs to line up the corrected portions of the arch. Photoshop has a better way: Guide lines (including the new Smart Guides found in Photoshop CS 2.0, which pop up when two objects are close to being aligned). This section uses the same basic perspective correction method you can use to fix a selection in your photo, but using Photoshop's Guides as an aid.

1. Open toledocathedral.jpg in Photoshop. The image will look like the one shown in Figure 2.6.

Figure 2.5 The final cropped image should look like this.

Figure 2.6 This bell tower also appears to be falling backwards, because of camera tilt.

2. As before, give yourself a little working space, choose Image > Canvas Size, and change the width of the image to 1500 pixels, and the height to 2500 pixels.

3. Choose View > Fit on Screen to allow the enlarged image to fit comfortably on your screen.

4. Choose View > Rulers to turn on display of Photoshop's measuring guides at the upper and left edge of your image.

5. Click in the ruler on the left side and drag a Guide out onto the picture area, aligning it with the right side of the tower. Repeat to create a Guide at the left side of the tower.

6. Choose View > Rulers again and turn off display of the Rulers. You won't need them any more. Your image will look like Figure 2.7.

Figure 2.7 Apply Guides to help line up your image as you change its perspective.

USING RULERS

You can move Guides at any time by pressing V to activate the Move tool, then dragging them to the position you want.

7. Use the Rectangular Marquee tool to select only the image of the tower, not the blank space you created around it.

8. Choose Edit > Transform > Distort to activate Photoshop's Distortion feature.

9. Hold down the Shift key and drag the upper-left and right-corner handles of the selection outward, using the guides to gauge the position of the tower walls. You'll broaden the top of the tower as you do this.

10. Hold down the Shift key and drag the lower-left and right-corner handles of the selection inward, narrowing it, and providing some fine-tuning as you straighten the walls. Your image should now look like Figure 2.8.

11. Crop the image to arrive at the final version, shown at right in Figure 2.9. The original, distorted picture is shown at left for comparison.

Figure 2.8 The tower has been straightened.

Figure 2.9 The final cropped image should look like the version at right.

Correction with the Crop Tool

Photoshop CS's Crop tool provides a third handy way to correct perspective distortion. You don't need to use Guides to fix images in this mode. All you must do is let Photoshop know what lines you want straightened out, and the image editor will square them up. Use the same Toledo Cathedral Tower for the following exercise, so you can compare the results you get with these significantly different methods.

1. Use a fresh, unaltered copy of the Toledo Cathedral Tower file.

2. Select the Crop tool (press C to make it active, or use the Tool Palette).

3. If values appear in the boxes on the Options bar (from previous use of the Crop tool), click the Clear button at the far-right end of the Options bar to remove those entries.

4. Drag a selection around the tower, as shown in Figure 2.10. If you're working with an image of your own, the object should be something that *would* be rectangular if not for the perspective distortion.

Figure 2.10 Drag a selection around a distorted object that should be rectangular.

Figure 2.11 Move the corner handles to align the marquee with the edges.

Figure 2.12 Drag the side, top, and bottom handles to enlarge the area to be fixed.

5. Mark the Perspective box in the Options bar.

6. Move the corner handles of the cropping marquee so the edges of the selection align with the edges of the object, as shown in Figure 2.11.

7. Because you don't want the image cropped down to just the selection, move the side handles at top, bottom, and either side outward to broaden the cropped area, as you can see in Figure 2.12. The perspective settings you've specified will be preserved as long as you don't move the center point of the cropping marquee.

8. Press the Enter/Return key, or click on the Commit button on the Options bar. Your image will be cropped to the boundaries you've specified, with the perspective corrected as you indicated by the marquee boundaries. Check out Figure 2.13 for the results. I've inserted some Guides so you can see how the sides of the tower now line up.

Figure 2.13 After cropping, your image will look like this.

Introducing the Lens Correction Tool

Photoshop CS 2.0 introduced a fourth method for fixing perspective problems, using the Lens Correction tool found in the Filters > Distort menu. I recommend using this tool only for fixing slight correction problems, because it provides less control than any of the three methods already described in this section.

The Lens Correction tool can do a lot more than fix perspective distortion, too. It can be used to correct chromatic aberrations, pincushion and barrel distortion, vignetting, and other problems. If you aren't sure exactly what these potential lens defects are, I'll describe them, along with tips on using the Lens Correction tool in the last section of this chapter. Rather than break the discussion into two parts, I'm going to address the use of this feature to fix perspective problems there, too.

Zoom

Zooming while making an exposure became popular in the 1960s as a way of adding movement to an otherwise static image. The technique is fairly easy to achieve with a conventional camera, especially one with manual controls: Simply take a picture using a shutter speed that is slow enough to let you zoom your lens during the exposure. Depending on how quickly you can zoom with your left hand on the lens barrel after you've pressed the shutter release with your right hand, a motion zoom of this type can be made successfully at speeds from 1/30th second or slower.

Zoom in or out as you prefer, and use a tripod with longer exposures if you want the smoothest effect. While the image will be blurred as it changes in size from the minimum/maximum zoom settings, there can be a relatively sharp image at some point in the zoom (usually the beginning or end) if you pause during the zooming. An electronic flash exposure, most easily made (automatically) at the beginning of the exposure, can also provide a sharp image to blend with your zoom blurs.

Figure 2.14 shows a zoom-during-exposure effect I created in-camera using a 4:1 zoom lens on a digital SLR camera that was mounted on a tripod. It's an interesting abstract picture, but I didn't have much control over the effect. I had to experiment, and then take what I got. Owners of digital point-and-shoot cameras would be left out in the cold most of the time when trying to get a picture like this because their motorized zooms aren't fast enough to produce a blur effect except for very long exposures.

Figure 2.14 Zoom-blur effects can be created in the camera if your zoom operates quickly enough.

But don't worry. Photoshop can overcome these limitations with its own built-in zoom-blur effect. Try the following technique:

1. Locate the basketball.jpg from the Course website, or use your own image. My sample image looks like Figure 2.15. The photo happens to be a cropped portion of a digital camera image taken under available light at about 1/500th second and f4. Notice how the girls' hands are a little blurry, but everything else is static and frozen in time. I thought it would be interesting to keep the basketball sharp, but add a little zoom blur to the players.

2. Press Q to activate Photoshop's Quick Mask feature, which allows you to "paint" a selection using ordinary brush tools.

Figure 2.15 The picture looks like this prior to adding the zoom effect.

CHOOSE MASK OR SELECTION

I usually choose Color Indicates Selected Areas, so I can paint my selection directly. You can change Photoshop's default (Color Indicates Masked (Unselected) Areas) by double-clicking the Quick Mask icon on the Tool Palette.

3. In Quick Mask mode, paint an area around the basketball using the Brush tool (press B to select it) and a soft, 100-pixel brush chosen from the drop-down palette at the left side of the Options Bar. Paint an area about 125 percent of the diameter of the ball itself.

4. Press Q again to exit Quick Mask mode.

5. We actually want to select everything in the image except the ball, so if you are in the habit of painting selections, like I am, invert the selection by pressing Shift + Ctrl/Command + I. That leaves the ball masked, and everything else selected.

6. Choose Filter > Blur > Radial blur from the menu to produce the Radial Blur dialog box shown in Figure 2.16. Choose 85 for the Amount, Zoom as the Blur method, and Best as the Quality level. While you can shift the point around which Photoshop will zoom by dragging the crosshair in the middle of the preview box, the sample picture already has the main subject centered right where the zoom will go.

7. Click on OK to apply the zoom. Your image will look like Figure 2.17.

8. Use the Edit > Fade control (or press Shift + Ctrl/Command + F) to reduce the amount of zoom-blur and restore some of the original image. That makes the blur effect less overwhelming, and makes your original image a bit more recognizable. I scaled back the blur to 71% to create the version shown in Figure 2.18.

9. Be a little creative if you like. I took the fully blurred image from Figure 2.17 and pasted it onto the original image from Figure 2.15. Then, I used an eraser with a large, soft brush to selectively erase part of the blurry layer, creating an image that is sharp in the center, and becomes dramatically zoomed everywhere else. You can see the final image in Figure 2.19.

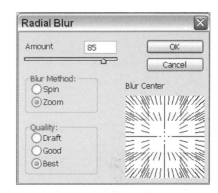

Figure 2.16 Choose your settings in the Radial Blur dialog box.

Figure 2.17 The zoom effect has been applied full-strength to the entire image except for the basketball.

Figure 2.18 Fading the zoom blur to 71% makes the image a little more recognizable.

Figure 2.19 Combining a blurred image with the original selectively gives you a picture that looks like this.

Zoom blurring works especially well with sports events, rock concerts, and other fast-moving situations where a little blur can liven up a photo.

OTHER BLUR EFFECTS

Photoshop CS 2.0 has other useful lens-like blur effects you can apply, including the Spin blur option in the Motion Blur filter, plus Lens Blur, Radial Blur, and Shape Blur.

Telephoto Effects

Photoshop can help you compensate for that long telephoto you can't afford, or which isn't available for your digital camera. Telephotos are great for bringing your subject closer when you can't get close physically. Telephotos also compress the apparent distance between objects that are actually more widely separated than they appear to be. Tele lenses are often used in those car-chase sequences you see in the movies. From the head-on view, it looks like the hero is weaving in and out of cars that are only a few feet apart. In real life, they were probably separated by 40 feet or more, and crammed together through the magic of a telephoto lens.

Unfortunately, most non-SLR digital cameras don't have really long telephoto lenses available. Some digital models may have skimpy 3:1 zoom lenses that simulate at their maximum the view you'd get with, say, a short 105mm or 135mm lens on a conventional 35mm camera. Some semi-pro models offer 10:1 and 12:1 zooms (or better) that still don't bring you close enough. The so-called "digital" zoom built into many models does offer more magnification, but they do nothing more than enlarge a selection of pixels in the center of the sensor to fill your entire image area. You don't actually gain any additional information. You can purchase add-on telephotos for most digital cameras, but these can cost hundreds of dollars and you might not use them very often. You might as well do the job in Photoshop, where you can enlarge and sharpen your image in real-time under your full control. If you have a digital camera with 5-6 megapixels or more, this can work quite well.

Of course, if you own a digital SLR and have deep pockets, you can add a longer lens. Economical zoom lenses in the 70–300mm range (which may equate to a 105mm to 450mm equivalent on a film camera at the typical 1.5X multiplier) are available, but those shooting sports, wildlife, and some other subjects may yearn for even longer optics.

Again, Photoshop can come to the rescue. The key to successfully mimicking a long telephoto with Photoshop is to start with the sharpest original picture possible. Follow these suggestions to get your best picture:

- Use the sharpest film (conventional camera) or lowest ISO setting (digital camera) you can, given the lighting conditions and your subject matter. That might mean using an ISO 100 film (or its digital equivalent setting) for a scenic photo, or an ISO 200–400 film or setting for an action picture. Whatever your digital camera's "base" ISO setting is will give you the best and sharpest results.

- If your camera has manual settings or can be set to shutter priority mode (in which you choose the shutter speed and the camera sets the lens opening) use the shortest shutter speed you can. I've found that even a brief 1/500th second exposure can still be blurred by camera motion in the hands of someone who isn't accustomed to holding the camera *really* steady. A short exposure will stop subject motion, too. While the brief duration of flash can also freeze your image, most flash units have a range of 20 feet or less, so they won't be useful for your long distance/long lens photography.

■ Consider using a tripod, if you have one available, to steady your camera. At the very least, try bracing the camera against a rigid object, such as a tree, building, or rail.

■ Use your longest lens or zoom setting to provide the most magnification you can in your original picture.

Figure 2.20 shows a true long-lens photo of the kind we want to simulate with Photoshop. It was taken with a digital SLR using a 400mm prime lens, which produces the same magnification as a 600mm lens (equivalent, after the multiplier factor was figured in; many dSLRs have sensors that are smaller than a full 35mm frame and provide a cropped image. The lens's focal length must be multiplied to arrive at the true equivalent). I added a 2X teleconverter attachment that increased the effective focal length again, to 1200mm. Photoshop lets you mimic this magnification in your image editor, although enlarging a moon shot like this one probably would be too fuzzy to use. We can get better results enlarging other kinds of scenes, which have lots of detail that masks the process. I use sports photos in the next example.

Figure 2.21 represents a combination of best possible/worst possible scenario. On the plus side, I managed front row seats next to the dugout on the first-base side for this professional baseball game, and I was armed with an awesome 14-megapixel pro-level digital camera. Unfortunately, when the action started, I had

Figure 2.20 This true telephoto shot can be mimicked in Photoshop.

a 28mm non-zoom lens mounted on the camera. So, I ended up with a "big picture" view that took in most of the infield and rendered the players a lot smaller than I would have liked.

Yet, because I had enough megapixels to play with, I was able to crop the photo and get the result you can see in Figure 2.22. It's not the best action picture, but it packs a lot more excitement than the original grab shot.

Figure 2.21 A great seat and a short lens provide this "big picture" view.

Figure 2.22 Cropping the image provides a telephoto effect.

For an absolutely worst-case scenario, check out Figure 2.23, which shows the view from the cheap seats at Jacobs Field in Cleveland, with a box drawn around the view I wish that I'd had. Fortunately, the rowdy gang of kids I'd brought with me couldn't tell the difference between these seats and the $40 Lower Box accommodations, so it was money better diverted to hot dogs, even if my photo opportunities suffered.

Figure 2.23 This is the sort of picture you can expect to take 380 feet from home plate.

The original was a full-frame digital image taken with a digital camera with a mere 3.3 megapixels. I zoomed in as far as I could with the 4X zoom lens, loaded the resulting image into Photoshop, and applied Photoshop's Filter > Sharpen > Unsharp Mask filter, which lets you "dial in" the amount of sharpness you want, using the dialog box shown in Figure 2.24.

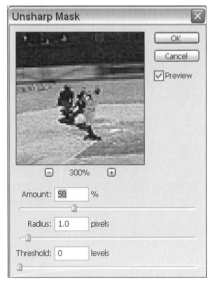

Figure 2.24 The Unsharp Mask dialog box allows you to dial in the amount of sharpness you want.

UNSHARP MASKING

Unsharp masking is derived from a conventional photographic technique, and, despite its name, is used to sharpen images. The technique was first applied to images made on 4 × 5 and larger sheet film. In the darkroom, a film positive is made from the original film negative, a sort of reversed negative in which all the parts of the image that were originally black are black, and all the parts that were white are white. This positive is slightly blurred, which causes the image to spread a bit (like any out-of-focus image). When the positive and negative are sandwiched together and used to expose yet another image, the light areas of the positive correspond very closely to the dark areas of the negative, and vice versa, canceling each other out to a certain extent. However, at the edges of the image, the blurring in the positive produces areas that don't cancel out, resulting in lighter and darker lines on either side of the edges. This extra emphasis on the edges of the image adds the appearance of sharpness. Figure 2.25 might help you visualize how this works.

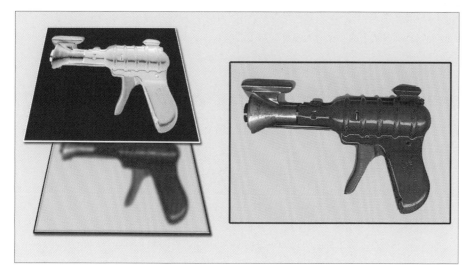

Figure 2.25 A blurred positive and negative image (left) are combined to produce a new, sharpened negative that can be used, in turn, to print an image like the one at right.

It's fairly easy for Photoshop to create the blurry positive "mask" and then match it with a negative image of the original picture. As a bonus, you end up with greater control over the amount of blur in the mask, the distance around the edges that are masked, and a threshold level (relative brightness) at which the effect begins to be applied. The Unsharp Mask filter is similar in many ways to the Sharpen Edges filter, but with this enhanced control. There are three slider controls:

■ The Amount slider controls the degree of edge enhancement applied. You can vary the sharpening effect from 1 percent to 500 percent, and view the results in the Preview window as you work.

- The Radius slider determines the width of the edge that will be operated on, measured in pixels, with valid values from .1 (very narrow) to 250 pixels (very wide). You can preview the results visually, but use a few rules of thumb to decide how much to move this control. The main thing to keep in mind is the original resolution of your image. Low-resolution images (under 100 dpi) can't benefit from much more than one- to three-pixels worth of edge sharpening, whereas higher resolution images (300 dpi and up) can accommodate values of 10 or more. You'll know right away if you have set your values too high. You'll see thick, poster-like edges that aren't realistic, accompanied by a high degree of contrast. You may, in fact, actually *like* the weird appearance, but you've left the realm of sharpening and ventured into special effects at this point.

- The Threshold slider sets the amount of contrast that must exist between adjacent pixels before the edge is sharpened. Sharpness is actually determined by how much the contrast varies between pixels in an area, as shown in Figure 2.26, a super-enlargement of the clock face in the tower that holds Big Ben (which itself is actually a bell) in London. Low contrast equals a blurry, soft image, whereas high contrast tends to mean a sharp, hard image. You can see that the pixels on either side of the enlargement are exactly the same size, but that the contrast between them is greater on the left ("sharper") side.

Figure 2.26 The pixels are the same size, so the resolution must be the same. Yet, the more contrasty half of the image, on the left, looks sharper than the lower-contrast image on the right.

When working with the Threshold slider, values from 0 to 255 can be used. A very low value means that edges with relatively small contrast differences will be accentuated. High values mean that the difference must be very great before any additional sharpening is applied. Normally, you'll need this control only when the default value produces an image with excessive noise or some other undesirable effect. To be honest, in all the years I've used it, changing the Threshold slider has produced effects that were hard to predict, because they varied widely depending on how the other two controls were adjusted, and the nature of the image itself. Your best bet is to set the Amount and Radius sliders first, then experiment with Threshold to see if you like the results any better.

Figure 2.27 shows my baseball picture after I experimented with the Unsharp Mask filter to optimize the sharpness. The view is still not as good as a front row seat, but then, I didn't have to pay a lot for my tickets or tote around a mammoth telephoto lens, either. If nothing else, Photoshop helped me create a souvenir of an exciting game.

Figure 2.27 Photoshop simulated a long telephoto lens by sharpening this tightly cropped image.

Compressing Distances

As I mentioned earlier, telephoto lenses are also used to compress apparent distances. The good news is that this effect, sometimes called "telephoto distortion" has nothing to do with the lens itself. It's simply an effect caused by moving farther away from a subject.

For example, if you are photographing a series of fence posts that are spaced 10 feet apart, and you're standing 10 feet from the first post, the second post will be twice as far away (20 feet), the third post will be three times as far away (30 feet), and the fourth post will be four times as far away (40 feet).

Now move 50 feet away from the first post. The second post will now be only 1.2X as far from you as the first post (60 feet instead of 50), the second will be 1.4X as far, the third will be 1.6X as far, and the fourth will be 1.8X the distance. The apparent distance between them will be much less in your photograph. However, the fence posts will be *waaay* down the road from you, so if you use a telephoto lens to bring them closer, you'll see the images as relatively compressed together, as shown in Figure 2.28. The exact same thing happens if you take the picture with a much shorter lens and enlarge it. The distances are relatively compressed. The figure shows an image of the town walls around the city of Avila, Spain, at left, and an enlargement taken with the same lens at roughly the same position, but cropped and enlarged in Photoshop so only the last six towers are

Figure 2.28 An enlargement of a portion of the photo at left produces a "compressed" image at right.

visible. You can see how compressed the distances between the towers appear when the picture is blown up.

Telephoto perspective can flatten images in which the distance between the objects is not so obvious. Figure 2.29 shows a wide view of the Spanish town of Segovia, taken from the tower of the city's famous castle (it's the one always shown in those "castles in Spain" posters). When the image is cropped to its center portion, buildings in the foreground that are 100 yards from the cathedral in the background appear as if they butted right up against its base. Photoshop helps you re-create this telephoto effect without the need for a telephoto lens.

Figure 2.29 A normal lens shot doesn't show the compression effect of a telephoto...

Figure 2.30 …but cropping the image more tightly does produce a compressed look.

Fisheye Lens

Fisheye lenses were originally developed as a way to provide a hemispherical view in unreasonably tight places, generally for technical reasons, such as examining the insides of a boiler, or for photographing things like the sky's canopy for astronomical research. Because of their specialized nature, they tended to cost a fortune to buy, but that didn't stop photographers of the 1960s who were looking for a way to come up with novel images. My own first fisheye lens was a second-generation Nikon optic, an improved 7.5mm lens that replaced the original 8mm Nikon fisheye, and which required locking up the single lens reflex's mirror and using a separate viewfinder. I later got Nikon's 16mm "full frame" fisheye lens, which did not produce a circular image like the original.

Today, fisheye lenses are available as prime lenses for conventional cameras, or as attachments for many digital cameras, but they're still not something you'd want to use everyday. So, you might want to try Photoshop's equivalent effect. Figure 2.31 shows you an image of a water tower in its original perspective (left) and transformed into a fisheye view with Photoshop (at right).

Figure 2.31 The water tower (left) and its fisheye version (right).

You can apply the fisheye effect in a more creative way. Try the following technique.

1. Load the toledoview.jpg file from the website, or use your own image. The sample image looks like Figure 2.32.

2. Use the Elliptical Marquee tool to create a circular selection in the center of the image. Hold down the Shift key as you drag to create a perfect circle.

3. Choose Filter > Distort > Spherize to produce the dialog box shown in Figure 2.33. Set the Amount slider to 100% to produce the maximum amount of spherization (to coin a term). Click on OK to apply the modification.

4. With the circular section still selected, copy the selection and paste onto a new layer (press Ctrl/Command + C to copy and Ctrl/Command + V to paste).

5. Use Image > Adjustments > Brightness/Contrast and move the brightness and contrast sliders each to the right to lighten the fisheye view and increase its contrast.

Figure 2.32 This is a view of a military academy located inside Toledo, Spain.

6. Use Filter > Sharpen > Unsharp Mask to sharpen up the fisheye view a bit.

7. Choose Layer > Layer Style > Outer Glow to add an eerie glowing effect around your fisheye view, adusting the various aspects of the glow to make it look a bit like a crystal ball.

8. With the circular area still selected, click on the original image layer and press Shift + Ctrl/Command + D to invert the selection so it includes only the area outside the fisheye view.

9. Use the brightness and contrast controls again to darken the area surrounding the fisheye, providing greater contrast. Your image should now look like Figure 2.34.

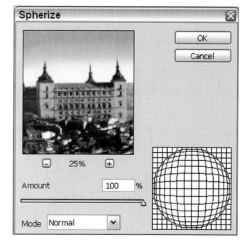

Figure 2.33 The Spherize dialog box lets you apply fisheye effects to an image.

Figure 2.34 After lightening the fisheye view and darkening the surroundings, the image looks like this.

Don't be afraid to experiment. Figure 2.35 shows the same picture with some additional tweaking. At top, I added a glass lens filter, like the one provided in Kai's Power Tools. For the bottom image, I applied the Spherize filter a second time to the first fisheye view, making it even more distorted.

Lens Flare

In computer terms, lens flare is a bug that became a feature. Like grainy, high-contrast film images, lens flare started out as an undesirable image defect that was eventually embraced as a cool artistic effect. As you might expect, Photoshop can duplicate this look with great versatility.

Lens flare is generally caused by light bouncing around within the elements of a lens in uncontrolled ways. A bright light source within the picture area, such as a spotlight or the sun, can generate flare. Very bright lights that are outside the area you've framed can also cause a kind of overall flare that reduces the contrast of your image. Lens hoods are designed to keep this stray light from reaching your lens' glass, thus improving contrast and making your images appear sharper and snappier.

Some kinds of lenses are more susceptible to lens flare than others. Telephoto lenses have a narrow field of view, and light from outside that view can be objectionable. That's why telephotos virtually always are furnished with a lens hood, usually one custom-designed to precisely exclude illumination from outside the intended perspective of the lens. There is less you can do with normal and wide-angle lenses, as

Figure 2.35 The image at top looks like a crystal ball, thanks to a glass lens filter. The image at the bottom has had the Spherize filter applied a second time, producing a more exaggerated look.

their much wider field of view automatically takes in every stray light source. However, lens hoods are a good idea for these lenses, as well. Even my ultra-wide 16mm fisheye has stubby fingers of a vestigial lens hood mounted on its outer edge.

The design of a lens also is a factor. Zoom lenses or any lens with many, many elements, as well as lenses with very large front surfaces are virtual magnets for image-obscuring stray light. With some lenses and certain shooting environments, flare is almost unavoidable. That may be why so many photographers have decided to grin and bear it by incorporating lens flare into their pictures as a creative element. Photoshop lets you put the lens flare exactly where you want it, with precisely the degree of flare that you desire. The algorithm the program uses is based on one developed by original Photoshop developer and Industrial Light and Magic guru John Knoll for his utility FlareMaker. Follow these steps to see for yourself how lens flare can be used.

1. Load the sunset.jpg file from the website. The image, a moody sunset picture, is shown in Figure 2.36.

2. The first thing to do is brighten the picture a little and give it more zip. Choose Image > Adjustments > Hue/Saturation. Move the Hue slider to −33 and the Saturation slider to +40. Click on OK and you'll end up with a more vivid image, like the one shown in Figure 2.37.

Figure 2.36 This sunset picture could use a little livening up.

Figure 2.37 Adjusting the saturation and hue of the image provides a bit more zip.

3. Choose Filter > Render > Lens Flare to produce the dialog box shown in Figure 2.38.

4. You can choose to imitate the lens flare typically produced by four different types of lenses, a 50–300mm zoom, as well as 35mm and 105mm prime (single focal length) lenses. The fourth choice was new to Photoshop CS: Movie Prime, which duplicates the flare effect of many motion picture camera lenses. Start off by selecting the 105mm prime lens. You can also adjust the amount of flare by moving the Brightness slider, and drag the cross hairs shown in the preview window around to precisely position the center of the flare.

5. Click on OK to apply the flare. Your image will look like Figure 2.39. You can see the effects of the 35mm and 50–300mm zoom lens settings in Figure 2.40.

Experiment with different brightness settings to achieve different effects. You can also apply the lens flare only to a selected portion of your image to keep the glare from obscuring some parts of the image.

Figure 2.38 The Lens Flare dialog box offers a choice of four different lens types.

Figure 2.39 Photoshop's 105mm Lens Flare filter inserts a setting sun into the photograph.

Figure 2.40 The 35mm Lens Flare (left) and 50–300 Zoom Lens Flare (right) options produce their own special effects.

Motion Blur

The goal of neophyte action photographers is to freeze action, stopping everything in its tracks. Once you learn some reliable ways to accomplish that miracle, it soon becomes evident that people or things frozen in time tend to look a little bit like statues, and not particularly realistic or exciting from an action standpoint. We *expect* a little blur in our sports photography, especially if the blur of motion is used effectively.

If you know what you're doing (or even if you don't), capturing images with just enough blur to make them look alive is not that difficult with either digital or conventional cameras. Among the techniques at your disposal:

- Choose just the right shutter speed for the action at hand. Don't use a speed that's so slow that your subjects will be terminally blurry, and avoid super-short shutter speeds that freeze everything. With experience, you'll learn which shutter speeds work with which kinds of motion.

- Learn to move your camera with the action (a technique called panning), which reduces the relative speed of your subject to the camera, allowing you to capture action with a slower shutter speed. As a bonus, panning often blurs the background enough to add the kind of motion blur you want to achieve.

- Understand the dynamics of motion. Objects crossing the camera's field of view blur more than those headed directly towards the camera. Some parts of an object, such as the wheels of a moving car or the feet of a running athlete, move faster than the rest of the subject, adding inevitable (or even desirable) blur. Subjects closer to the camera blur more than those located farther away.

Understanding these concepts can help you duplicate them within Photoshop, too, as another example of how photographic experience can help you when it comes time to edit your images. Try the exercise which follows to see some of the ways in which you can add motion blur to your images.

1. Load the soccerblur.jpg image from the website. The original image is shown in Figure 2.41.

Figure 2.41 This image is sharp and unblurred and looks as if the soccer players were statues.

2. Select the soccer ball using the Elliptical Marquee tool. Hold down the Shift key to select a perfect circle. Press the cursor arrow keys to nudge the selection a bit, if necessary, so it encompasses the entire soccer ball.

3. Choose Filter > Blur > Radial Blur, shown in Figure 2.42. This is the same filter you used earlier to produce a zoom effect. This time choose Spin as the blur type, and move the Amount slider until the soccer ball has a bit of a blur to it, as shown in Figure 2.43.

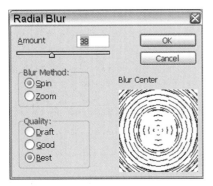

Figure 2.42 The Radial Blur filter adds some motion effects.

Figure 2.43 First, add some radial blur to the soccer ball, as if it were spinning.

4. Press Q to enter Quick Mask mode, and using a 65-pixel soft brush, "paint" a mask onto the right halves of the bodies of the players on each side of the kicker. These players are running towards the left side of the frame, so we want to add a little blur to the right sides of their bodies.

5. Press Q again to exit Quick Mask mode, then choose Filter > Blur > Gaussian Blur to invoke the dialog box shown in Figure 2.44. Move the Radius slider to about 3 pixels and click on OK to apply the blur.

6. The relevant portion of your image should now look like Figure 2.45.

7. Repeat steps 4 and 5, only paint over the entire body of the girl at the left side of the frame, to apply blur over her form completely. The finished shot looks like Figure 2.46.

Figure 2.44 The Gaussian Blur dialog box lets you choose the amount of blurring to add.

Figure 2.45 Next, add some motion blur to the players who appear to be running towards the left.

Figure 2.46 Finally, add overall blur to the girl at the far left to produce this final image.

Keep in mind the dynamics of motion when applying blur. In some cases, you might want to blur only your subjects' feet and/or hands. Add some blur to the wheels of a locomotive to give it a feeling of speed and power. Put streaks behind a skyrocket rising into the heavens.

Selective Focus

Selective focus is one of the most valuable creative tools at your disposal, allowing you to isolate or feature various parts of your composition. For example, by throwing the background out of focus, you can place emphasis on the subject in the foreground. The techniques of selective focus, using depth-of-field (the amount of the image that is in relatively sharp focus), should be familiar to every photographer.

- Use longer lenses, which inherently have less depth-of-field, to give yourself great control over what's in focus and what is not.

- Move in close to take advantage of the reduced depth-of-field at near range.

- Use larger lens openings to reduce the amount of depth-of-field.

- Use manual shutter speed settings or the aperture priority mode of your camera to allow use of those larger lens openings.

- Filters, slower films or ISO settings, and other aids can help control the lens opening you use and, thus, the amount of depth-of-field you're working with.

- Learn the dynamics of focus, such as how two-thirds of the depth-of-field at any particular distance and lens opening is applied to the area behind your subject, and only one-third to the area in front of it.

- Preview the amount of area in focus using your single lens reflex camera's depth-of-field preview, or your digital camera's LCD screen.

SELECTIVE FOCUS AND DIGITAL CAMERAS

Photoshop is a lifesaver for digital camera users eager to apply selective focus techniques because digital camera lenses inherently provide much more depth-of-field for a given field of view than a conventional film camera.

The depth-of-field bonus of digital cameras comes from the relatively short focal length lenses they use. The maximum "telephoto" setting of a typical non-SLR digital camera may be 32mm (producing the same field of view as a 150mm lens on a 35mm camera). However, the depth-of-field provided by the digital camera at that setting is much closer to that of a wide-angle lens than to a telephoto lens. As a result, it may be very difficult to use selective focus with a digital camera, unless you're taking a picture very, very close to your subject. Photoshop CS can fix that!

Photoshop added a new Lens Blur filter which debuted in the first CS version, with lots of amazing options. First, I'll explain how to apply selective focus the old-fashioned way, useful for versions prior to Photoshop CS. Figure 2.47 is a digital camera picture of a kitten, taken at close range. The background is already fairly blurry, but it's still distracting and we can do better. For this image, I used the Quick Mask mode we've already deployed several times in this chapter, and painted a selection that included only the cat, taking special care around the edges of the feline.

Then, I applied Photoshop's Unsharp Mask filter to sharpen the cat even more, and followed that with an application of Photoshop's Blur tool to the non-cat portions of the image to increase the out-of-focus appearance of the background. As a final touch, I put the Dodge tool to work to lighten the cat's eyes. You can see the final image in Figure 2.48.

The Photoshop CS Lens Blur feature can do much the same thing, except producing a more realistic effect. Lens blur uses something called a *depth map* to decide which pixels in a "flat" image belong "in front" and which belong "in back," so blur can be applied only to the portion we want. This depth map can be a stored selection (which Photoshop calls an *alpha channel*) or a *layer mask*, which is a type of selection/alpha channel that's associated only with a particular layer, and which applies only to that layer.

Figure 2.47 Even digital cameras can achieve selective focus when shooting close up. But we can do better.

Figure 2.48 Blurring the background while sharpening the cat produces a more dramatic selective focus effect.

For Photoshop's purposes, the darker pixels in the alpha channel or layer mask are treated as though they reside in the foreground of your photo, while the lighter pixels are treated as if they are in the background. I'll provide an example that should make this clearer. Figure 2.49 is a digital camera photo which, like most digital camera photos, has a plethora of depth-of-field. Everything in the foreground and background is as sharp as the subject herself.

To show how Lens Blur works, I created a Layer Mask and applied a black-white gradient to it. (I'm not going to explain how Layer Masks work here, as Lens Blur effect is the main point at the moment.) You can see the Layer Mask I created in Figure 2.50. When the Lens Blur is applied using that black (bottom) to white (top) gradient, the blurring shown in Figure 2.51 results. Everything at the bottom of the frame is sharp and gradually gets more blurry as you move towards the top of the frame.

If that's all Lens Blur could do, it wouldn't be much, because you can accomplish the same effect using Photoshop's Blur filter. But wait, there's more. We'll work with the same image, but in a different way. You can follow along using teryn.jpg found on the website. I'm going to produce an exaggerated effect for this exercise so you can see exactly how this feature works.

Figure 2.49 Everything is sharp in this digital camera shot.

Figure 2.50 The Layer Mask provides a gradient for the blurring effect.

Figure 2.51 When Lens Blur is applied using the Layer Mask, the image gradually gets sharper as you move from top to bottom.

Creating the Alpha Channels

We're going to use alpha channel selections to perform the magic. As you follow these steps, keep in mind that, unless you change the values using a control I describe next, the *darker* the pixels in the alpha channel/selection, the blurrier the corresponding pixels will be after the filter is applied. Let's get started. First, let's define the area to be blurred using two separate alpha channels, one for the far background we want heavily blurred, and one for the near background and foreground we want partially blurred.

1. Press Q to enter Quick Mask mode.

QUICK MASK MODE'S MODES

Quick Mask can operate two ways: You can paint the selection or mask, or you can paint the unselected, unprotected portion of your image. It doesn't matter which mode you use, but many Photoshop veterans prefer to paint the selection itself, so that's what I'll assume you're using throughout this book. When I tell you to enter Quick Mask mode and tell you what to paint, you'll be painting the selection. You can switch back and forth between these modes by double-clicking the Quick Mask icon in the Tool Palette and in the Color Indicates area choosing either Masked Areas or Selected Areas. Here's where you can also change the mask "paint" from red to another color (useful when you're masking a subject that itself contains lots of red), and select a transparency for your mask paint other than the default 50 percent.

---

2. Press B to select the Brush tool, and choose a brush in a fairly large size from the Brush Palette in the Options bar. I selected a 200 pixel brush so I could paint large areas in a few swipes.

3. Paint the far background area behind the young girl with the brush. If you get some paint on the deck railing, use a hard-edged Eraser to remove it. Don't worry about the background areas between the deck railing's spindles. If you were going to use the photograph for something, you might want to attend to them, but this is just a tutorial exercise, so the extra work isn't required. The selected area is shown in Figure 2.52.

4. Press Q to exit Quick Mask mode, and then choose Select > Save Selection, and give the selection a name such as Background.

   We want the far background area of the image to be the most blurry, so this selection applies the selection "paint" in full force. Areas closer to our subject (just behind her, or just in front of her) only partially should be blurry, so we need to paint them as a slightly less opaque selection. (Remember, for this exercise, less opaque means less blur is applied.)

Figure 2.52 First select the background with an opaque mask.

5. Press D to cancel the current selection, then Press Q to enter Quick Mask mode again.

6. Choose a soft fuzzy brush, because we want the blur effect to "fade out" gradually. Set the Opacity of the brush to 50% in the Options bar, so that the brush strokes you apply will be partially transparent (thus producing less blur).

7. Paint the gazebo area that appears just to the right and behind the girl with this 50% transparent brush. Dab a bit around the railing that's in front of her, too. Your selection will look like Figure 2.53.

8. Save this selection under another name, such as Partial Blur. I had you create the fully blurred and partially blurred masks as two separate alpha channels because it was easier to manage them that way. The next step is to combine them into one alpha channel.

9. With your Partial Blur alpha channel still selected, choose Select > Load Selection, and pick the Background alpha channel from the Channel dropdown list. Click the Add to Selection button so that this additional alpha channel will be added to the Partial Blur channel.

Figure 2.53 Then, select the near background and foreground with a semi-transparent mask.

10. Save the combined alpha channel under a new name, such as Both. Because you've also stored the channels individually, you can edit them independently later on if you need to (say, because accidentally you've blurred something you'd rather not have blurred).

Applying the Lens Blur Filter

Next, we'll use the alpha channels you just prepared to apply the Lens Blur filter. Just follow these steps.

1. Choose Filter > Blur > Lens Blur to produce the dialog box shown in Figure 2.54. You'll see the numerous options at the right side of the dialog box, and a preview image at the left side. If you're using a relatively slow computer, you can set the Preview option to Faster, which will cause Photoshop to produce a preview more quickly, instead of More Accurate (which gives you a better idea of how the effect will look).

2. In the Depth Map area, choose the combined alpha channel, Both, from the drop-down list.

3. For now, leave the Blur Focal Distance set at 0. This control sets the mid-point of the blur effect.

Figure 2.54 Set your options in the Lens Blur dialog box.

SETTING BLUR FOCAL DISTANCE

This control helps determine how the blur is applied. That is, pixels become blurrier the farther their brightness is from the distance value you set. Confused? Consider this example: If you set the Blur Focal Distance to a value of 128, pixels at that point (a middle gray) will be sharpest. Pixels that are black (with a value of 0) or white (with a value of 255) will be completely blurred. Amount of blurriness would decrease, then, as you move from 0 toward 128 or from 255 towards 128. This is a useful feature, but we're not going to use it right now, allowing our blurriness "gradient" to go straight from 0 (blurry) to 255 (unblurred).

4. Set the Radius slider in the Iris area of the dialog box to a value of 35. As with a real camera, the nature of the blur effect can depend on the characteristics of the "iris" (like the iris surrounding the pupil of your own eye). After you've been using Lens Blur for awhile, you can experiment with different shapes and blade curvature using the sliders in the Iris area of the dialog box. For

now, we'll work only with the Radius slider, which, to oversimplify a bit, controls the amount of blurring applied.

5. You can make brighter pixels blur more strongly, which is what happens in real life. Slide the Brightness control in the Specular Highlights area to a value of 55. The Threshold slider adjusts how bright a pixel must be to be affected by this option. Leave it at 255 for now, but you can play with the slider to see how it affects the image, if you like.

6. Blurring tends to remove the normal "grain" of an image, which is unrealistic. Set the Noise slider to a value of about 7 to replace some of the grain that the Lens Blur filter is removing. Choose the Gaussian option to randomize your noise, and mark the Monochromatic box to ensure that the noise will add grain only, and not change the colors of your image.

7. Click on OK to apply the Lens Blur effect. The final result is shown in Figure 2.55. It's a little exaggerated so the blurring will show up on the printed page, but you get the idea.

I love Photoshop CS's Lens Blur effect. It's much more flexible than the old way I showed you first, and can create some extraordinary looks.

Figure 2.55 The finished effect looks like this.

Photoshop CS Photo Filters

Photoshop CS has a Photo Filters effect hidden in the Image > Adjustments menu. It's primarily of use to photographers who want to apply familiar filter effects to their image, rather than use the program's color correction facilities. Or, it can be used to quickly add filter-like color for special effects.

For example, films are produced (even today) balanced for a particular kind of light source. The most common films are designed to produce accurate colors when exposed under daylight illumination, but a few professional films are balanced for the much more orange light produced by incandescent lamps. Back in the olden days, most photographers owned a set of filters that would convert one kind of illumination to the other (at the cost of an f-stop or two of exposure). A tungsten-balanced film can be exposed under daylight if a Kodak Wratten 85B filter is used to correct the light.

Even if you're not using film, you can get this kind of wrong color if your white balance is set incorrectly. If you manually set your white balance for incandescent light and then take pictures under daylight, you'll end up with the same bluish pictures a film photographer gets when using indoor film in outdoor illumination.

In both cases, Photoshop's Photo Filter adjustment can provide a quick fix. You can also add Wratten 80- and 82-series filters to go the other way, correcting outdoor film (or white balance settings) for incandescent illumination. The Image > Adjustments > Photo Filter dialog box looks like Figure 2.56.

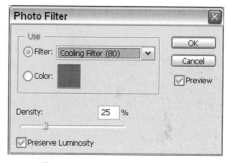

Figure 2.56 The Photo Filter dialog box has 20 different color filters from which to choose.

You can choose any of 18 different filters, or click the color patch in the dialog box and select a custom hue from Photoshop's Color Picker. You can also specify the degree of density for the filter (increasing or decreasing the effect) and direct Photoshop to change only the color, while preserving the brightness of the original image. Figure 2.57 shows an action picture taken under incandescent illumination, and then corrected using Photoshop's 80-series Photo Filter. While I think Photoshop's traditional color correction techniques (described more completely in Chapter 6) are the most versatile, you can have some fun with this new Photo Filter capability.

If you know in advance that you want a special color effect, you can sometimes apply color filters using a digital camera's built-in effects filter capabilities. Check out your camera's instruction manual to see if you have that option.

Figure 2.57 Shot under incandescent illumination, this photo has been (partially) corrected using Photoshop's Photo Filter capability.

Lens Distortion Correction

Here's something you *can't* readily do with your lenses, but which Photoshop CS 2.0 makes a snap: correcting the most common varieties of distortion found in many types of optics. I introduced this tool earlier in this chapter. Now we're going to explore some of its capabilities. First, I'll start off with a brief description of common lens distortions, and why they need to be corrected.

No Perfect Lens

As you probably know, there are no perfect lenses. Even the most sophisticated lens design, developed for costly ($8000 or more!) interchangeable lenses for digital and film SLRs are, at best, compromises of some sort. Lens designers depart from the theoretical "perfect" lens design to add features that photographers demand. Perhaps the lens is intended for low-light photography, so the designer makes a trade-off here or there to allow a wider maximum aperture. Or, the lens must be developed so it is physically shorter, lighter, or can be attached to an SLR camera without interfering with the mirror.

Some lenses are designed so they can better work with ultraviolet illumination for scientific purposes, or optimized for close-up photography. The most challenging lens design of all may be the zoom lens, which with a continuous series of focal lengths, is many lenses in one. There are lots of tricks optical magicians can work with, including non-spherical lens surfaces, special coatings, and combinations of lens elements that move in strange ballets to improve your results. There are even lenses that jostle their elements in response to camera movement to stabilize the image when the shutter speed isn't fast enough.

Because of all the compromises that must be made in building a lens, various types of distortion and aberrations are unavoidable. Photoshop's new Lens Correction filter helps you fix some of them. Here's a description of the most common types of distortions:

- **Chromatic Aberration.** This is an image defect, often seen as green or purple fringing around the bright edges of an object, caused by a lens failing to focus all colors of a light source at the same point.

- **Barrel Distortion.** This is a lens defect that causes straight lines at the top or side edges of an image to bow outward into a barrel shape.

- **Pincushion Distortion.** The opposite of barrel distortion, this defect causes lines at the top and side edges of an image to bend inward, producing an effect that looks like a pincushion.

- **Vignetting.** If a lens is unable to provide even illumination out to the corners of the image area, the result can be dark corners. This is often found in wide-angle zoom lenses at their widest setting, and when a lens is mounted on an SLR that has a larger sensor size than the lens was designed for. Vignetting can also be produced by using a lens hood that is too small for the field of view, or generated artificially using image-editing techniques.

- **Perspective Distortion.** This is not, strictly speaking, a defect of a lens but, rather, a result of tilting the camera to take in more of a tall subject, throwing the alignment of the subject and camera focal plane out of whack. I discussed this effect in more detail earlier in the chapter. I've included it here because Photoshop's Lens Correction filter can correct for this kind of distortion.

Fixing Chromatic Aberration

This one's a toughie because chromatic aberration may be difficult to see and evaluate, and is difficult to fix. The effects differ from camera to camera and lens to lens, too. So, your results will generally vary from mine. I'm going to provide you with the basics so you can experiment on your own.

Figure 2.58 shows an image that's been enlarged so you can see the chromatic aberration, which is most noticeable as the blue/yellow (green) fringing around the shoulders of the softball player's jersey. To partially fix this problem, I used Filters > Distort > Lens Correction to produce the Lens Correction dialog box shown in Figure 2.59. Then, in the Chromatic Aberration area of the dialog box, I moved

Figure 2.58 Chromatic aberration shows up in this shot as green fringing.

Figure 2.59 The Lens Correction filter has removed the green fringing.

the Blue/Yellow Fringe slider all the way to the right. (I unchecked the Grid box at the bottom of the dialog to produce an unobstructed view of the original image, too.) While this didn't fix all the color fringing problems in the image, it did eliminate the green fringe in the jersey's shoulders.

As you might guess, you'll need to experiment with this tool to see if it's suitable for your particular camera, lens, and subject matter.

Correcting Barrel and Pincushion Distortion

These defects are sometimes so slight that you don't notice them at all in your pictures, unless your subject matter happens to have straight lines near the edges that obviously bow outwards towards the edges of the frame, or inwards, towards the center. Figure 2.60 shows an image that has been exaggerated in both directions so you can clearly see the barrel and pincushion distortion.

Figure 2.60 Pincushion distortion (top) and barrel distortion (bottom) can be fixed in Photoshop.

To use this tool, follow these steps:

1. Choose Filters > Distort > Lens Correction to produce the dialog box.

2. If you want to use the tool's grid to help you align the image, make sure the Grid box at the bottom of the dialog is marked.

3. Press D to activate the Remove Distortion tool, and then drag portions of the image to correct for the kind of distortion your image requires. Or, use the Remove Distortion Slider (your best choice for ease of use, plus if you want to apply the same amount of correction to several different images).

4. As you correct the image, it will change in the preview window, and the Remove Distortion slider will show how much correction is being applied. Movement of the slider to the left indicates adding a barrel effect (to counter pincushion distortion), whereas moving it to the right counteracts barrel distortion. Figure 2.61 shows correction of a pincushioned image, while Figure 2.62 shows repair of an image with barrel distortion.

5. Note that the boundaries of your image will change as you apply correction. It's most noticeable when countering barrel distortion, because your fixed image will bow inwards, leaving blank areas outside its original boundaries. In the Edge area of the dialog box you can choose whether Photoshop leaves the area outside the new edges transparent, fills it with the background color, or extends the current background to fill up the area.

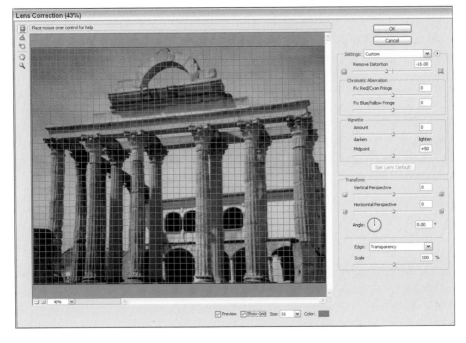

Figure 2.61 Correcting a pincushioned image.

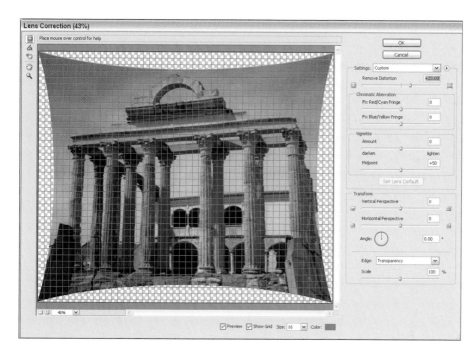

Figure 2.62 Fixing an image with barrel distortion.

Your best choice is to select a large enough area for correction that you can crop out the distorted edges and not need to worry about what they look like at all. If your image has areas at the edges that have few important details (for example, sky), you can try extending the current background. Otherwise, use the Transparent or Background Color options and crop.

6. If you want to use the same correction on other images, choose Save Settings from the fly-out menu in the Settings area, and give your corrections a name (such as 43–86 Zoom At 43mm).

7. Click OK when finished.

MODIFYING THE GRID

You can turn the grid overlay on or off, change the spacing of the grid to make the pattern of squares larger or smaller, and use the Move Grid tool (press M to activate it) to drag the grid around the image area so it aligns more closely with vertical or horizontal lines in your image. Double-click the Color box to change the grid from its default gray to another hue that may contrast better with your subject matter. For example, if you're modifying an image that's heavy in neutral grays, you might want to select a vivid magenta color for the grid.

Correcting Vignetting

This is two features in one! Not only can you remove vignetting in the corners of your image, but you can *add* some darkness rather quickly and efficiently if you *want* dark corners (or lighten the corners, too, if that's what you prefer).

To use Photoshop's vignetting correction feature, follow these steps. If you want to try this feature out on your own, use one of your images for practice. It really doesn't matter what photo you work with; the vignetting effect can be seen with any image that isn't already completely dark or completely light in the corners.

1. Choose Filters > Distort > Lens Correction to produce the dialog box.

2. If you want to get rid of the distraction of the grid, make sure the Grid box is unchecked.

3. In the Vignette area of the dialog box, move the Amount slider to the right to darken the corners of the image, or to the left to lighten them.

4. If you find the area being affected needs to be enlarged or reduced, move the Midpoint slider. Moving to the right increases the size of the vignette, while sliding to the left decreases it.

5. Click OK when finished. Figure 2.63 shows an image being processed.

Figure 2.63 Remove—or add—vignetting quickly.

Correcting Perspective

The Lens Correction tool's perspective-fixing features can be useful with images that need a minor amount of correction. Figure 2.64 shows an image taken with an ultra-wide-angle lens tilted way back to include the top of the building. It exhibits the typical "falling backwards" look that perspective distortion produces. We can partially compensate for the distortion and improve this photo.

Figure 2.64 This image has way too much distortion for a complete fix, but we can improve its lines.

You can use taylorhall.jpg from the website, or work with your own photo.

1. Choose Filters > Distort > Lens Correction to produce the dialog box.

2. To make the grid a little easier to view, change the spacing to 64, and click the Color box and change to a bright magenta color, as you can see in Figure 2.65.

3. Click the Straighten Tool (or press A to activate it) and drag along the lower edge of the railing at the base of the columns. This tells the tool that you want to rotate the image so this line becomes horizontal.

4. Move the Vertical Perspective slider to the left (roughly to the –43 point) so that the center column is vertical.

5. Move the Horizontal Perspective slider to the left (again, about to the –43 position), providing some side-to-side correction.

Figure 2.65 Straighten out the vertical lines to more closely align with the grid.

6. Click OK when finished. The perspective correction won't be perfect (try one of the other methods described earlier in this chapter if you're fussy), but, with a little cropping to remove the transparent areas of the image, this drastically distorted image will look a *little* more normal.

HELP WITH STRAIGHTENING IMAGES

You'll find that the Straighten tool will help you rotate any image just enough to align an edge that *should* be vertical or horizontal, but which isn't.

Next Up

We'll encounter other lens and camera techniques in some of the other chapters. But next, it's time to venture into the digital darkroom to learn how to reproduce time-honored processing techniques with the new and improved Photoshop.

3

Darkroom Techniques with Photoshop CS 2.0

One of the things I miss the most, and the least, about photography from the pre-digital age is the fun and drudgery of laboring in the murk of a musty darkroom, surrounded by humid, acid-tinged odors and an eye-straining pale yellow glow. Despite an environment that would drive a claustrophobe nuts, miracles are created in the darkroom, and magical images often emerge from behind the heavy black curtain.

Fortunately, there's no need to throw the spectacular images out with the stopbath water. Photoshop includes a whole raft of features that let you re-create the most useful darkroom techniques quickly and repeatedly, without risk of wasting film, paper, or chemicals. You can even manipulate your digital "negatives" using your digital camera's RAW format.

This chapter will show you some of the advanced darkroom techniques that you can put to work using Photoshop's awesome capabilities.

Manipulating Digital Negatives

Although you still may be working with images scanned from film or print, it's more likely today that much of your Photoshop fodder will come from pictures captured with a digital camera. Digital cameras now outsell film cameras by a hefty margin, and a huge number of the prints that are made are created from digital "negatives."

So, you probably already know that your digital camera may be capable of producing three different types of image files, all of which are well-suited for enhancing within Photoshop CS. You can learn more about them in my book *Mastering Digital Photography.* In this section, I'll provide a summary of some of the information detailed there.

All newer digital cameras produce, by default, JPEG files, which are the most efficient in terms of use of space. JPEG files can be stored at various quality levels, which depend on the amount of compression used. You can opt for tiny files that sacrifice detail or larger files that preserve most of the information in your original image.

Many cameras can also save in TIFF format, which, although compressed, discards none of the information in the final image file. However, both JPEG and TIFF files are quite different from the original information captured by the camera. They have been processed by the camera's software as the raw data is converted to either JPEG or TIFF format and saved onto your flash memory card or other camera media. The settings you have made in your camera, in terms of white balance, color, sharpening, and so forth, are all applied to the raw image data. You can make some adjustments to the image later using Photoshop CS, but you are always working with an image that has *already been processed*, sometimes heavily.

The information captured at the moment of exposure can also be stored in a proprietary, native format designed by your camera's manufacturer. These formats differ from camera to camera, but are called Camera RAW, or just RAW for convenience. These "digital negatives" contain all the original information grabbed by your camera's sensor with no compression, sharpening, or other processing.

Each camera vendor's products save images in a proprietary RAW format, which, in some cases (such as Nikon and Canon) are TIFF files with special information embedded. Other cameras produce more esoteric RAW files. All RAW files require special software provided by the camera vendor or a third-party application that can interpret the files. However, because RAW files are generally smaller than TIFF files and include a great deal more information, only a small number of digital cameras (mostly higher-end models) produce TIFF files today. RAW has replaced the TIFF option in most digital cameras.

Photoshop's RAW Support

Photoshop CS now includes a Camera RAW plug-in (which was formerly an extra-cost option with Photoshop 7) that works quite well. It can be used only with the particular digital cameras that Adobe supports, typically from Nikon, Canon, or Konica Minolta and quite a few other vendors. In addition, Camera RAW supports the new Adobe Digital Negative (DNG) format. DNG is Adobe's attempt to create a common RAW format that can be used by all the different camera types.

The list of supported cameras at the time this book was published is a long one, shown in Table 3.1. You can also expect that camera models introduced after Photoshop CS from the same vendors are also supported. For example, although the Canon EOS 350 XT and Konica Minolta A200 debuted after the original Photoshop CS, their RAW formats are similar to their predecessor models and are fully supported. You can find the latest updates that list compatible cameras at **www.adobe.com**.

Table 3.1 RAW Camera Formats Supported by Photoshop CS

Camera Vendor	Models Supported
Canon	EOS-1D, EOS-1Ds, EOS-1D Mark II, EOS-1Ds Mark II, EOS 10D, EOS 20D, EOS D30, EOS D60, EOS 300D (Digital Rebel/Kiss Digital), EOS Digital Rebel XT, PowerShot 600, PowerShot A5, PowerShot A50, PowerShot Pro 1, PowerShot S30, PowerShot S40, PowerShot S45, PowerShot S50, PowerShot S60, PowerShot S70, PowerShot G1, PowerShot G2, PowerShot G3, PowerShot G5, PowerShot G6, PowerShot Pro70, PowerShot Pro90 IS
Contax	N Digital
Epson	R-D1
Fujifilm	FinePix F700, FinePix S5000 Z, FinePix S7000 Z, FinePix S2 Pro, FinePix S20 Pro, FinePix S3 Pro
Kodak	DCS 14n, DCS Pro 14nx, DCS 460, DCS760, DCS Pro SLR/n
Konica Minolta	DiMAGE A1, DiMAGE A2, DiMAGE A200, DiMAGE 5, DiMAGE 7, DiMAGE 7i, DiMAGE 7Hi, Maxxum 7D/Dynax 7D
Leaf	Valeo 6, Valeo 11, Valeo 22
Leica	Digilux 2
Nikon	D1, D1H, D1X, D2X, D100, D2H/D2Hs, D70, D70s, D50, Coolpix 5000, Coolpix 5400, Coolpix 5700, Coolpix 8700, Coolpix 8400, Coolpix 8800
Olympus	E-10, E-1, E-20, C-5050 Zoom, C-5060 Zoom, C-8080 Wide Zoom
Panasonic	DMC-LC1
Pentax	*ist D, *ist Ds
Sigma	SD9, SD10
Sony	DSC-F828

Using the Camera RAW Plug-In

Photoshop's Camera RAW plug-in is one of the import modules found in the File menu. To open a RAW image in Photoshop CS, just follow these steps:

1. Transfer the RAW images from your camera to your computer's hard drive.

2. In Photoshop, choose Open from the File menu, or use Photoshop's File Browser or Bridge.

3. Select a RAW image file. The Camera RAW plug-in will pop up, showing a preview of the image, like the one shown in Figure 3.1.

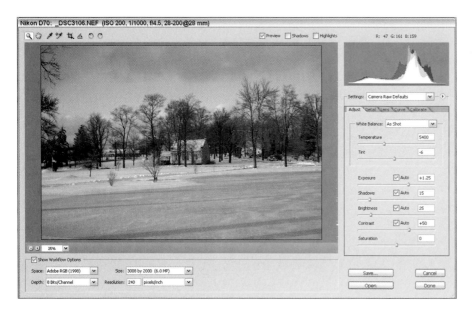

Figure 3.1 Photoshop's Camera RAW filter provides a wealth of options.

4. If necessary, rotate the preview image using the Rotate Preview buttons.

5. Zoom in and out using the Zoom tool.

6. Adjust the RGB levels using the Histogram and RGB Levels facilities.

7. Make other adjustments (described in more detail below).

8. Click on OK to load the image into Photoshop using the settings you've made.

Photoshop's Camera RAW plug-in lets you manipulate many of the settings you can control within your camera. I'm using the Nikon D70 as an example here. Your camera probably has similar RAW file settings that can be worked with. Here are some of the most common attributes you can change. This is an overview only. Check your Photoshop Help files for more detailed information on using these controls. I'll also be providing you with information on color correction, exposure compensation, saturation, and other parameters in later chapters of this book. I'll address these topics with respect to Photoshop CS, but the same concepts apply to the manipulations you can make within the Camera RAW plug-in.

- **Color Space.** It's possible your digital camera lets you choose from among several different color space profiles, such as Adobe RGB or sRGB. The RAW file will be saved by the camera using the camera's native color space. You can change to another color space using the Space drop-down list shown at lower left in Figure 3.1.

- **Depth.** Here you'll choose 8 bits or 16 bits per color channel. Photoshop CS 2.0 now supports more functions using 16-bit channels through its new High Dynamic Range (HDR) capabilities, so you might want to preserve the extra detail available with the 16-bit option if you plan on using HDR.

- **Pixel Size.** Usually, you'll choose to open the image at the same resolution at which it was recorded. If you plan to resample to a larger or smaller size, you might find that carrying out this step on the RAW file yields better results because of the new algorithm incorporated in this version of the plug-in.

- **Resolution.** This is the resolution that will be used to *print* the image. You can change the printing resolution to 300 or 600 pixels per inch (or some other value) to match your printer.

WHAT ARE 16-BIT CHANNELS?

You'll learn more about color depth later in this book, but you're probably already wondering about Photoshop CS's improved 16-bit features, which allow saving 16-bits of color information in the program's native PSD file format, and manipulating that information with layers, channels, and other tools. As you may know, a 24-bit full-color RGB image contains 8 bits of information for each of the red, green, and blue channels (8+8+8 bits=24 bits). A 24-bit image can include any of 256 colors for each of the RGB layers, and a total of 16.8 million possible colors for the entire image. However, many digital cameras and scanners are able to (theoretically, anyway) capture 16 bits of information per channel, resulting in 65,535 different colors each for red, green, and blue, and roughly 281 trillion possible colors in the image. (The actual number is 281,474,976,710,655, but who's counting?) As you might imagine, being able to work with such an extraordinary amount of colors seems like overkill, but serious Photoshop workers will find that this capability provides better control over colors in the darkest areas of the image, thanks to the expanded dynamic range. You'll learn more about this as we go along.

Photoshop CS 2.0 has five tabs of additional options (up from the four available with Photoshop CS 1.0). The most-often used settings are found on the Adjust tab shown in Figure 3.1. You'll learn more about how to use these settings, including working with histograms, later in this chapter.

- **White Balance.** You can change this to a value such as Daylight, Cloudy, Shade, Tungsten, Fluorescent, or Flash, or leave it at As Shot, which would be whatever white balance was set by your camera (either automatically or manually). If you like, you can set a custom white balance using the Temperature and Tint sliders.

- **Exposure.** This slider adjusts the overall brightness and darkness of the image. Watch the histogram display at the top of the column change as you make this adjustment, as well as those for the four sliders that follow.

- **Shadows.** This slider adjusts the shadows of your image. Adobe says this control is equivalent to using the black point slider in the Photoshop Levels command.

- **Brightness.** This slider adjusts the brightness and darkness image, similarly to the Exposure slider, except that the lightest and darkest areas are clipped off, based on your Exposure and Shadow settings, as you move the control.

- **Contrast.** This control manipulates the contrast of the midtones of your image. Adobe recommends using this control *after* setting the Exposure, Shadows, and Brightness.

- **Saturation.** Here you can manipulate the richness of the color, from zero saturation (gray, no color) at the −100 setting to double the usual saturation at the +100 setting.

The Detail tab has these controls, shown in Figure 3.2:

- **Sharpness.** This slider applies a type of unsharp masking using a sophisticated algorithm that takes into account the camera you're using, the ISO rating you used, and other factors. If you're planning on editing the image in Photoshop, Adobe recommends not applying sharpening to the RAW image.

Figure 3.2 The Detail tab lets you adjust sharpness and noise attributes of your image.

■ **Luminance Smoothing/Color Noise Reduction.** Both these sliders reduce the noise that often results from using higher ISO ratings. Each control works with a different kind of noise. Luminance noise is the noise caused by differences in brightness, whereas color noise results from variations in chroma. Because Photoshop CS 2.0 also has a powerful Reduce Noise filter, you might prefer to use the additional controls available with that module, rather than apply noise reduction here.

The Lens tab, shown in Figure 3.3, includes controls for adjusting chromatic aberration and vignetting. These options function the same as the Lens Correction filter discussed in Chapter 2.

Figure 3.3 The Lens tab has settings for technical lens corrections.

■ **Chromatic Aberration.** As you'll recall from Chapter 2, in digital photography, two kinds of chromatic aberration are possible. One variety is caused by the inability of a camera lens to focus all colors of light onto the same plane. Because the problem is caused by the lens, it can plague film photographers, too. Digital photographers have their own type of chromatic aberration, caused by the overload of oversaturated pixels that overflow their excess photons onto adjacent pixels, producing a purple fringing effect around backlight objects. You can fix some of these problems in the Camera RAW module, or choose to work with the Lens Correction filter within Photoshop itself.

■ **Vignetting.** This is generally the darkening of corners of the image, either because the lens is unable to provide even coverage of the entire image area, or because a lens hood is too small and is intruding on the image. Both effects can appear in film and digital images. You can fix them here, or work with the Lens Correction filter in Photoshop.

The Curve and Calibrate tabs, shown in Figures 3.4 and 3.5, let you make calibrations in the way the Camera RAW plug-in adjusts hues, saturation, or shadow tints. If you consistently find your images need some tonal adjustment, end up too red, blue, or green, or have a color cast in the shadows, you can make an adjustment here. You'll learn more about working with curves and adjusting colors later in this book, and the knowledge you pick up can be applied to these tabs.

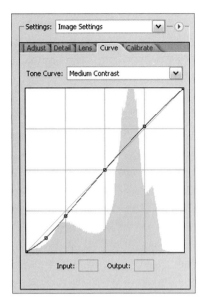

Figure 3.4 The Curve tab offers control of image tonal values.

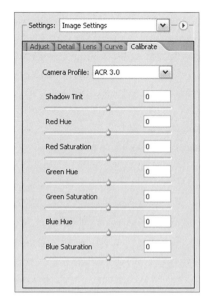

Figure 3.5 The Calibrate tab provides a way for calibrating the color corrections made in the Camera RAW plug-in.

Film Development Techniques

Some of the most interesting, and, unfortunately, permanent, visual special effects can be achieved by doing abusive things to your film during development, including exposing your latent images to light, boiling the film, overdeveloping it, or plunging it into icy cold water. Back when film was popular, these techniques found their way into many darkroom workers' repertoire. As you might guess, none of these processes are very forgiving. Developing the film a few seconds too long, exposing it to a bit too much light during processing, raising the temperature of the developer a few degrees too much, or any of a dozen other "errors" can change the results you get dramatically. After you've tried out the effects that follow, you'll wish you had Photoshop's Undo features available for conventional film processing.

Solarization

Solarization is a process which, like the reticulation technique discussed in the next section, started out as a disastrous error that some photographers soon adopted as a creative technique. Wildly popular as a means of adding a psychedelic look to photos of rock bands in the late '60s, solarization lives on as a creative tool in Photoshop. Adobe's flagship image editor offers several different ways to create solarization effects, and I'm going to show you all of them. But first, a little refresher for those who may have seen traditional solarization many times, but are a little uncertain on how it is achieved. You may be a little surprised.

First of all, what we usually call solarization isn't necessarily the same phenomenon as what was initially given the solarization tag at all. First discovered in the 19th century, solarization was originally a particular appearance caused by extreme overexposure, which reversed some tones of an image, such as the glare of the sun reflecting from a shiny object. No chicanery in the darkroom was required. In the 20th century, some photographers, including Ansel Adams and Man Ray, took advantage of this technique to produce some memorable pictures in which the brightest object in their images, the sun, appeared as a completely black disk. At the time those innovators worked, an exposure of five to ten times normal was required to create the solarization effect. Modern films are designed to resist solarization and require an exposure at least 10,000 times as strong to generate the effect, making overexposure solarization something of a rarity.

A somewhat different look, sometimes called the *Sabattier effect* to differentiate it from overexposure solarization, was discovered to occur when partially developed film or paper is exposed to light and then more completely developed. This happens frequently when a clumsy third party (or the chagrined photographer) accidentally turns on a light at the wrong time. The resulting image is part positive and part negative, an interesting mixture that gives it a psychedelic look. Color or black-and-white film as well as prints all can be solarized, but finding the right combination of development and "accidental" exposure is tricky and difficult to repeat. For that reason, in the conventional photography realm you'll most often see descriptions of how to solarize prints, because, if you spoil a print, you can easily make another and solarize it as well. However, the most striking solarization effects come from manipulating film, and that can get expensive very quickly. Fortunately, Photoshop lets you experiment to your heart's content, and takes all the error out of trial and error.

Using Photoshop's Solarize Filter

Follow these steps to solarize an image using Photoshop's Solarize filter. Start with the Clown Filter image from the website (**www.courseptr.com/downloads**). I chose this particular image, shown in Figure 3.6, because it has lots of bright, saturated colors that clearly demonstrate the effects of solarization.

1. Choose Layer > Duplicate layer to create a new layer to work with.

2. Next, select Filter > Stylize > Solarize. This filter is a single-step filter with no dialog box or settings to make.

3. You'll get a dark, murky image with some tones reversed. Immediately apply Image > Adjustments > Auto Levels to produce the more viewable picture shown in Figure 3.7.

Figure 3.6 This image has lots of bright colors, making it great for solarization effects.

Figure 3.7 This solarized image has its colors reversed.

4. The black background is still a little disconcerting, so you might want to use the Magic Wand selection tool to select the background, then click inside the black areas within the largest filter on the right side of the image, too. Then choose Image > Adjustments > Invert to convert the black background to white, as shown in Figure 3.8.

Figure 3.8 Inverting the colors produces a more viewable image like this one.

5. Although the Solarize filter doesn't have any controls, you can still customize your solarization. Choose Image > Adjustments > Hue/Saturation (or press Ctrl/Command + U) to produce the Hue/Saturation dialog box shown in Figure 3.9.

6. Move the Saturation slider to the right to increase the richness of the colors, according to your taste.

7. Move the Hue slider to the left or right to modify the colors to get an effect you like.

8. Click on OK to apply your changes.

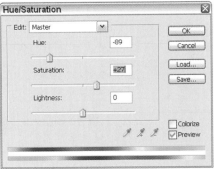

Figure 3.9 Use the Hue/Saturation dialog box to enrich the colors.

Using Photoshop's Curves to Solarize

This next section will show you a more flexible method of creating solarizations using Photoshop's Curves command, which allows you to manipulate the amount of each of the primary colors in an image based on the lightness or darkness of the tones. Because the traditional Sabattier effect affects the midtones of an image most strongly, manipulating Photoshop's Curves gives you much the same look with a lot more flexibility than the image editor's built-in Solarize filter. The best part of this technique is that you don't have to learn exactly how manipulations made to the color curves of an image produce a particular effect to use it. Because you're not trying to correct color but, instead, create new colors, feel free to play around. Just follow these steps, using the same Clown Filter image you worked with earlier.

1. Choose Layer > Duplicate again with the image you just worked with to create a new, fresh version to work on, while retaining the original in case you need to start over.

2. Select Image > Adjustments > Curves to produce the dialog box shown in Figure 3.10.

3. Grab a point on the left side of the curve in the graph preview and drag it upwards. Your image will become washed out, and the colors will start to change.

4. Drag other points on the curve up or down, creating a series of hills in the curve. You'll get a variety of effects, one of which is shown in Figure 3.11.

These steps operate on your image's red, green, and blue color layers at the same time. You can also select one color layer from the drop-down Channel list, and manipulate that color individually. Feel free to play around with the colors to get the exact solarization effect you like best.

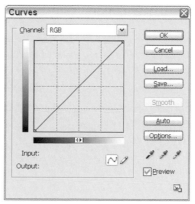

Figure 3.10 Photoshop's Curves dialog box lets you adjust tonal values for grayscale and color images.

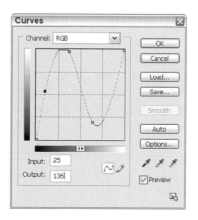

Figure 3.11 Create a series of hills and valleys to change the colors in a dramatic way.

WORKING WITH CURVES

Photoshop has three main ways of adjusting the tones of an image, and we'll use all of them in this chapter. The Brightness/Contrast dialog box lets you change an image globally, with no differences among the way the changes are applied to the highlights, midtones, and shadows. Use these controls only if you want to make some brightness or contrast adjustments in the worst way (because this *is* the worst way). The Levels command adds more control, allowing you to change the shadows, highlights, and midtones, separately. The Curves command, used next, goes all out and lets you change pixel values at any point along the brightness level continuum, giving you 256 locations at which you can make corrections.

You can see the Curves dialog box in Figure 3.10. The horizontal axis maps the brightness values as they are before you make any image corrections. The vertical axis maps the brightness values after correction. Each axis represents a continuum of 256 levels, divided into four parts by finely dotted lines. In Photoshop's default mode, the lower-left-hand corner represents 0,0 (pure black) and the upper-right-hand corner is 255,255 (pure white).

Whenever you open the window, the graph begins as a straight line, because unless changes are made, the input will be exactly the same as the output, a direct 1:1 correlation. As you change the shape of the curve, you adjust the values in the image at each point along the curve. If you haven't used Curves before, it's easier just to play with the curves to see what your manipulations do.

Reticulation

Reticulation is another one of those darkroom processes that can either ruin your film or generate some "I meant to do that"-style images. It results from rapid temperature changes during development. As you probably know, conventional photographic film consists of a silver-rich (and relatively soft) gelatin emulsion coated on a thin, but tough substrate such as polyester. When developing, black-and-white film is moved from a warm developer to a significantly cooler solution, the soft gelatin warps in strange-looking patterns, and the grain in the image increases dramatically. The result is an interesting texture that can be used as a creative tool.

Like solarization, reticulation effects are difficult to plan or duplicate. In the darkroom, a slow-working developer is used at, say, 100 degrees instead of the more usual 68 to 75 degrees, and its action is stopped by plunging the film into ice-cold water or acidic stopbath, prior to normal fixing and washing. Done properly, and with a bit of luck, you'll end up with some interesting film effects. With bad luck, you may end up with emulsion that slides right off your film substrate, as has happened to me a few times.

There's no such danger when using Photoshop to produce reticulation. While this effect is considered a black-and-white process (rapid changes in temperature ruin color film in ways that are rarely artistic), I'm going to show you a way to get the same look in full color. We're going to use an image called Tower, shown in Figure 3.12, which you'll find on the website. When you've loaded it into Photoshop, just follow these steps.

1. Create a duplicate layer of the tower image (Layer > Duplicate Layer), to give you a fresh canvas with which to work.

2. Choose Filter > Sketch > Reticulation to produce the Reticulation dialog box shown in Figure 3.13.

Figure 3.12 Start with this image to begin the reticulation process.

Figure 3.13 Change the Density, Foreground Level, and Background Level controls.

3. Change the Density slider to a value of 9, Foreground Level to 22, and Background Level to 22 (although you're free to experiment with different settings).

4. Click on OK to apply the filter. You'll find that the texture looks very much like real reticulation. If you'd like to see reticulation in color, you need to merge this reticulated black-and-white version with the original color image in the layer below.

5. To create a color reticulation, make sure the black-and-white reticulated layer is selected in the Layers Palette, then choose Color Dodge from the drop-down layer modes list at the left side of the palette, as shown in Figure 3.14. This merging mode allows the color of the underlying layer to show through, while retaining the reticulated texture of the layer on top.

6. Merge the two layers (Layer > Merge Layers or Ctrl/Command + E) to produce the finished image.

Figure 3.14 Use Color Dodge to merge the black-and-white reticulated image with the color image in the layer below.

Cross-Processing

Weird color effects, like those produced with cross-processing, are often used because they produce unusual and unique looks, until eventually the point is reached that everybody is using them and they're no longer novel. In the latter years of the last millennium so many images with cross-processing were used in advertising that I began to wonder if perhaps evil photo labs were at work trying to undermine our color perception. Now, more than five years later, the technique has fallen out of favor again, so I'm including it in this book in case you need a retro-punk look for an image you're working on.

Cross-processing is nothing more than a technique in which color film is processed in the wrong chemicals. For example, color negative film can be developed in solutions intended for color transparencies, yielding a dark blue-tinged positive image. Or, color slide film can be processed in color negative chemicals, creating an interesting negative image. Of course, the resulting negatives-cum-slides are much too dark to be used as slides, but they can be successfully reproduced in books and magazines. Likewise, the slides-cum-negatives lack the orange mask found in normal negative films, but still can be printed or reversed by a skilled darkroom technician. In both cases, the results are images with colors unlike any scenes found in nature or nightmare.

There are several methods for creating cross-processed images in Photoshop, but this is one of the easiest. Just follow these steps.

1. Open Cross Process from the website. The basic image looks like the one shown in Figure 3.15. It's a light image with bright skin tones, a combination that works well with Photoshop cross-processing techniques.

Figure 3.15 Start with this image.

2. Use Layer > Duplicate to create a copy of the background layer.

3. Choose Image > Adjustments > Curves to produce the dialog box shown in Figure 3.16.

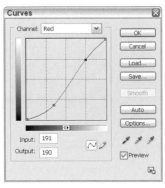

Figure 3.16 Adjust the Red channel first.

4. Select Red from the Channel drop-down list.

5. Click on the curve at the fourth vertical line from the left on the graph and drag to the position shown in the figure, making the Input and Output levels 191 and 190, respectively.

6. Click on the curve between the second and third vertical line and drag to the position shown. The Input and Output boxes should read about 82 and 46, respectively. This change gives the image a distinct cyan cast in the midtones.

7. Select Green from the Channel drop-down list.

8. Click on the curve at the positions shown on the third vertical lines from the left on the graph and drag to the positions shown in Figure 3.17, resulting in Input and Output figures of 125 and 127. Then drag a point on the fifth vertical line to positions that equal Input and Output values of 255, 203, respectively.

9. Select the Blue channel from the drop-down list.

10. Drag the point on the fifth vertical line down to the position shown in Figure 3.18, producing Input and Output figures of 255 and 162, respectively. Then drag a point between the second and third vertical lines upward to create Input and Output values of about 94 and 109.

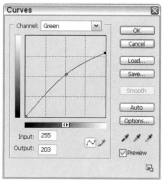

Figure 3.17 Adjust the Green channel next.

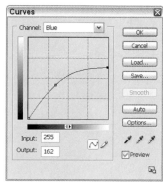

Figure 3.18 Finally, adjust the Blue channel.

11. Click on OK to apply the changes.

12. Next, choose Image > Apply Image, and select Hard Light from the Blending Mode drop-down list.

13. Set Opacity to 50%, as shown in Figure 3.19, and then click on OK to apply the change.

14. Use Image > Adjustments > Brightness/Contrast to lighten the image a little more and add some contrast, according to your taste. The final image will look something like Figure 3.20.

Figure 3.19 Select Hard Light to blend the image.

Figure 3.20 The final image will look like this.

High-Contrast Images

Many years ago, some well-meaning soul discovered that super-high-contrast images had an interesting, minimalist look that stripped images down to their bare bones. Andy Warhol, although not best known as a photographer, used this effect in his work, including his famous Marilyn Monroe series. Indeed, high contrast images are easy to achieve simply by using lithographic films intended for reproducing line art.

Litho films have a built in "threshold" that must be exceeded before an image is formed. That is, if a portion of an image is below the brightness threshold of the film, it won't register at all. If the portion of an image is above that threshold level, it is recorded as black. Figure 3.21 shows a black-and-white image at left, with a high-contrast version at right. While this example could have been produced using lithographic film, Photoshop lets you do much the same thing without resorting to special films and litho developers.

Figure 3.21 A normal black-and-white image (left) and a high-contrast version (right).

High-contrast images can be created in color or black and white, and can consist of just two or three tones (for example, black and white, or white and a color or two) or may encompass more tones to create a poster-like effect. The important thing to remember when choosing a subject for a high-contrast image is to make sure that the most important part of the subject matter has one of the lightest tones in an image. As the contrast is boosted, the dark tones and most midtone areas will become black, while the very lightest tones will remain white. If your key subject matter is too dark, it will turn black along with the other mid- and deep-tones and not be visible in your finished image.

You can easily create high-contrast images by manipulating Photoshop's brightness and contrast controls. Select Image > Adjustments > Brightness/Contrast, and then manipulate the brightness and contrast sliders to get the effect you want. The contrast control determines the number of different tones in the final image. A typical black-and-white image contains up to 256 different tones; moving the contrast slider to the right reduces that number gradually until, when it reaches 100%, you're left with only black and white. The brightness control adjusts the lightness of all the tones in an image, making the darkest tones brighter and the lightest tones gradually so bright they merge into white. Figure 3.22 shows a series of six versions of the same image, with the contrast set at 25%, 35%, 50% (top row), and 65%, 75%, 85% (bottom row). If you compare the individual images side by side, you can see how details are gradually lost as the increase in contrast moves them across the threshold boundary, and they change from gray to black or white.

In Figure 3.23 you can see the effect of adjusting the brightness control. The image at top left is the basic head shot at the 50% contrast level. The next three have brightness set for 25%, 50%, and 75%. Learn to use these controls to provide the exact look you want. Often, a 100% black/white image is not the best looking one.

Figure 3.22 Here are six versions of the same image with the contrast set at 25%, 35%, and 50% (top row), and 65%, 75%, 85% (bottom row).

Figure 3.23 Here, the brightness has been adjusted from 25 to 75%.

High Contrast with Levels

You can use Photoshop's Levels dialog box to give yourself a lot more control over your high-contrast image than the Brightness/Contrast controls alone. This can be especially important when you're working with a color image, as you can adjust the contrast of each of the three primary RGB colors separately.

The Levels dialog box, shown in Figure 3.24, provides a different way of adjusting brightness and contrast. The graph is called a histogram and is used to meas-

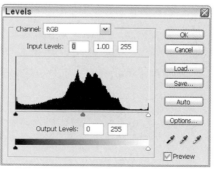

Figure 3.24 The Levels dialog box is used to adjust brightness and contrast using a histogram.

ure the numbers of pixels at each of 256 brightness levels. Each vertical line in the graph represents the number of pixels in the image for each brightness value, from 0 (black) on the left and 255 (white) on the right. The vertical axis measures that number of pixels at each level. There are three triangles at the bottom of the graph, representing the black point (darkest shadows), midtone point, and white point (the brightest highlights). How these are used will become clearer shortly.

This histogram shows that most of the pixels are concentrated in the center of the histogram, with relatively few very dark pixels (on the left) or very light pixels (on the right). If we wanted to make the best use of the available tones, we'd move the black triangle on the left to a point that better represents where the darkest pixels are in the image, and the white triangle on the right to a point that represents where the image actually contains some light pixels, as shown in the upper dialog box in Figure 3.25. The result would be a "better" image, producing a histogram more like the lower one shown in the figure. Notice that the tones are spread more evenly in the graph.

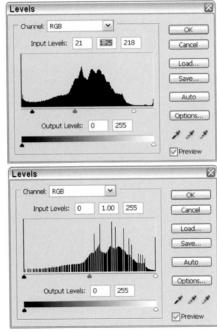

Figure 3.25 Adjusting the black, midtone, and white points distributes the tones more evenly.

Ah, but when working with high-contrast images, the concept of "better" differs slightly from the ideal. Instead, if we pulled the three triangles together, as shown in Figure 3.26, the brightest and darkest tones in the original image are ignored, and the emphasis is placed on a narrow range of midtones, producing the results you see. Move the white, midpoint, and black sliders to experiment with different effects. Concentrating them at the left side of the histogram produces a high-contrast, very light image, while bunching them up at the right side of the histogram produces a high-contrast, dark image, as you can see in Figures 3.27 and 3.28.

 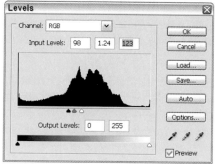

Figure 3.26 Clustering the black, midtone, and white point triangles together produces a high-contrast image.

 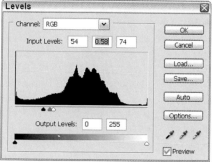

Figure 3.27 Clustering the points on the left side produces a high-contrast, light image.

 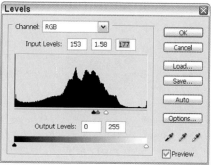

Figure 3.28 Clustering the points on the right side produces a high-contrast, dark image.

You can see that experimenting with the Levels controls can produce a wide variety of high-contrast results. You can even apply the level adjustments to each of the individual red, green, and blue color channels to create spectacular color effects even as you adjust the contrast.

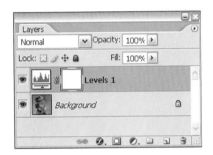

Figure 3.29 Access an Adjustment layer by clicking its icon in the Layer Palette.

WORKING WITH ADJUSTMENT LAYERS

For maximum flexibility, create an Adjustment Layer using Levels as the control (select Layer > New Adjustment Layer > Levels) to let you play with the levels without making any permanent changes in your image. The Adjustment Layer appears in the Layer Palette with a special icon, shown in Figure 3.29. You can access the layer's Levels dialog box at any time by double-clicking the icon. When you're satisfied with the result, flatten the image before saving to make the changes permanent. Adjustment Layers can be used with the Curves and Brightness/Contrast controls you've also used in this chapter.

High Contrast with Photoshop's Posterize Command

Photoshop's Posterize command can also be used to create high-contrast images. Its dialog box (accessed by choosing Image > Adjustments > Posterize) has only one parameter: You type in the number of different tones in your final image. In practice, once you include more than about 16, the image tends to look like an ordinary photograph. Figure 3.30 shows our clown rendered in 4, 8, 12, and 16 different levels.

Figure 3.30 Photoshop's Posterize command produces effects like these at 4, 8, 12, and 16 different levels of color.

Grainy Images

Film grain is an inescapable fact of life in conventional photography, as clumps of silver grain are roughly the equivalent of the pixel in digital imaging. Generally speaking, the larger the grains of silver in a film, the more sensitive that film is to light, and the better able it is to capture images in reduced lighting or with faster shutter speeds and/or smaller lens openings. In the never-ending quest to increase the exposure "speed" of films, grain has been a frequent byproduct. Given the "if you can't beat 'em, join 'em" attitude of photographers, grain itself has found a place as a creative tool. Grain can mask defects in a person's face and, like high contrast (which often goes hand-in-hand with grainy pictures) reduces an image to its bare essentials.

In conventional photography, extra grain can be produced in several different ways. You can use a faster, inherently grainier film, or underexpose your film and then use longer processing times to make the grains that were exposed (usually the largest, clumpiest grains) visible. Warm developer solutions or even "grainy" overlays used to add grain to an image as it is printed are other options.

Photoshop offers several different ways of creating grain effects. Figure 3.31 shows the dialog box for the Film Grain filter, which is available by choosing Filters > Artistic > Film grain, or from the Filter Gallery (Filter > Filter Gallery). All these filters work best with black-and-white images, as adding grain effects to color photos generally produces unnatural-looking results. You'll learn more about filters in Chapter 8.

Figure 3.31 The Film Grain filter is included in the Filter Gallery.

Film Grain

This filter has three slider controls. You can adjust the amount of Grain, the size of the Highlight area, and the Intensity of the highlights. The Grain setting controls the density of what appears to be random little black grains that are sprinkled throughout your image. The higher the value, the more details of your image obscured by the grain overlay. Since the Film Grain filter applies more grain to the highlights than to the shadows and midtones, the Highlight Area slider determines how many tones are considered highlights; at higher values, virtually the entire image is given the full treatment. The Intensity slider controls how strongly the grain is applied to the highlight areas.

Grain

While the Film Grain filter adjusts the amount of grain and how the granules are applied to highlights, the Grain plug-in works with contrast (the darkness of the grain in relation to the image area surrounding it) plus the shape of the granules. You can also control how much grain is added. The ten available types of grain cover several varieties often seen in photographs, plus some new ones that offer imaginative artistic effects. You can choose from regular, soft, sprinkles, clumped, contrasty, enlarged, stippled, horizontal, vertical, or speckle grain patterns. It's sometimes difficult to tell the difference between some of these effects. For example, the Stippled effect uses foreground and background colors to create grain, while Sprinkles uses just the foreground color.

WHY TWO GRAIN FILTERS?

Why does Photoshop include two filters called Film Grain and Grain, rather than one? In practice, each operates a little differently than the other, producing different effects, but we can thank the free enterprise system for their existence. Photoshop's current Film Grain filter was originally part of a third-party set of 16 compatible plug-ins called Aldus Gallery Effects, which sold for $199. These filters proved so successful that Aldus Corporation followed up with a second set of 16, which included the slightly different Grain filter. Soon after Aldus released the third Gallery Effects library, Adobe acquired the company (adding PageMaker to its product line along with Gallery Effects). The filters were sold by Adobe for a time, but disappeared as a separate product when they were folded into Photoshop 4.0.

Add Noise

The Add Noise filter (Filter > Noise > Add Noise) has one slider, a pair of radio buttons, and a checkbox. You can select an Amount from 1 to 999 (the default value is 32). This value is used to determine how much the random colors added to the selection will vary from the color that is already present (or from the gray tones, if you're working with a monochrome image).

Choose either Uniform or Gaussian distribution of the noise. Uniform distribution uses random numbers in the range from 0 to the number you specified with the Amount slider. The random number is then added to the color value of the pixel to arrive at the noise amount for that pixel. Gaussian distribution uses a bell-shaped curve calculated from the values of the pixels in the selected area, producing a more pronounced speckling effect.

Mark the Monochromatic box to apply the noise only to the brightness/darkness elements of the image without modifying the colors themselves. This can reduce the "color specks" effect that often results from applying noise to a color image.

Mezzotint

The Mezzotint filter (Filter > Pixelate > Mezzotint) is another technique borrowed from traditional printing, in which a special overlay is placed on top of a photograph to add a pattern during duplication. Digital filters offer much the same effect with a little less flexibility, since the range of mezzotints you can achieve with Photoshop is fairly limited. Only dots (fine, medium, grainy, or coarse), lines, or strokes (in short, medium, and long varieties) can be applied. You can rotate your image, apply this filter, and then rotate it back to the original orientation if you want to change the direction of the lines or strokes.

Figure 3.32 shows examples of grain effects produced by the Film Grain, Grain, Add Noise, and Mezzotint filters.

Diffuse Glow

My favorite of all Photoshop's "grain" effects is the Diffuse Glow filter, which can produce a radiant luminescence in any image. The glow seems to suffuse from the subject and fill the picture with a wonderful luster, while softening harsh details. It's great for romantic portraits, or for lending a fantasy air to landscapes. Diffuse Glow works equally well with color and black-and-white images, using the dialog box controls shown in Figure 3.33.

You can get a variety of effects by manipulating the filter's controls, such as the examples shown in Figure 3.34. The Graininess slider adds or reduces the amount of grain applied to an image. A large amount obscures unwanted detail and adds to the dreamy look of the image. The Glow Amount control adjusts the strength of the glow, as if you were turning up the voltage on a light source. The higher the

Figure 3.32 Various film grain effects. In the top row (left to right), the original image; Film Grain filter with Grain, Highlight Area, and Intensity all set to values of 5; Film Grain filter with settings of 10, 5, and 7. In the bottom row (left to right), Grain filter set to Speckle; Add Noise filter; and Mezzotint filter in Fine Dots mode, then faded to reduce the effect slightly.

Figure 3.33 The Diffuse Glow dialog box lets you control the amount of Grain, Glow, and Clear areas in your image.

setting, the more glow is spread throughout your picture. The Clear Amount slider controls the size of the area in the image that is not affected by the glow. You can use this control with the Glow Amount slider to simultaneously specify how strong a glow effect is produced, as well as how much of the image is illuminated by it. The current background color becomes the color of the glow. That's an important point. Beginners sometimes forget this, and then wonder why their glow effect looks weird. If you want a glowing white effect, make sure the background color is white. Anything else will tint your image. You can use this feature to good advantage, by selecting background colors with a very slight tint of yellow, gold, or red to add a sunny or warm glow to your image.

In the examples, the portrait in the upper right has the Graininess control set to 5, the Glow Amount control set to 10, and the Clear amount set to 20. At lower

Figure 3.34 The original photo (top left) with three variations on the Diffuse Glow filter.

left the diffusion is less obvious, and the contrast not quite as high, producing a romantic fuzziness that doesn't take over the entire picture. I used Graininess, Glow amount, and Clear amount settings of 1, 4, and 12, respectively. Finally, for the example in the lower right I concentrated the attention on the model's eyes by using settings of 7, 10, and 15, and then merged the layer with a copy of the original, unmodified layer, using the Layer palette's Merge drop-down list set to Lighten. In that mode, Photoshop looks at each pixel in the two layers and uses the lightest pixel for the final image. The resulting picture is very washed out and grainy with an interesting high-contrast appearance.

Black-and-White Infrared Film

The look of black-and-white infrared films is not a darkroom effect but, instead, is a result of using, in conventional situations, specialized films that are intended to capture a bit of the infrared spectrum along with the normal visible light. Despite the common misconception, widely used infrared films don't image "heat" as we think of it. Instead, they are simply more sensitive to light that's even redder than the reds we capture with ordinary films, light in the near infrared portion of the spectrum.

Because infrared films see light that the unaided eye cannot, these pictures look quite a bit different from a standard black-and-white image. Anything that reflects infrared illumination especially well, such as clouds, foliage, or human skin appears much lighter than it does to the naked eye. Subjects that absorb infrared, such as the sky, appear much darker than normal. You can't predict ahead of time what an infrared photo will look like (because the image is affected by light you can't see), so these pictures are often surprising and mysterious looking.

Infrared film is difficult to use, too. Light meters don't accurately measure the amount of infrared light, so exposures may vary quite a bit from your meter reading. You should bracket exposures on either side of the "correct" reading to increase your odds of getting a good picture. Infrared film must be loaded and handled in total darkness, too, and your fancy new autofocus lens might not focus properly with infrared film. Fortunately, faking an infrared photo with Photoshop is simple to do.

Use the infrared.pcx photo (or another color photo of your choosing) from the website . Photoshop needs to see the various colors in the image, just as an infrared film or digital camera recording with an infrared filter attached does, so you must start with a color picture. Just follow these steps.

1. First, select the sky area of the image. Press Q to enter Quick Mask mode, and paint around the sky area with a soft brush, as shown in Figure 3.35. Use a small brush to paint the edges of the selection around the castle and trees.

Figure 3.35 First, paint around the sky area in Quick Mask mode to select it.

2. Press Q again to exit Quick Mask mode, then press Ctrl/Command + C to copy the sky. Then press Ctrl/Command + V to paste it down in its own layer. Double-click the layer to activate Photoshop's renaming mode, and name the layer Sky.

3. Press Ctrl/Command + S and save the file as infrared.psd to preserve your work so far.

4. Double-click the background layer and name it Castle.

5. Choose Layer > New Adjustment Layer > Channel Mixer, and click on OK when the New Layer dialog box appears. The Channel Mixer dialog box should pop up, as shown in Figure 3.36.

Figure 3.36 Use the Channel Mixer to apply an infrared look to the greens of the image.

6. To mimic the infrared effect, we want everything that appears as green in the image to appear much lighter than normal (because living foliage reflects a lot of infrared light), but in black and white. Click on the Monochrome button to apply the changes we're going to make to a grayscale version of the layer.

7. Lighten the green portion of the image by boosting the Green channel to 200 percent (the maximum allowed by Photoshop). Move the Green slider all the way to the right.

8. Reduce the amount of red by moving the Red slider to the left, to about −80%. Click on OK to apply the change. The image will now look like the one shown in Figure 3.37.

Figure 3.37 After adjusting the Red and Green channels the image will look like this.

9. Click on the Sky layer and Choose Layer > New Adjustment Layer > Channel Mixer to create an adjustment layer for the sky.

10. Move the Red slider to the right, to about 90%, and then click on OK to apply the change.

11. Save the image with the adjustment layers intact. You can reload the image at any time and make further modifications with the adjustment layers.

12. Flatten the image and save it under a new name. Figure 3.38 shows a comparison of the original image converted to grayscale, and our "fake" infrared image.

Figure 3.38 Darken the sky to complete the faux-infrared look.

Color Infrared Film

If you have some genuine digital infrared photos to work with, Photoshop can turn them into stunning false-color images. The technique known as channel swapping can give a basic infrared picture an interesting other-worldly look.

First you need a digital infrared image to work with. This is an image editing book and not a photography techniques tome, so I'll provide only the basics. You can find more complete discussions of how to take infrared photos in my books *Mastering Digital Photography* and *Mastering Digital SLR Photography.*

To take the original photo, you'll need a camera that can "see" infrared (take a picture of your TV remote control in action to see if a dot shows up from the sending end), and a filter that blocks visible light and passes infrared, such as the Hoya R72. Mount your camera on a tripod, because infrared photos may need exposures well below 1/30th second, and venturing into the multi-second range (that makes non-moving landscape subjects your best bet). You'll also want to set the white balance control of your digital camera manually, preferably using an expanse of grass as your "neutral." With any luck, you'll end up with an infrared photo like the one shown in Figure 3.39.

Figure 3.39 An unprocessed infrared photo looks like this.

Load the photo into Photoshop (you'll find IR Landscape on the website) and follow these steps:

1. Choose Image > Adjustments > Autolevels. The image will now look like the one in Figure 3.40, which is interesting in its own right.

2. Next, choose Image > Adjustments > Channel Mixer. With the Red output channel selected, you'll see that the Red slider is set at 100% and the Green and Blue sliders are both at 0%, as shown in Figure 3.41.

3. Set the Red slider's value to 0% and the Blue slider's value to 100%.

4. Choose Blue Output Channel, and set the Red slider to 100% and the Blue slider to 0%. In effect, you've swapped the red and blue channels and left the green channel untouched, as you can see in Figure 3.42.

5. Click OK to apply the change.

6. Choose Image > Adjustments >Hue/Saturation.

7. In the Edit box choose the Green channel.

Figure 3.40 Autolevels adjustment transforms the photo into this version.

Figure 3.41 Swap the blue channel for the red channel.

8. Slide the Saturation slider to 0 and click OK. Desaturating the green channel often improves some color infrared shots, but your results will vary. Your final image will look like Figure 3.43.

Figure 3.42 Swap the red channel for the blue channel.

Figure 3.43 Your results will look like this.

Printing Techniques

The fun doesn't stop when the film is developed and hanging from clothespins. There are many different things in the darkroom that you can do to your images while they are being printed. Those of us who rely on digital output hardcopies can still enjoy the pleasure of fine-tuning pictures in the digital darkroom. Here are a few techniques to work with.

Dodging/Burning

Color and black-and-white prints are traditionally made using an enlarger, which casts an image of the film onto a photosensitive sheet of paper for a carefully calculated number of seconds. For about as long as photographers have been making prints, they have also been sticking their fingers, hands, or other objects in the light path to reduce the relative exposure of one part of an image (dodging) while increasing it in another (burning). The result is an image in which the light and dark tones are more evenly balanced or, in some cases, deliberately changed to provide a different appearance (as with vignetting, discussed next).

Cupped hands with a gap between them are often used to burn parts of an image. The darkroom worker is able to keep the hands moving, varying the size and position of the opening, to blend the burned areas with their surroundings. A hand can also be used to hold back or dodge part of an image, but it's more common to use a homemade dodging tool (such as a piece of cardboard fastened to a length of coat hanger wire) so the adjustment can be made only to a portion of the image in the center portions.

Because the image being exposed on the paper is visible, and the length of the overall exposure known, the printer is able to adjust the tones quite precisely. For example, with a 60-second exposure, a portion of the image that needs to be lightened or darkened can be dodged or burned in roughly 5 or 10 second increments by viewing the enlarger's timer while working. The amount of dodging or burning required comes from experience, usually gained by redoing a print that hasn't been manipulated properly.

It also was widely believed that some small changes could be made in black-and-white prints by fiddling with the paper development, usually by controlling how the paper went into the developer, by rubbing portions of the paper with the fingers (to generate heat and "faster" development of that portion), as well as through mystical incantations and applications of alchemicals like ferricyanide.

Today, you can do the same magic with Photoshop. You can use the image editor's built-in dodging and burning tools, or create a selection mask and adjust the brightness using controls like Brightness/Contrast. Open the file lighthouse.pcx from the website and follow these steps. The original image looks like Figure 3.44.

1. Use Layer > Duplicate Layer to create a copy of the background layer.

2. Choose the Burn tool from the Tool Palette, and make the following adjustments in the Options bar: Choose a 65-pixel soft brush, set the Range drop-down list to Highlights, and set the Exposure slider to 15%. This will let you darken the brick wall in front of the lighthouse gradually by painting carefully. The low exposure setting means the changes won't be dramatic, and by choosing Highlights as the range, your darkening will be applied mostly to the lightest areas of the wall. Figure 3.45 shows how your screen will look before you start burning, while in Figure 3.46 you can see the results you can expect.

3. You can also darken by painting a selection mask in Quick Mask mode and using Photoshop's Levels or Brightness/Contrast controls on the selected portion. Press Q to enter Quick Mask mode and paint the left side of the lighthouse.

4. Press Q again to exit Quick Mask Mode.

Figure 3.44 The original lighthouse photo looks like this.

Figure 3.45 Darken the wall in front of the lighthouse with the Burn tool.

5. Choose Image > Adjustments > Brightness/Contrast and adjust the sliders to darken the left side of the lighthouse. Don't move the brightness slider too far to the left, or you'll eliminate the dramatic lighting entirely. We just want to reduce the excessive contrast. I used a value of −17 percent.

6. Use the Dodge tool to lighten the front face of the lighthouse, producing the result you see in Figure 3.47 at right. The original image is shown at left.

Figure 3.46 After burning, the wall will look like this.

Figure 3.47 After the walls of the lighthouse have been dodged and burned, the image should resemble the one at right. The original is shown at left for comparison.

Vignetting Revisited

Here's a quickie. Vignetting, in which the corners and edges of an image are significantly darker than the center, can be produced in a number of ways outside the darkroom. A lens hood that is too small for the field of view of the lens it is used with can produce a vignette effect unintentionally. The same thing can happen if your lens doesn't fully cover the image area. The photographer can shoot through a hole or other aperture to create a vignette, too. Or, you can dodge the image while it's being printed to achieve the same end. Photoshop is as good an option as any, and better than most, especially if you want a fine degree of control over your vignettes.

There are two ways to create a vignette in Photoshop, and I showed you one way in Chapter 2, using the Lens Correction filter. If you want more control over the size and shape of your vignette, you'll want to try this alternate method. Just use the Quick Mask tool to paint a selection mask, and then use the Brightness/Darkness controls to darken the edges. However, you'll get a more regular, feathered mask if you use the following technique:

1. Use the file ghouly from the website, or work with a photo of your own.

2. Select the Elliptical Marquee tool and drag an oval selection like the one shown in Figure 3.48.

3. Invert the selection by pressing Shift + Ctrl/Command + I.

4. Choose Select > Feather (or press Alt/Option + Ctrl/Command + D), and type in 80 as the pixel value for feathering your selection.

5. Create vignette by filling the selection with black, as shown in Figure 3.49.

Figure 3.48 First, drag a selection oval to outline the vignette boundaries.

Figure 3.49 After feathering the selection, fill it to create the vignette look.

Sepia Toning

In one sense, color photography predated black-and-white photography by a number of years. Early photographic processes like the daguerreotype all had sepia or bluish tinges to them. It took a while before truly color-neutral black-and-white photography became possible. We still equate sepia toning with old-timey photography. Who hasn't donned Civil War attire to pose for a family portrait reproduced in rich browns and light tans? While in modern times it's been necessary to use special toning solutions in the darkroom to achieve a warm sepia look, Photoshop can do the same thing with very little trouble. Try out the effect using the image sepia.pcx from the website, or use your own photo. Just follow these steps.

1. Start with a black-and-white image, like the one shown in Figure 3.50.

Figure 3.50 Start with a black-and-white image, convert it to color, and then use Photoshop's Hue/Saturation controls to add a tone.

2. Convert the image to color using Image > Mode > RGB Color.

3. Choose Image > Adjustments > Hue/Saturation, or press Ctrl/Command + U to produce the Hue/Saturation dialog box.

4. Click the Colorize button, and then move the Hue slider to the 20 position for a sepia tone, or any other position on the scale for a blue, green, or yellow tone, as you prefer.

5. Move the Saturation slider to enrich or mute the tone. Click on OK to apply the toning effect.

6. Use Photoshop's Brightness/Contrast controls to give the image a somewhat washed-out, old-timey look if you like. The finished photo should resemble Figure 3.51.

Figure 3.51 Finish the effect with some extra contrast to give the photo an old-timey look.

You can also get a toned effect using Photoshop's Duotone feature.

1. While in Grayscale mode, choose Image > Mode > Duotone.

2. When the Duotone Options dialog box pops up, choose Duotone from the Type drop-down list.

3. Click the colored box next to Ink 2 to select a custom color for the second shade.

4. Click the spectrum in the center of the Custom Colors dialog box to choose a particular color range, then click on the exact color swatch you want from the patches on the left side of the dialog box, as shown in Figure 3.52.

5. Click on OK twice to apply the duotone.

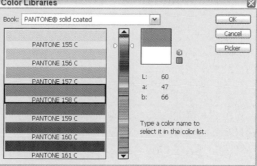

Figure 3.52 Duotones are another way of creating an interesting toned look.

Automatically Crop and Straighten Photos

Photoshop CS added a great automation tool called Crop and Straighten, which can be a lifesaver if you capture a photo with your scanner and then discover that the picture wasn't squarely lined up on the scanner bed. You can also use this tool to fix digital photos you might have taken with the camera held askew. This one's so easy that I'll simply provide a list of the steps to carry out. There are no dialog boxes to mess with, or any other parameters to choose. Just follow these steps:

1. Load the image you want to realign into Photoshop. I used the portrait shown at left in Figure 3.53. The feature works best with images that have clearly defined horizontal and vertical lines at the edges.

2. Use Image > Canvas Size and add some space around the photo to give Photoshop some working room.

3. Choose File > Automate > Crop and Straighten Photos. Photoshop rotates your image to straighten it, then crops around the vertical and horizontal borders it used to align the image. What could be simpler?

Figure 3.53 At left, a slightly skewed photograph. At right, Photoshop CS has straightened the image out and cropped it to fit.

Next Up

Retouching is another time-honored photographic endeavor that's part art and part craft. Photoshop gives all of us a fighting chance to do some decent retouching, as you'll learn in the next chapter.

4

Secrets of Retouching

Retouching is the digital equivalent of plastic surgery and Botox, except the results look more natural and life-like. For many of us, our first exposure to photo retouching came in high school, when we exchanged wallet-sized senior portraits with friends and noticed that none of our classmates looked anything like their pictures. Once adolescence passes, the only time you may give any serious thought to the topic of retouching is when you see your passport picture or drivers' license, or enlarge one of your prize photos up to 11 × 14 or larger and see that tiny dust spots that weren't apparent at 5 × 7 now appear as big as boulders. Any of these events can cause you to stop and say, "Can't we do something about this?"

With Photoshop, you can. Retouching is a common technique now, and one that's become particularly easy with Photoshop CS 2.0, which has some new tools to help you. Indeed, manipulating photos has become so simple that "photoshopped" (lowercase) has become *au currant* as a verb, much to the dismay of Adobe's trademark department. Anyone can transform their photos into something that more closely resembles what we'd like to think of as reality, and I'll provide you with some tips in the next two chapters.

To simplify things, I'm going to divide what you may think of as retouching into two parts, to account for two very different kinds of picture-manipulation procedures. This chapter will deal with methods for correcting defects in an image, such as eliminating dust or other artifacts, fixing small problems with your subject matter, or adjusting minor tonal variations. More dramatic manipulations, as when you add entire objects or people, combine two images to create one, or make other major changes will wait for the next chapter, "Combining Images with Compositing."

The easiest way to understand the difference is to think of your Aunt Mary. If you use Photoshop to reduce the wrinkles around Aunt Mary's eyes, touch up her hair a little, and change her skin color from a ghastly pale to a more healthy-looking ruddy glow, that's retouching. If your improvements to Aunt Mary's appearance involve replacing her head with that of Cameron Diaz, that's compositing.

Should you want to learn more about retouching (and compositing), check out my book *Digital Retouching and Compositing: Photographers' Guide* (ISBN: 1932094199), also from Course Technology. When I finished writing the first edition of *Photoshop CS: Photographers' Guide*, I realized that most of the individual sections in this chapter and the next one could be expanded into entire chapters of their own in a more specialized treatment of image manipulation. So that's what I did. However, I think you'll find plenty of food for thought right here.

Retouching, the Old Way

Even in the pre-Photoshop, manual labor era, retouching was a lot more common than you might think. The end product of advertising photography—ads and commercials—involves millions of dollars in media fees, so a few thousand dollars for retouching is small change. An art director might have sketched a layout on a piece of translucent media that was then placed on the focus screen of a large format camera and subsequently used by the photographer to arrange the subjects just so. Then, the finished transparency (or, more likely, a duplicate of it) might be painstakingly retouched with dyes so the colors are perfect and to remove every small defect. It's not an exaggeration to say that every important advertising still image you've seen has been retouched in some way.

Retouching has also been common in portraiture, because few faces are perfect, and even visages that *are* perfect don't necessarily photograph that way. Retouching is a convenient way to touch up portraits without resorting to irreversible camera techniques, such as using detail-obscuring filters or other tricks.

Another kind of retouching, called "spotting," is used to touch up the inevitable dust spots and other artifacts that appear in enlargements, particularly those made from small negatives. Any time you make a print larger than 5 × 7 of, say, a 35mm negative, tiny spots that weren't invisible on the original film will loom as huge as Godzilla when blown up ten times or more. It's always a good idea to clean your film before printing it, but there's a cleanliness point of diminishing returns after which a few seconds with a spotting brush or pen can fix things quickly.

Until retouching at all professional levels went completely digital, three types of photographic media were commonly retouched: negative film, transparencies, and prints. Here's a brief description of each of these procedures. I'm including more detail than you really need to know to demonstrate just how technically demanding old-fashioned retouching can be. You'll appreciate the magic of Photoshop all the more.

Retouching Negatives

With negative film, it makes sense to retouch the original before you make prints, because all the changes will be reflected in each of the resulting prints. Black-and-white negatives, because they consist of a single image layer, can be retouched using etching knives, reducing chemicals and bleaches, as well as pigments. Color negatives consist of separate layers for each color of the image, so those remedies are not practical. However, color negs can be retouched with colored dyes, black lead, colored pencils, or a combination of dyes and pencils. Because color negatives have an overall orange or red tint to them (masks which optimize color reproduction), and all negatives have their colors and tones reversed, retouchers often must make a proof print to use as a guideline. Even experienced retouchers may have to view a color negative through different colored filters to evaluate areas being retouched. I can't emphasize how much skill negative retouching requires. For example, to correct prominent veins in a portrait, the retoucher has to learn to look for yellow-orange lines on the subject's face, and obscure them with cyan dye or blue pencil, because clear areas on negatives represent shadows, dark areas represent highlights, and colors are reversed.

Retouching Transparencies

Color transparencies ("chromes," as the pros refer to them) are a little easier to retouch, because the image looks more like the subject it is supposed to represent. Chromes can be retouched using bleaches, dyes, or both (although when using both, the bleaching needs to be done first). It's possible to use selective bleaching to remove one color at a time (there are special bleaches for each color). Overall bleaching reduces each of the three colors in an image by an equal amount, and total bleaching removes all the colors in an area. Bleached areas can even be partially restored ("regenerated" is the term), which makes the process a little forgiving. Cyan, magenta, and yellow dyes can be used to retouch transparencies, too. Special dyes that match the original transparency dyes both visually and when the chrome is reproduced must be used. In days of yore there were additional hair-raising retouching techniques that involved major surgery on the transparency (quite literally) using cutting knives and butting portions of the transparency together.

Retouching Prints

Color and black-and-white prints can be retouched, and often are, if the original negative is too small for the detailed work that must be done. Dyes, pencils, airbrushes, or any other way of applying tone can be used for retouching prints. If a pigment will stick to paper, it's probably been used to retouch prints.

Retouching has always involved a great deal of artistic skill as the retoucher painted or drew changes on the film or paper, and the training required to achieve that skill could easily be as extensive as for any other area of photography. Photoshop doesn't eliminate the need for artistic skill, but it does make any retouching change you make more easily reversible. So, even those of us whose sketches look like we had the pencil taped to our elbows can spend as much time as we need to make our images look their best.

Retouching, the New Way

Today, virtually all the retouched images you see reproduced in advertising and magazines have been manipulated digitally. Indeed, Photoshop has become the tool of choice for virtually all retouching. The most common application for traditional retouching skills today is in the field of hand-coloring, using the venerable Marshall's Photo Coloring System of pigments, photo oils, spot colors, retouch pencils, and other products. However, Photoshop is becoming a mainstay in that arena, too.

I'm going to show you some of the most common applications for retouching, and then take you through a typical project. Most images will require more than one type of retouching, so fixing several problems with a single photo is a more realistic way of demonstrating these techniques. Let's look at the most common problems first, before moving on to the solutions. I'll use two different photos to give you a broader experience.

Figure 4.1 shows the high-school senior portrait I took of my middle son (prior to his blue hair period). This is the unretouched version, and while it might look okay to you thanks to the inevitable loss of detail wrought by the offset printing process, there were lots of things that needed to be done to it before it was ready to be framed and set on the mantel.

Figure 4.1 This basic portrait has plenty of room for improvement.

Dust Spots

Even the most carefully printed photos will always have a few white dust spots that need touching up. If you then digitize your print using a scanner, you'll probably pick up a few dust spots from the scanner bed's glass, as well. Scanned transparencies will show black spots instead of white. The dust is actually the same color in both cases, and varies only because the image is captured by reflected light in the former case, and transmitted light in the latter. Digital cameras are not immune to "dust" spots, either. You may pick up artifacts in your digital image from a defect in your camera's sensor or other mysterious electronic phenomena. Figure 4.2 shows a close-up of the portrait with lots of dust showing. You probably won't have to eliminate quite so much dust, but dust spots are quite common, and have to be dealt with.

Figure 4.2 Your photos probably won't be this dusty, but some photos are.

Double Catchlights

Photographers know that catchlights in the eyes are the key to making a portrait subject look alive and vibrant. It's the moisture on the cornea catching reflections from the lights that give eyes their sparkle. Without catchlights, even a smiling portrait looks wooden and unrealistic. We may not even know what's wrong until it's pointed out to us. Figure 4.3 shows our portrait with the catchlights removed. Compare it with Figure 4.4, and you'll see what I mean.

The original photo does have catchlights. The problem is it has too many of them, as you can see in Figure 4.4. Although the portrait is an informal one, it was shot in a studio, and if you look closely, you can probably make out the outlines of the two umbrella reflectors I used to light the picture. You'll see quite a few octagonal photo umbrellas reflected in the eyes of portrait subjects as catchlights. Sometimes the reflections are used as a creative element, showing up as a glamorous studio-oriented element in the lenses of wrap-around sunglasses.

In theory, we're most accustomed to seeing square, window-shaped catchlights in eyes, but, in practice, the round catchlights aren't especially distracting. Two catchlights do look

Figure 4.3 No catchlights at all mean dead-looking eyes and a dull appearance.

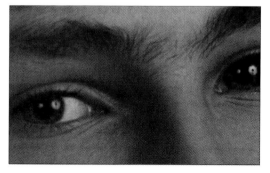

Figure 4.4 Dual catchlights are almost as bad as none at all.

wrong, however, so if you have a pair this obvious in your own photos, you'll want to learn how to remove them during digital retouching.

Other Defects

Other common defects in photographs that are susceptible to retouching include skin blemishes (in portraits), areas that are too dark or too light, and objects that need to be removed. Many photos have many or all of these. Indeed, it's common to mark up a proof print with a grease pencil, as shown in Figure 4.5, so the retoucher will know exactly what needs to be done.

The finished, retouched portrait looks like Figure 4.6, with all the suggested fixes applied. It's not perfect (I still wish I'd used a touch of a hair light and some background lighting when I took the picture), but it's a great improvement.

Figure 4.5 You may want to mark up a proof print to make sure you don't miss any areas that need retouching.

Figure 4.6 After retouching, the portrait looks like this.

MARKING UP DIGITAL IMAGES

You don't need a grease pencil to mark up your digital images. If your photograph was taken with a digital camera or already has been scanned, you can use Photoshop's layers and annotation features to mark up your image. Press N to select the Annotation tool in the Toolbar, click in an area you'd like to comment about, and type your comments. You can collapse a comment down to a sticky-note icon when you don't need to view it. Choose different color notes for the various meddlers working with the photo. Should your instructions be *really* complicated, Photoshop includes an audio annotation feature. If you need to "draw" directly on the image, say, to mark cropping, create a new empty layer and draw on that. Make the layer invisible when you no longer need to view the instructions on the comment layer. Figure 4.7 shows a typical marked up digital image.

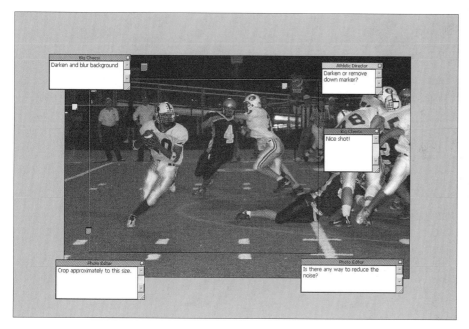

Figure 4.7 Digital images can be marked up, too, using Photoshop's annotation features.

Tackling a Retouching Project

I'm going to show you how to retouch a typical picture using a different photograph, which is included on the website at **http://www.courseptr.com**. You can use my image, Mardi Gras, or one of your own, if you like. You'll be spotting dust, removing objects, and performing other retouching magic in no time. But first, learn how to save yourself some time.

Avoiding Retouching

The best martial arts choreographer and philosopher of my generation, Li Xiaolong, espoused the "art of fighting without fighting." Bruce Lee's approach works equally well in the photographic realm. The most effective way to retouch an image is to avoid the need for it in the first place. Here are some tips to help you minimize your retouching efforts.

- **Work with "clean" images.** Use your digital camera's best resolution and optimum ISO speed setting to produce images with the least amount of noise and artifacts that will need to be cleaned up. If you're working from conventional photographic images, use a lab that won't add dust to your negs or slides. If you have your lab convert your images to digital format, let them do the scan on the first visit, before your film has had a chance to pick up dust and dirt. If you scan your images yourself, clean off the print or film before scanning, and make sure your scanner glass is clean.

- **Watch your lighting when you take a photo.** High contrast lighting accentuates defects in your subject, as does light that comes from the side. You may not always want to use soft, front lighting for your images, because of creative reasons, but keep in mind that high contrast effects can mean extra retouching later.

- **Check out your background and other parts of the picture before you shoot.** One of the most frequent needs for retouching arises from "mergers" where a tree or some other object appears to, say, grow out of the top of someone's head.

- **Double-check your composition.** If you have everything arranged the way you want, you won't need to move things around in Photoshop.

Many of the things we'll work on with our Mardi Gras picture could have been avoided if the photographer hadn't been looking specifically for a bad photo to use as a "before" picture for this book. The original image is shown in Figure 4.8. There is an entire panoply of things to fix in this picture, most of them easily discerned by the unaided eye. We'll tackle them one at a time.

Figure 4.8 A bad background is only one of the problems with this photo.

Cropping

The first thing to do is crop the photo a little better to remove some of the extraneous stuff at all four sides of the photo. While you can simply make a rectangular selection with the Rectangular Marquee tool, and then choose Image > Crop, there's a better, more flexible way. Just follow these steps.

1. Choose the Crop tool from the Tool Palette (or press C to switch to it).

2. Place the cursor in one corner in the image where you'd like to start cropping, and drag to the opposite corner. When you release the mouse button, a selection rectangle with handles in each of the four corners and midpoints of the selection lines appears, as you can see in Figure 4.9. The area outside the rectangle is darkened to make it easier to see what your composition will look like cropped.

3. To fine-tune your cropping, drag the handles in any direction to enlarge or reduce the size of the cropped area.

4. When you're ready to apply the cropped area, press Enter (Return on the Mac).

Figure 4.9 The Crop tool helps you visualize how your trimmed image will look.

Removing Dust and Noise

Photoshop includes several ways to remove dust spots, noise, and other artifacts from an image. Three of them, the Reduce Noise, Despeckle, and Dust & Scratches filters, don't lend themselves to this particular image, so I'll describe them and get them out of the way first.

Reduce Noise

Noise shows up in conventional photographs as grain, although that kind of graininess comes from the silver halide clumps in the photosensitive media when the photo is taken and processed. Noise can be *added* to a film image or print as it is scanned and converted to digital form, because electronic noise is an inherent part of the digital process. Any time an electronic signal is converted from analog form to digital, or is amplified, some random information gets mixed in with the actual picture data in the form of noise.

Noise is often removed by the electronic gadget, such as a digital camera, that produces it. The process involves comparing the image data with a "blank" image exposed under the same conditions. Certain kinds of fuzziness that appear in the blank version *and* the image can be assumed to be noise and safely removed. Photoshop has its own noise reduction function, which can be summoned using the Filters > Noise > Reduce Noise command. The dialog box shown in Figure 4.10 pops up.

Figure 4.10 The Remove Noise filter softens random noise that appears in digital images.

Both Basic and Advanced modes are available. The Advanced mode has an additional tab that lets you apply noise reduction separately to individual channels. That's a valuable capability, because some cameras are particularly poor performers at high ISO settings (ISO 800 and above) in particular channels. If you learn that your digital camera needs noise reduction in, say, the green channel, you can do it with the Reduce Noise filter in Advanced mode.

The basic noise reduction features include sliders for setting strength (the amount of noise canceling applied); how much detail you're willing to lose as the filter removes what it deems to be "noisy" pixels; how much color noise (those multi-color specks you see in noisy digital images); and how much to sharpen detail (which can tend to cancel the noise-removal effects). There's also a checkbox for removing JPEG artifacts, which are little clumps that appear in images, often in the shape of little spiders, as supposedly redundant image information is discarded during JPEG compression.

If you're working with my test image, you'll see there isn't much noise to remove, so we'll move on. However, your own photos may have enough noise to benefit from this filter.

Despeckle

Despeckle is a clever filter that examines the pixels in your image, looking for areas with a great deal of contrast between them. In an image, such areas generally mark the boundaries of edges. When the Despeckle filter finds these edges, it leaves them alone and, instead, blurs other parts of the image. That produces lower overall sharpness in most of your image (the non-edge parts), which tends to blur any speckled areas so the speckles blend in. However, because the edges remain sharp, your image may still look acceptable. The Despeckle filter is a quick way to mask a lot of dust in images that contain many different spots, or to minimize the halftone screen of pictures that already have been printed in a book or magazine. It works best in images that are fairly sharp to begin with, especially those that may have a bit of noise that can benefit from the blurring. It works worst with images that are not very sharp, because the blur effect can be objectionable.

This filter has no controls to adjust. Simply select it from the Filter > Noise menu and see if it does the job. If not, choose Edit > Undo, or Edit > Fade to fully or partially reverse Despeckle's effects.

Dust & Scratches

The Dust & Scratches filter is a smarter tool that actively seeks out areas of your image that contain spots and scratches. Photoshop performs this magic by looking at each pixel in the image, then moving out from that pixel radially, searching for abrupt transitions in tone that might indicate a dust spot on the image. If a spot is found, only that area is blurred to minimize the appearance of the defect. This filter has two controls, shown in Figure 4.11.

The Radius slider adjusts the size of the area searched for the abrupt transition, measured in pixels. You can select from 1 to 16 pixels. If your image is full of dust spots, you might find a value of about four pixels useful, but for most pictures either a one or two-pixel radius should be sufficient. The larger the radius you select, the greater the blurring effect on your image, so you should use the smallest radius you can. The Threshold slider tells the filter just how extreme a transition must be before it should be considered a defect. Set the radius slider to the lowest setting that eliminates the spots in the Preview window, and then adjust the Threshold slider up from zero until defects begin to reappear. The idea is to eliminate dust and scratches without adding too much blur to your image.

Figure 4.11 The Dust & Scratches filter dialog box has two sliders and a Preview window.

Using the Clone Stamp

Our sample picture was taken with a digital camera and doesn't have dust spots. It does have some white spots that were possibly caused by some bad pixels in the sensor. If the spots had been gray or black and we were using a digital single-lens reflex (SLR) camera, it's likely that they were caused by dust on the sensor. Usually, you can blow off this dust to avoid leaving dark spots on every digital photo you take. (Sensor cleaning can be tricky; you can find more information on this topic in my book *Mastering Digital SLR Photography*, from Course Technology.)

We can erase these white spots just as if they were dust spots; the same technique applies to both kinds of defects. With conventional photography, dust spots are covered up with spotting brushes or pens, and if the pen happens to match the color of the background, the process can be quick and easy. With Photoshop, the process is even easier, because the Clone tool can be used to create a pen that automatically matches the color and texture surrounding the spot you are removing. That's because the Clone tool paints copies of those actual pixels. The Healing Brush tool and Spot Healing Brush, discussed later in this chapter, do an even better job, but the Clone Stamp is fine for the following task, because it works much faster.

1. Use the Zoom tool (press Z to activate it) and click in the image multiple times to zoom in so you can see the spots good enough to work on them.

2. Next, choose the Clone Stamp tool (press S). Make sure the Aligned box is checked in the Option bar, and then choose a 13-pixel soft brush from the drop-down Brush menu.

3. Place the cursor near a spot that contains some image area with the same tone and texture as the area surrounding the spot, and click while holding down the Alt/Option key. Photoshop will now use the point where you clicked as the "source" for its cloning action.

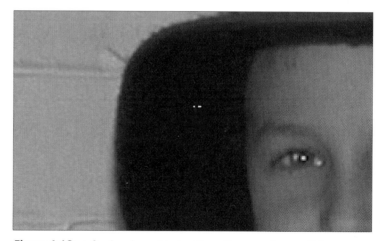

4. Paint with the Clone Stamp's brush until you've covered up the spots, as shown in Figure 4.12.

Figure 4.12 A few brushes with the Clone Stamp and most of the spots are invisible. A few more dabs, and the last two you can see in the hat will vanish, too.

Fixing Dual Catchlights

Here are those dual catchlights again, as shown in Figure 4.13. The brightest catchlight was caused by the electronic flash used to take the picture. The secondary catchlight can be blamed on a bright window behind the photographer. It's sometimes difficult to previsualize a picture well enough to realize that double catchlights are going to result (the main catchlight doesn't appear until the flash goes off, for example), so the easiest solution is simply to remove one of the reflections in Photoshop. Again, for a simple fix like this, the Clone tool is the best choice,

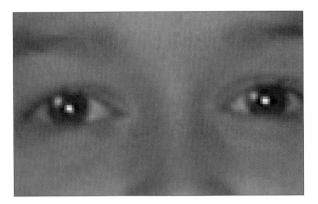

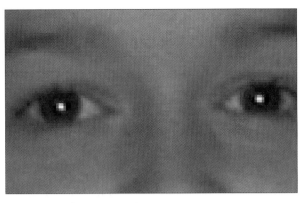

Figure 4.13 Dual catchlights need to be fixed.

Figure 4.14 With the dual catchlights removed, the eyes look more normal and lifelike.

because the Healing Brush uses complex algorithms
to perform its magic, and that sort of effort is not needed for this simple task. All
we need to do is blot out the offending reflection. Follow these steps.

1. Press S to select the Clone Stamp tool.

2. Choose the brush size to the smallest fuzzy brush (the 5-pixel model), set
   Opacity to 66 percent, and make sure the Aligned box is marked.

3. Choose an origin point somewhere below the second reflection and
   Alt/Option click it.

4. Paint out the redundant catchlight. Because Opacity has been set to 66%, you
   can blend the pixels in smoothly so the cloning is not so obvious.

5. Repeat with all four kids to remove all their catchlights. Their eyes will look
   something like Figure 4.14.

ALIGNED/UNALIGNED

When the Aligned box is marked, Photoshop copies pixels from the point that you
first marked as the source (by pressing Alt/Option when you clicked) to the point
in the image where you begin cloning. Then, as you move away from that point,
Photoshop uses the distance and direction the cursor moves from the cloning point
to determine which pixels to copy. For example, if you move 1/4 inch up and to
the left of the first point where you start painting, the Clone tool will copy pixels
that are 1/4 inch up and to the left of the origin point. It doesn't matter if you stop
painting and start again. Unless you Alt/Option click again somewhere else, the
origin point will be used as the reference point. When the Aligned box is not
checked, each time you begin painting again, the origin point is used in the new
location. Figure 4.15 shows what happens. In both cases, I clicked on the girl's shoe

to set the origin point, and then began painting at a point above her knee. Then, I stopped painting, and resumed cloning at a point a little to the left. With the Aligned box checked, the soccer ball, located to the left of the girl's foot at the origin point, is cloned. With the Aligned box not checked, the Clone stamp begins painting her foot again.

Begin Painting Here

Figure 4.15 You can see the difference between Aligned and Unaligned cloning.

Resume Painting Here   *Alt/Option+Click Here*

Removing Unwanted Objects

I chose the best background that was available when I snapped this picture. However, there are still some objects in the picture that should be removed. The Clone Stamp can help by painting parts of the wall, or other subject matter, over the portions we want to remove or hide. Follow these steps to learn how to remove your ex-brother-in-law from those family reunion photos, or in this case, delete a picture that was securely taped to the wall.

1. Press Z to choose the Zoom tool, and zoom in on the boy's face with the picture on the wall behind him, as shown in Figure 4.16.

Figure 4.16 Zoom in on the image area you are going to work on.

2. Press Q to activate Quick Mask mode, and then B to choose the Paintbrush tool. Use the hard-edged 19-inch brush and paint a mask around the edge of the boy's hat, as you can see in Figure 4.17. This will protect the hat from accidentally being cloned onto.

3. Press Q again to exit Quick Mask mode. If you have Photoshop set to paint a selection while in Quick Mask mode, press Shift + Ctrl/Command + I to invert the selection so that everything is selected *except* the area of the hat that you painted.

4. Press S to choose the Clone Stamp tool, and then Alt/Option + click somewhere in the area of the wall to the right of the boy's head. Make sure the Aligned box is checked. You should have Opacity set to 100%.

5. Use a soft-edged brush to paint the blank wall area into the part of the image occupied by the picture on the wall. Your image will begin to look like Figure 4.18. Try to choose your origin point and the spot where you begin painting so the lines on the wall will line up properly in the cloned area.

6. When you're finished, remove the other extraneous objects from the image, using this same technique, as indicated in Figure 4.19. Figure 4.20 shows the finished image with the extra image area cloned out. The instructions to lighten parts of the image will be handled in the next section.

Figure 4.17 Paint a mask to protect the hat from the cloning operation.

Figure 4.18 Clone the blank wall into the area where the picture on the wall resides.

Remove picture   Remove flower   Remove reflection on lip

Figure 4.19 Here are some other extraneous objects to be removed.

Delete pipe and wall outlet   Lighten faces   Darken shirt   Move feather from face

Figure 4.20 The retouched image looks like this, with the extra objects removed.

Darkening and Lightening

Only a couple of fixes remain, and they don't require a great deal of instructions. To lighten the faces, all you need to do is enter Quick Mask mode, paint a selection over each of the three left-most faces and the girl on the right's shirt, then exit Quick Mask and use Photoshop's Brighten/Contrast controls to lighten the three faces on the left to match that of the girl on the right. Figure 4.22 shows the final image with the brightness/contrast adjustments, plus the final movement of the boy on the left described below. Choose Image > Adjustments > Brighten/Contrast to access these controls. You'll learn more about how to use them later in the book.

Moving Boy Over

It's difficult to get your models to stand exactly where you want them. The most frequent error amateur photographers make in group shots like this is to fail to have the subjects standing close enough together. Even seasoned pros can fall victim, especially when the subjects include a lively quartet of second-graders in which one or more of the boys doesn't especially want to *touch* one of the girls. Luckily, Photoshop makes it easy to move our subjects closer together, as I did in this case.

1. Use the Lasso selection tool to create a selection around the boy at the left. Select some of the wall area behind him to make it easier to blend the boy back into the picture.

2. Press Ctrl/Command + C to copy the boy's figure, then press Ctrl/Command + V to paste him down in a new layer.

3. Press E to select the Eraser tool, and then remove part of the area surrounding the boy. Use a soft-edged eraser brush on the wall area at the right side of his head, and a harder-edged brush to erase his sleeve, so he can overlap the girl. Figure 4.21 shows what the partially erased layer should look like.

4. Use the cursor arrow keys to nudge the boy closer to the girl.

5. Flatten the image when you're satisfied, producing the final image shown in Figure 4.22.

Figure 4.21 After pasting the boy into his own layer, erase the area around him so he'll blend in.

Figure 4.22 The final image looks like this.

Repairing Images with the Healing Brush and Patch Tools

So far, we've concentrated on the Clone Stamp tool in this chapter, because it is a basic, versatile tool that's quick to learn and easy to use, and you should be comfortable with it. However, Adobe introduced two tools with Photoshop 7, the Healing Brush and Patch tools, and added yet another handy aid, the Spot Healing Brush, with Photoshop CS 2.0. The advantage of the Healing Brush is that it takes into account the lighting, texture, and other aspects of an image when you clone from one layer to another within or between images or parts of images. That simplifies fixing defects without totally masking the underlying area. Where the Healing Brush works like a brush, the Patch tool applies pixels based on areas that you select to clone over other areas, while preserving as much of the underlying detail as possible.

The Spot Healing Brush is similar to the Healing Brush, but works better with small areas. There's no need to take a sample of the area you want to use as the basis for the healing. This brush automatically samples pixels surrounding the area you're working on, and takes into account the texture, lighting, shading, and transparency of those nearby pixels when doing its work.

Why do we need these tools? The chief drawback to the Clone tool is that it's "dumb." The Clone brush ignores the pixels you're painting over, and covers them completely with the pixels you're copying from another location. That means you must be fairly clever about where you Alt/Option + click to create an origin point for the Clone tool. Ideally, you should select an area that is fairly close to the destination pixels in color, tone, and texture. If you can't do that, there are various work-arounds, such as changing the Opacity of the Clone brush to less than 100 percent to allow some of the underlying pixels to show through. You can also clone onto a new, empty layer and merge that with the original image pixels using one of Photoshop's cryptic blending modes.

The Healing Brush and Patch tools perform all those calculations for you automatically. When you use either one, they copy pixels from the location you specify to the destination you indicate. But, before the pixels are merged, Photoshop examines the texture, lighting, and shading of the destination pixels and matches the copied pixels to them. As a result, the new pixels merge more smoothly with the old, avoiding the complete obliteration of the detail that was there originally. These implements are very smart, and do a good job. As I mentioned, the Spot Healing Brush doesn't require choosing a sampling area.

These tools are best applied to subjects that truly need "healing" of small areas that need to be blended in with the areas around them. Figure 4.23 shows the kind of situation in which you would not want to use either one. In this case, I applied

Figure 4.23 The Patch tool doesn't lend itself to patching large areas with very different textures.

a patch of wall over the picture taped to the wall. The Patch tool used the underlying pixels in the original picture and modified the patch so that it blends with the picture, rather than obscures it.

A better choice is the image shown in Figure 4.24. This photo of a prairie dog was scanned from a 35mm slide, and, as a result, has a few black spots from the dust that wasn't removed from the transparency. In addition, the creature has a scar on his "forehead," possibly from an old injury, that the Healing Brush or Spot Healing Brush are perfect for.

Figure 4.24 This photo has many small defects that can be fixed with the Healing Brush or Patch tools.

If you'd like to work on this image yourself, locate the prairiedog image on the website and follow along with the steps that follow.

1. Zoom into the forehead area of the prairie dog.

2. Click the Healing Brush tool in the Tool Palette (or press J to activate it). Unlike the most common Photoshop brush tools, the Healing Brush doesn't have a selection of preset brushes from which to choose. In fact, the Brush Palette is deactivated while the Healing Brush is in use.

3. Set your brush characteristics from the drop-down dialog box available in the Options bar, as seen in Figure 4.25. You can choose the brush size, hardness (how hard or fuzzy the brush is), brush shape, and other parameters. Choose a 27-pixel brush, and leave the hardness set at 0, producing a medium-sized soft brush.

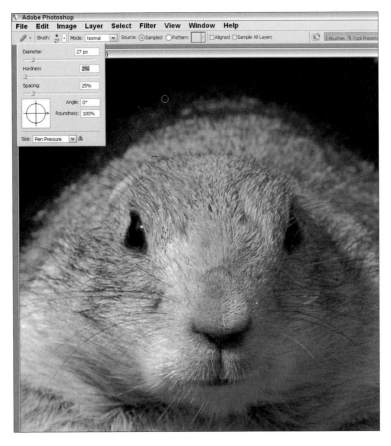

Figure 4.25 Set the Healing Brush characteristics from the drop-down dialog box.

4. Make sure the Source box is checked. That tells Photoshop to use the area where you Alt/Option + click as the source for the cloned pixels. If you mark the Pattern box instead, you can heal an area with a pattern of your choice.

5. Alt/Option + click in the area of the forehead to the left of the scar, and paint over the blemish with the Healing Brush. The defect will vanish.

6. Use the drop-down dialog box to reduce the size of the Healing Brush to about 15 pixels, and repeat the operation on each dust spot, wrinkle, or other defect you see.

If the area you are working on is small, you can use the Spot Healing Brush, and not bother with selecting an area to sample. This tool is smart enough to produce good results on its own.

The Patch tool works in a similar way to the Healing Brush, except that you make a selection in your image of an area to be used as a patch, and then apply the patch to the destination area of the image. Scroll down to the right cheek area (your right, not the model's) and zoom in. Then, follow these steps.

1. Activate the Patch tool from the Tool Palette. Mark the Destination box in the Options bar. This indicates that you'll be selecting an area that will be used as a patch. You'll see exactly how this works shortly.

2. The tool cursor turns into a crosshair, which you can drag to define the area to be used as a patch, shown in Figure 4.26.

3. Once you've defined the patch, place the cursor inside it and drag to the area you'd like patched. The patch blends in with the area smoothly, as you can see in Figure 4.27.

4. Use either the Patch tool or Healing Brush to fix the other dust spots and problem areas in the image.

Figure 4.27 After patching, the image looks like this.

Figure 4.26 Define the area of the patch first, then drag it to the area to be patched.

> **Note**
>
> You can also reverse the order of the patching process by defining the area you want to fix first as a selection, then dragging that area to the source for the pixels to be used for the patch. Just click the Source button instead of the Destination button in the Options bar. How do you decide which way is better? If you think you'll have a problem creating a patch that fits exactly over the problem area, define the problem area as a selection first with the Source button marked. If you'd rather select the area used as a patch first and aren't fussy about the area you're patching, mark the Destination button and define the patch area instead.

Canceling Red Eyes

Photoshop CS 2.0 borrowed a trick from Photoshop Elements, in the form of a very sophisticated red-eye removal feature, called the Red Eye tool. Apparently this tool, which was an Elements exclusive, proved too useful not to adopt for the "professional" application, Photoshop.

This tool is highly automated. It allows you to click or paint away those glowing pupils that affect any wide-eyed human who is close enough to the camera to reflect light from their eyes directly back into the camera lens. Unfortunately, it doesn't work with the yellow or green eyes sometimes produced by animals. Use Enhance > Color > Replace Color instead. (You'll learn more about that feature in Chapter 6.) Just follow these steps to put the Red Eye Brush to work.

1. Open the picture to be de-demonized.

2. Click the Red Eye tool in the Tool Palette (it's nested with the Healing Brush, Spot Healing Brush, and Patch Tool) to activate it (it has a crosshair cursor and eyeball icon). Then apply any appropriate options: Adjust the Pupil Size parameter to control the size of the "brush" you'll be using to paint over the red eyes. Set the Darken Amount control to adjust the degree of darkening applied to the red eyes.

3. Click in the area that includes the red eye effect.

   The tool automatically seeks out the red tone and darkens it, creating more natural-looking eyes.

4. If both eyes are glowing (they usually are), you can repeat this process for the second eye. Figure 4.28 shows some red eyes (before and after) and the Options Palette for this tool.

Figure 4.28 Before and after red-eye correction.

Next Up

In the next chapter, we're going to explore compositing, which is a much more complex type of retouching that involves combining pieces of images into one whole work of art. You'll get to use most of what you know about working with Photoshop Layers, Selections, and then some.

5

Compositing in Photoshop CS

Compositing was thrust into the public attention in a big way early in 2005, when a certain home economics tycoon was released from prison and *Newsweek* published a jubilant photo of her on the cover—except that it was actually only Martha's *head* superimposed on a model's body. Photoshop had done it again! Whether the photo is an Oprah Winfrey/Ann-Margaret hybrid (*TV Guide*, August, 1989) or nudging two pyramids closer together (*National Geographic*, February, 1982), when compositing is deemed to mislead, it's often castigated and condemned.

Fortunately, compositing is perfectly fine if you're not a news organization or corporation charged with presenting a truthful image. After all, what are you to do when a hated ex-brother-in-law mugging in the center of a treasured family portrait ruins the photo for generations to come? Do you want a photograph of the Eiffel Tower in downtown Wichita, Kansas? Would that Little League photo of your kid be a little more interesting if you could show a baseball intersecting the bat? Compositing is the perfect solution.

You can do the same thing as tabloid magazines, which regularly picture Hollywood celebrities out on "dates" when, in fact, they may never have met. Even more legitimate magazines, like the late *Picture Week* managed to picture Nancy Reagan and Raisa Gorbachev having a friendly chat that never took place. Journalists have some serious ethical considerations when creating composited images. (Robert Gilka, former director of photography at *National Geographic* magazine says that significantly manipulating images is an oxymoron on the order of "limited nuclear warfare.") The rest of us, however, can happily modify and combine images to our heart's content, as long as we're not attempting to defraud anyone.

This chapter concentrates on the tools and techniques you need to create composites. Sometimes, your goal will be to create realistic images; other times, you'll simply want to combine several pictures in interesting ways, even if the end result is obviously a fantasy. If you want to learn more about compositing, check out my book *Digital Retouching and Compositing: Photographers' Guide*, from Course Technology. You'll find the topics covered in this chapter in much more detail in that guidebook. You can find information on that book on my website: **www.dbusch.com.**

Your Compositing Toolkit

Ads for photographic-oriented products like image editors and printers are one venue in which creating outlandish image combinations is definitely okay. In fact, if you look closely at some of the ads for Epson printers in the past few years, you'd think that high-end image editing programs and photo-quality printers are used primarily to print images of trees made out of human bodies.

However, compositing also has more mundane applications that involve nothing more than blending several photos with no overt intention to deceive. The goal here is to combine the best features of four or five flawed images to produce a post-card-quality photo that doesn't scream *fake* until you look at it very closely. To make this chapter even more interesting, we'll work with some out-take photos. Some of them were dark, blurry, or otherwise defective in ways that would ordinarily keep them out of the shoebox (or the digital equivalent, the archive CD). I kept these rejects for the same reason the miser kept a box carefully labeled "Pieces of string not worth saving." You never know when an odd image can come in handy!

Figure 5.1 shows three vacation photos that range from interesting to boring. Figure 5.2 shows the result of one of the exercises in my *Digital Retouching and Compositing: Photographers' Guide* book (if you need more details on how it was done). I moved the Spanish castle to the rugged shores of Ireland, enriched the colors, and added some clouds. Figure 5.3 shows the same photos given a different, more outlandish treatment. These obvious fantasy photos don't stand up under close scrutiny.

Figure 5.1 These three photos weren't stunning on their own.

Figure 5.2 Combining them produced an image that doesn't exist in real life.

Figure 5.3 Going over the top can produce an even more outlandish image.

By eliminating the fantasy element, you can come up with more realistic photos that most viewers won't even question. Figure 5.4 shows a car parked in a grungy driveway (top) and a more attractive setting (bottom). Some careful compositing, which even included simulating shadows on the surface of the vehicle, produced a more realistic picture, as you can see in Figure 5.5.

First, let's look at exactly what you need to know to do effective compositing. The main tools you need to master are the selection tools. If you've been working with Photoshop for a while, you've already used the selection tools extensively, and the good news is that there have been virtually no changes to these tools in Photoshop CS 2.0. To grab portions of an image for realistic compositing, you need to be able to select precisely the object or area that you need. Because the ability to make selections is so crucial, I'm going to spend some time reviewing the key tools before we begin actually butchering a few photos later in this chapter.

Figure 5.4 These two photos can be combined into one…

Figure 5.5 ...producing a composite that most viewers would accept as the real thing.

Selection Refresher Course

In order to facilitate making changes or to copy only part of an image, Photoshop allows you to make selections. A selection is the part of the image inside the crawling selection border (called marching ants and various other names) when you define an area with one of the selection tools. Once you've created a selection, you can do the following things with the selected area:

- Copy the area to the Clipboard and paste it down in a new layer of its own, surrounded by transparency.

- Paint or fill selected areas with color or pattern using all the painting tools in any of the available modes.

- Fill selections with the contents of other selected areas (for example, pasting one image into another).

- Mask selected areas to prevent them from being changed.

- Apply a filter to a selected area.

- Edit a selection: scale its size, skew or distort its shape, change its perspective, flip it horizontally or vertically, rotate it, add to or subtract from it, and combine it with another selection.

- Save selections in channels or layers for later use.

- Convert selections to vector-oriented paths that you can manipulate using the Pen tool.

When you create a selection in Photoshop, you are essentially doing what airbrush artists do when they cut masks out of film: You define an area in which painting (or another process) can take place. Photoshop allows you to make masks with three kinds of edges: anti-aliased (smoothed), feathered (fading out gradually), and non-anti-aliased (jagged edged). In addition, masks can be opaque, semi-transparent, or graduated in transparency. You can use Photoshop's selection tools, described next, or actually "paint" a selection using Quick Mask mode, which we've already worked with earlier in this book (so I won't be reviewing it in this chapter).

PC AND MAC KEYBOARD SHORTCUTS

As you work through this chapter and those that follow, keep in mind that some keyboard shortcuts are different for the PC and Macintosh. Most tools from the Tool Palette can be selected by pressing the appropriate alphabetical key on the keyboard, *except* when the Text tool is active. So, you can switch to one of the Marquee tools by pressing M on both PCs and Macs. Press Shift + M to cycle through the alternative versions of that tool, the Elliptical and Rectangular Marquees. Use the same technique to select the Lasso tool and its variations (use L), as well as all the other tools on the palette. Learn the keyboard shortcuts and use them.

Some shortcuts use keys in combinations, and you'll need to keep in mind that the PC and Mac have the Shift keys in common, but other keys have different names on the two platforms. In this book, I'll separate the equivalent keys with a slash, so when you see Ctrl/Command or Alt/Option you'll know to press the Ctrl and Alt keys on the PC and Command and Option keys on the Macintosh. The Mac also has a Control key (not to be confused with the PC's Ctrl key), which serves the same function as a right-click with the mouse on the PC. So, right-click/Control-click are the same command sequence on the two platforms. And, the Mac has a Return key rather than an Enter key.

Making Rectangular, Square, Oval, and Circular Selections

The easiest way to make rectangular, square, oval, and circular selections is with the Rectangular and Elliptical Marquee tools. To make such a rectangular selection, just choose the tool (press M to select it), then drag in your image, releasing the mouse when the selection is the right size. To deselect any selection at any time, press Ctrl/Command + D or click anywhere on the screen with a selection tool outside of the selection border. If you click outside the border with another tool, this shortcut will not work. Hide a selection by pressing Ctrl/Command + H. Here are some of the options you should learn when using the selection tools.

- Click at the point where you want the rectangle or ellipse to begin, and then drag in any direction. The selection will grow from that point in the direction you drag.

- Hold down the Alt/Option key and click a point, then drag in any direction. The selection will radiate outward, with that point as its center.

- To draw a perfect square or circle, click and hold down the Shift key while you drag. Hold down both the Shift and Alt/Option keys when you first click, and the selection will radiate from the centerpoint where you clicked.

- Choose Fixed Aspect Ratio from the Style drop-down list in the Option bar, shown at the top in Figure 5.6. Leave the Width and Height values at their default 1, and forget about holding down the Shift key. You'll draw only perfect squares or circles every time you click and drag when this option is active.

- Type other values into the Width and Height boxes to create selections with other proportions. For example, using 8 and 1, respectively, will force the Marquee tool to create only selections that are eight times as wide as they are tall.

- Choose Fixed Size from the Style drop-down list in the Option bar and type in dimensions, in pixels, for your selection. Say you had an image that was 800 × 600 pixels and wanted to grab a 640 × 480 pixel chunk of it. Once you've typed the target dimensions into the Width and Height boxes, clicking with the Rectangular Marquee produces a selection in that size that you can drag around the screen to the part of the image where you want it to be.

Figure 5.6 Choose selection options from the Option bar.

Creating Single-Row and Single-Column Selections

Choose the single row and single column selection tools, which reside in the same icon as the other marquee tools. Position the mouse pointer in the window, then click and drag. You will select a single line, which extends across the entire window. If you had chosen the single-column option, you would have drawn a single vertical line. These lines, horizontal and vertical, have properties of selections and therefore can be filled with paint, rotated, and manipulated in many other ways.

Making Freehand Selections with the Lasso Tool

With the Lasso tool you can make freehand selections of a part of an image. Select the tool and drag around the outline of the area you want to select. This tool has three modes. The default mode draws a selection as if you were sketching it with a pencil. The Polygonal Lasso tool lets you create selections in straight lines by clicking, dragging to the next point and clicking again, and then repeating this process until you click back at the origin point to close the selection. The Magnetic Lasso tool examines the image area as you drag, and attempts to "hug" the edges of the area as closely as possible, using parameters you type into the Option bar, shown at the bottom in Figure 5.6. You can see the Magnetic Lasso at work in Figure 5.7.

The options available with the Magnetic Lasso include:

- **Detection Width.** An area, measured in pixels, which the tool will use to search for high contrast areas in the path of the selection border to "hug" to.

- **Edge Contrast.** The amount of contrast required in the area (from 0 to 100 percent) to qualify as an "edge."

- **Frequency.** The spacing between magnetized points. The higher the number (from 0 to 100) the more frequently Photoshop will add points.

- **Pen Pressure.** Allows you to draw thicker lines when you press harder with a stylus on a pressure-sensitive tablet.

Figure 5.7 The Magnetic Lasso "hugs" the edges of an area at the point of greatest contrast.

Use large width and higher-edge contrast settings with a higher frequency to create a selection that has well-defined images. Use a smaller width, reduced contrast settings, and a lower frequency to trace a softer-edged selection.

Other Selection Tips

Here are some more tips that apply to the selection tools:

- When any selection tool is active, you can drag a selection anywhere on the screen.

- Mark the Anti-aliased box in the Option bar to smooth the edges of an elliptical or freehand selection. Rectangles don't need anti-aliasing, so this option is grayed out when the Rectangular Marquee tool is active.

- Type a value into the Feather box in the Option bar to create a selection that fades out gradually over a range of the number of pixels you specify.

Adding, Subtracting, or Combining Selections

Once you've made a selection, you can modify it by adding, subtracting, or combining. Here's a refresher of the options at your command.

- Choose a selection tool and add to an existing selection by holding the Shift key while you drag. You can also click the Add To Selection icon in the Option bar to temporarily make adding to the selection the default action.

- Choose a selection tool and subtract from an existing selection by holding the Alt/Option key while dragging. Or, click the Subtract from Selection icon in the Option bar.

- Click the Intersect with Selection icon in the Option bar, then create a selection that overlaps the original selection. Only the portion that overlaps the two will be selected. This useful technique can help you do things like create a particularly shaped selection. Figure 5.8 shows the results of adding, subtracting, and intersecting selections.

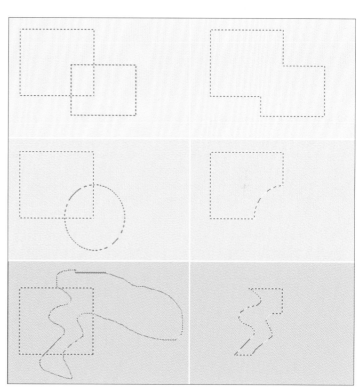

Figure 5.8 At top, adding the two selections at left produces the final selection at right; middle, subtracting the circular selection from the rectangular selection at left produces the final selection at right; bottom, Intersecting the squiggly selection at left with the rectangular selection produces the final selection you can see at right.

Other Selection Tools

There are other tools you can use to make selections within Photoshop. Here is a brief refresher for those tools, too.

Magic Wand

The Magic Wand, which you can activate by pressing the W key, selects all pixels that are similar in hue and value to the pixel you first clicked on. Originally, the Magic Wand would select only the pixels that touched each other (were contiguous), but now this capability is an option (albeit, the default). If you turn off the contiguous parameter in the Option bar, the Magic Wand will select all the pixels in an image that are similar in hue and value to the first pixel.

You tell the wand how choosy to be by setting its tolerance, from 0 to 255. Based on the tolerance set, the wand extends the selection outward until it finds no more pixels with the color values within the limits you've specified. For example, if the tolerance was set to 40 and you clicked with the wand on a pixel that had a value of 100, the Magic Wand would select all pixels with values between 60 and 140. (Both hue and luminance are figured into a special equation as the wand decides which pixels it can and cannot select.) A high tolerance will select a wider range of pixels. A low tolerance will select a very narrow range of pixels.

If you want to select a wide range of a color, from bright to dark, set the tolerance higher than the default (32) and click the wand in the middle of the range of color values. If you click in an area of the color that is very dark or very light, you are giving the wand less latitude. (Remember, color values can range from 0 to 255.)

The Magic Wand's selections can be smoothed (anti-aliased) or rough, depending on whether you've marked the Anti-alias box in the Option bar, and you can also check the Use All Layers box, in which case the Magic Wand will select pixels based on color information in all the layers of your image, rather than simply from the active layer. For Figure 5.9 I took a simple close-up photo (made with a lowly 2-megapixel camera, by the way), and set the Tolerance first at 12 (at top) and then at 32 (bottom), clicking with the Magic Wand in the brightest part of the orange in both cases.

The Select Menu

You can change a selection using choices from the Select menu.

- **Select All** (everything in an image; also Ctrl/Command + A), **Deselect** (cancel all selections; also Ctrl/Command + D); **Reselect** (the last selection made; also Shift + Ctrl/Command + D); and **Inverse** (reverse the selection; also Shift + Ctrl/Command + I).

Figure 5.9 The Magic Wand's Tolerance control was set to 12 at top, and 32 at bottom.

- **Select Color Range.** Using the dialog box shown in Figure 5.10, make a selection based on colors you specify using the Eyedropper tool.

- **Feather.** (fade out a selection; also Alt/Option + Ctrl + D) Type in a pixel value for the desired width of the fade zone.

- **Modify.** Change the selection boundary to a border of a pixel width you specify; smooth the rough edges of the selection border; expand the selection border outward by the number of pixels you specify; contract the selection border inward by the number of pixels you specify.

- **Grow.** Adds adjacent pixels that fall into the brightness range specified by the Magic Wand tool's options.

- **Select Similar.** Adds pixels anywhere in the image that fall within the Magic Wand tool's tolerance setting.

- **Transform Selection.** Produces a set of handles you can use to modify the selection using Photoshop's transformation tools. Right/Control (on the Mac) + click the selection to choose one of the transformation options, such as Scale, Rotate, Skew, and so forth.

- **Load/Save Selection.** Allows you to save the current selection, or load one you've previously saved.

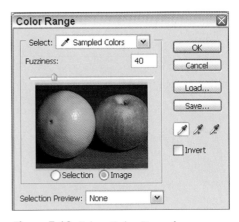

Figure 5.10 Select Color Range lets you create a selection based on hues in your image.

Making Selections with the Paths Palette

If you have used an object-oriented illustration program, you will recognize the Pen tool as a Bézier (Bez-ee-ay) curve drawing device. With the Pen tool you can create lines and shapes that can be fine-tuned, saved as paths, filled with color or outlined (stroked), and used as the basis for selections. Conversely, you can change selections into paths and edit them with the tools on the Paths Palette. The smallest part of a path is a segment—the line connecting two anchor points. Several segments, linked, make a subpath, and subpaths combine to form paths. A path can be a line or a closed shape or a series of lines, a series of shapes, or a combination of lines and shapes. You can stroke and fill subpaths as well as paths. Importantly, paths can be converted to selections, which is useful when you want to select an area of an image that can be closely approximated by a path.

Here's a quick refresher on the Pen tool. Open an empty document and try out the individual tools and options to make sure you're up to speed. There are considerably more options and techniques for using the Pen tool and Freehand Pen tool than I've outlined here. If you find the Pen especially useful for making selections, you'll want to brush up on them.

Drawing Straight Lines

Here's how to draw straight lines:

1. Select the Pen tool. Click in the window to set an anchor point. It is called an anchor point because it will anchor one end of a line. Release the mouse button. Click again a distance away to create a second anchor point; a line will be drawn between the two.

   Notice that a new anchor point is darkened as it is created, indicating that it is selected. At the same time, the previous anchor point lightens, meaning that it is deselected, as shown in Figure 5.11. Release the mouse button and click to create a third anchor point and second line.

2. Release the mouse button and move the pen on top of the first anchor point. A small loop appears to the side of the Pen tool icon, letting you know that clicking will close the path. Click on the first anchor point to close the triangle. Photoshop will create this new shape in its own shape layer, called Shape 1 by default. Each new object you create with the Pen tool will be created in its own layer, too.

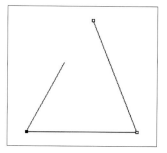

Figure 5.11 The dark anchor point is the one that is currently selected.

Be certain that you do not drag the mouse as you create any of these lines. If you do, you will create curved lines, not straight-edged ones. Press Delete twice to eliminate all lines before going on to the next part of the exercise.

Hold down the Shift key to constrain the placement of an anchor point to a 45 degree angle or a multiple of 45 degrees, such as a 90 degree angle. This also works to constrain the angle of a direction line to 45 degrees or a multiple thereof. Both constraints are helpful for drawing some geometric shapes.

Drawing Curves

Here's how to draw curves:

1. Click the pen once in the window to create an anchor point in a new shape layer, and holding down the mouse button, drag at an angle to form the first part of a curve. As soon as you begin dragging, the pen will turn into an arrow.

   The lines that emerge as you drag are called direction lines. The slope of the curve is the same as the slope of its direction lines, and the height of the direction lines determine the height of the curve. There are two dark dots at the end of each direction line. These are direction points.

2. Release the mouse button to finish drawing the first part of the curve.

3. Position the pen a short distance from the first point. Click, keeping the mouse button held down. A slightly curved line will form between the two anchor points.

4. Still keeping the mouse button down, drag in the direction away from the first anchor point. This action will shape the curve connecting the two anchor points, making it more exaggerated, as shown in Figure 5.12.

5. Release the mouse button and click again, in line with the first two anchor points, and drag in the direction away from the second anchor point. Another curve is formed. You can continue in this way, building a gently curved line.

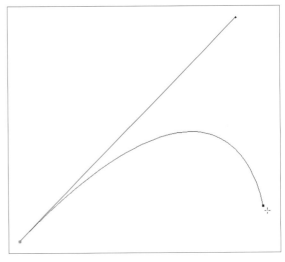

Figure 5.12 Drawing curves with the Pen tool.

PREVIEW

Before you add an anchor point, you may want to preview the curve it will be making. This is especially helpful when you're outlining an image. To use this preview option, click the down-pointing arrow in the Option bar and mark the Rubber Band checkbox. Thereafter, when you release the mouse button, but move the pen to set your second anchor point, a curved line will follow it. You can use this feature to assist you with anchor point placement as you outline an object.

Moving an Anchor Point or Direction Point to Change the Shape of a Curve

You can change the shape of a curve:

1. Draw a simple path with the pen: one anchor point with direction lines, connected by a curve to a second anchor point.

2. Select the arrow from the palette and place it on the first anchor point. Click on the point and drag it. The shape of the curve will change as you do.

3. Now place the arrow on one of the direction points (at the end of a direction line), and drag it back and forth. This is another way to change the shape of a curve. When you select the pen again, you can continue drawing from where you left off.

Making a Selection from a Pen Tool Path

Here's how to transform your path into a selection:

1. Select the path you want to transform by making its layer active.

2. Right/Control + click the path and choose Make Selection from the pop-up menu shown in Figure 5.13.

3. In the Make Selection dialog box you can set the feather radius for the selection border and, if you want, you can choose the Anti-aliased option.

4. Choose whether you want a new selection, or add, subtract, or intersect a current selection.

5. Click on OK to change the path to a selection.

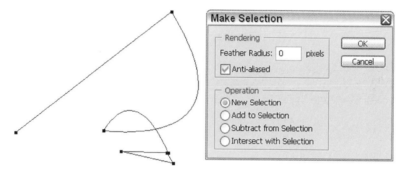

Figure 5.13 Change a path to a selection.

Creating a Simple Composite

Now it's time to use your selection skills, plus some other techniques we'll pick up as we go along, to create a simple composite. This section will help you learn not only the Photoshop tools you need to create realistic composites, but also some of the visual considerations. You can follow along using the Soccer Ball and Soccer Kick images from the website at **http://www.coursptr.com**, or work with a similar photo of your own. The techniques can be applied broadly.

I warned you earlier in this chapter that we'd be working with out-takes. The goal for this particular exercise is to take a photo reject, and make it more presentable. Figure 5.14 shows the original photo we'll work with. It's not razor sharp, but it's not a bad action photo, particularly if you happen to be the parent of one of the players pictured. The chief problem is that the soccer ball is all washed out and excessively blurry, and, unfortunately, merges with a bit of light-colored background showing through the trees behind, making it look like the ball has a knob growing out of the bottom. A simple composite can improve this photo while offering the opportunity to make other changes, as well.

Figure 5.14 This action photo can be improved, a lot.

Follow these steps to create the transformation.

1. The first thing we can do is make the picture more dramatic by raising the young girl an extra two or three feet off the ground. Use the Lasso to select her, and paste her down onto a new layer. Then use the Move tool to nudge her up higher in the picture, as shown in Figure 5.15. (I've dimmed the original image background to make the pasted selection more obvious.)

2. Use a soft eraser brush to erase around the edges of the figure on the new layer so she'll blend in with the background behind.

3. Go back to the original background layer and use the Clone Stamp to remove the extra shadow that appears under the player's feet, leaving only the original shadow beneath her. Use the Clone tool to put part of the background image on any portions of the original player figure that show through. The image will look like Figure 5.16. (The background is no longer dimmed, so you can see how smoothly the background and pasted image merge.)

Figure 5.15 Give the young soccer player a lift to add to the excitement.

Figure 5.16 Blend the elevated portion of the image so it merges smoothly with the background.

4. Next, load the Soccer Ball photo from the website, and use the Elliptical Marquee tool to select it. You can hold the Shift and Alt/Option keys, click the approximate center of the ball, and drag to create a perfect circle with the ball centered in the selection. If necessary, nudge the selection and/or expand or contract the selection (as you learned to do earlier in this chapter) until only the ball is selected, as shown in Figure 5.17.

5. Copy the ball and paste it down in the original photo on top of the original soccer ball.

6. Resize the ball in its new layer so it's exactly the size as the ball it replaces.

7. Use the Clone Stamp tool to erase the original ball from the background image.

Figure 5.17 Select only the soccer ball from the second photo.

8. Make the replacement ball match the photo a little more closely by performing these modifications:

- Use Image > Transform > Rotate to rotate the ball a little counterclockwise so its brightest surface is upwards, matching the direction of the sunlight in the original photo (almost exactly overhead, but a little to the right).

- Use the Burn tool with a soft brush to darken the underside of the soccer ball.

- Use Image > Adjustments > Brightness/Contrast to adjust the brightness and contrast of the ball so it looks more natural in the image. You'll need to judge the amount of brightness and contrast to apply visually. Just move the sliders until the ball looks "best."

- Use the Filter > Blur > Motion Blur filter, with the Distance setting at 11 pixels to give the ball a little blur.

The finished photo will look like Figure 5.18. In Chapter 8 you'll learn how to do other interesting things with photos like these, such as add motion blur streaks to the players themselves.

Stitching Two Photos Together

Ordinary panoramic pictures are the penultimate wide-angle photograph (the ultimate being either a 360-degree panorama or, perhaps, a picture that would encompass a complete sphere, with the camera at the center). In practice, 100- to 120-degree panoramas are easier to achieve simply by taking multiple pictures and stitching them together with Photoshop. This next project will show you how to do it, using Photoshop CS's Photomerge feature as well as a time-tested technique

Figure 5.18 The finished photo is a lot more interesting with the new, composited elements and added blur.

that can be used with earlier versions of the image editor. But first, a little background.

Traditionally, panorama photos have been produced using several different methods. One elegant solution has been a special panorama camera, which uses a lens that rotates from left to right in concert with a moving shutter, thus exposing a long strip of negative with a very wide-angle view of the subject, something like the one shown at top in Figure 5.19. Such cameras tended to be expensive and required working with a tripod for best results.

Another solution is the one used by now-discontinued and not-much-lamented APS (Advanced Photo System) cameras, which let you switch back and forth between three different aspect ratios, including a panorama view. This system works by taking an ordinary frame and simply ignoring the top and bottom portions, enlarging a thin strip in the middle of the frame to create a panorama. There

Figure 5.19 Special panorama cameras expose a wide image on a long strip of film (top). Or, you can simply crop the top and bottom out of an image (bottom).

are advantages and disadvantages to this approach. One advantage is that you don't need a tripod; any picture you care to take can be transformed into a panorama by flipping a switch on the camera. The most important plus to this system is that photofinishers are set up to handle such panorama photos automatically. The APS camera marks the film's magnetic strip with a code that labels a panorama picture as such. The photolab's automated printing equipment reads this code and prints out your wide photos using the panorama area previewed in the camera's viewfinder.

The chief disadvantage is that such panoramas don't use all the available film area, and that's probably one of the reasons why the APS system failed (cheap digital cameras being another reason). You get a wide-angle shot by enlarging only a center strip of the film. Your 4 × 10-inch panorama picture is actually just an 8 × 10 with two inches trimmed from the top and bottom. That's cheaper and faster than snipping an 8 × 10-inch print yourself, but you're not getting the sharpest possible picture. At the bottom of Figure 5.19 you can see how such a panorama might be derived from a full-frame photograph.

A third way to create panoramas is with one of the newer digital cameras with this feature. When you switch to panorama mode, the digital camera shows a ghost image of the edge of your last picture in the LCD panel on the back of the camera. You then use this ghost image to line up your current image so that the two overlap. You can repeat this step as many times as you want to create sweeping panoramas. Of course, each portion of the panorama is created as a separate digital image. You'll still need to stitch them together in Photoshop. (Digital cameras with the panorama feature often are furnished with special utilities that can stitch the images effectively.)

A fourth way to create panoramas is to take several full frame photos with a digital or film camera, lining them up as best you can by eye, and then stitching them together to create one very wide photo. Such photos have been pasted together in the past, and then rephotographed and printed, but Photoshop makes it easy to mate a series of photos digitally. The advantage of this method is that each picture contains the maximum resolution possible with a full frame digital or film camera image. Another plus is that it's not necessary to shoot with a wide-angle lens, which tends to load the image up with foreground and sky, while pushing the important subject matter way, way back. You can move to a good vantage point and take your set of pictures with a normal lens or telephoto, then join them to create one seamless image. The chief disadvantage of this method is that it's tricky to produce the original images, and time-consuming to join them.

However, if you plan out your panorama as you shoot, you can avoid many of the problems. Here are some tips for shooting good panoramas.

- Minimize the number of photos you take to reduce the number of images you have to stitch together. If you really, really want a 360-degree panorama you can take one, but plan on spending a lot of time combining images.

- There are specialized software programs you can buy, but I recommend seeing how well Photoshop works for you before buying one of these.

- Use a tripod with a panning head as a way to keep all your images level. Adjust the tripod (use an actual level if necessary) and swivel through your panorama to make sure the transitions will be smooth before taking the first photo. Some panheads have markings in degrees to help you align the camera.

- Try to keep exposures, including lens opening and shutter speed, the same between pictures so they'll match more easily.

- Remember to overlap your images slightly so you'll be able to blend each photo into the next.

■ You should know that, technically, the camera should rotate around the optical center of the *lens*, not the center of the *camera body* to produce the most realistic perspective. Some panorama attachments for tripods include a plate that includes a tripod mount under the lens center, rather than in the usual location under the camera body. Figure 5.20 shows the right and wrong locations for your center of rotation.

Figure 5.20 Ideally, a camera should swivel around the optical center of the lens when creating a panorama.

This next exercise will introduce you to the basics of stitching, using only two pictures to start. Load the Toledo Left and Toledo Right photos from the website. These two pictures were taken on a hill outside Toledo, Spain, at the exact spot where the artist El Greco stood in the 16th century to craft his immortal painting *View of Toledo*. Unfortunately, the location is so far from the town that a wide-angle picture of the entire panorama displays more hillside and sky than actual town. Reaching out with a telephoto lens to grab the medieval city on its perch above the Tagus River yields a minimum of two pictures, shown in Figures 5.21 and 5.22. I'm going to show you two ways to create a panorama, using pre-Photoshop CS techniques (the hard way) and the Photomerge feature introduced with Photoshop CS 1.0.

Figure 5.21 The left side of the panorama.

Figure 5.22 The right side of the panorama.

Merging Photos the Hard Way

It's useful to learn how to create panoramas the hard way, because there are times when merging photos entirely using manual techniques is the way to go. For example, you might find that some sophisticated color matching or sharpening needs to be done on each photo to make them match smoothly. Photomerge might not provide the cleanest transition, so you might choose to do it using the technique I'll describe next.

1. Create a large, empty document, approximately 3,000 pixels by 1,500 pixels, then copy and paste the left and right versions of the Toledo picture into the new document.

2. Try to align them so they overlap. You'll see that the right picture is rotated slightly relative to the left picture, and offset vertically. That's because these photos were taken handheld, without benefit of a tripod. You can see the ill fit in Figure 5.23.

3. Rotating the right photo clockwise, as shown in Figure 5.24, lines the photos up better. Click the Rotate tool at the left side of the dialog box, and then drag the images. Focus your attention on the building that overlaps both photos at the edge, rotating until left and right sides of the building are lined up. Figure 5.25 shows how the two pictures will be oriented when you've finished rotating them.

Figure 5.23 Unfortunately, the pictures don't fit exactly together, even though they overlap.

Figure 5.24 Rotate the right photo clockwise to line up the pictures.

Figure 5.25 Now the images match more closely.

4. If you like, you can use the Clone Stamp to copy some of the sky in to the area above it. Or, you can copy sky sections and paste them in, as you can see in Figure 5.26. This will let you crop the picture a little "taller" once you've merged the photos.

Figure 5.26 Paste or clone some sky area to fill in empty portions of the photos.

5. Using a soft brush eraser, erase some of the overlapped area from the right side image, which you should have placed on top of the left side image. The image will begin to blend seamlessly.

6. Finally, use the Brightness/Contrast controls (if necessary) to blend the two images together. Use the Clone Stamp tool to copy parts of the sky over the edges of the sky portions you've added.

7. Flatten the image, which should look like Figure 5.27.

Figure 5.27 Flattened and cleaned up, the finished panorama looks like this.

Merging Photos the Easy Way

Now, let's merge the same two pictures using Photomerge. You'll see just how much easier the whole process can be when you let Photoshop CS handle most of the work for you.

1. Choose File > Automate > Photomerge. The dialog box shown in Figure 5.28 appears.

2. Select the files you'd like to merge. You can choose the files to combine in three ways, using the drop-down list labeled Use.

   ■ Choose Open Files from the list to select from files already open in Photoshop.

   ■ Select Files from the list to browse for files on your hard disk.

   ■ Select Folders from the list to choose files in a particular folder.

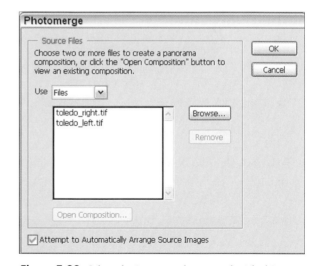

Figure 5.28 Select the images to be merged with this dialog box.

3. Mark the Attempt to Automatically Arrange Source Images check box if you think the images have enough overlapped area that Photoshop can match them up. It does no harm to try, because if Photoshop can't match them up, it will simply leave that step to you.

4. Click on OK to start the process. Photoshop will examine the images and attempt to match them. If it cannot, you'll see the dialog box shown in Figure 5.29. Click on OK, and then drag the images onto the Photomerge workspace, as shown in Figure 5.30.

Figure 5.29 If Photomerge can't match up your images automatically, you'll get this warning.

Figure 5.30 Use the workspace to line up the images manually if you need to.

5. If you're manually lining up images, each image will become semitransparent as you drag so you can line up its overlapping area with the image underneath. Photomerge has tools at the left side of the workspace that can be used to move, rotate, or zoom in on the image.

6. Mark the Normal box on the right side of the dialog. You'd use the Perspective choice instead if you needed to adjust the tilt of the images. Our test images are a good match perspectivewise, so Normal works just fine.

7. Mark the Snap to Image box. This tells Photoshop to go ahead and move one or more of the images being merged to more closely line up the common areas. Other options include Advanced Blending, which may be needed to

smooth the transition between images that don't match well; and Keep As Layers, which tells Photoshop not to flatten the final image. You might want that option when you plan to make other changes to the merged images later.

8. Click on OK to merge the images.

9. Crop the image at top and bottom to produce the panorama shown in Figure 5.31.

Figure 5.31 Your final image will look like this.

Creating a Fantasy Landscape

By now you should be ready to tackle a major project. We're going to create a fantasy landscape similar to the one in Figure 5.2, only better. We'll use a stack of photos, each with various defects, and combine them into one over-the-top composite.

You'll be using various skills that already have been exercised in previous projects, so I won't provide detailed step-by-step instructions for everything. Instead, I'll explain in general terms what needs to be done, focusing on any new or difficult tasks.

We'll start with the photo shown in Figure 5.32, and end up with one that looks like Figure 5.41 (it's okay to peek ahead). The major center of interest was supposed to be the medieval castle perched at the top of the darker green mountain in the middle of the photo. Unfortunately, the castle is too far away to show up well, and the cluttered foreground includes an automobile tire retailer, some electrical poles, and a group of non-medieval homes and other structures. The plain blue sky is a little bland, too. We can fix all of that.

Figure 5.32 The mountains look nice, but we can add some new elements to the image.

In this exercise, you'll learn all the different things that must "match" for a composite image to look realistic. These include:

- **Lighting.** In general, all the illumination must appear to come from the same general area. In the finished composite, the "sun" is high in the sky, just above the upper-right corner of the picture, so most of the shadows are cast towards us. I took some liberties with the mountain picture, in which the illumination is coming from the upper-left corner, instead, because the mountains looked better lit that way, and we tend not to notice lighting discrepancies for objects located that far in the distance.

- **Color.** The colors should match in hue and degree of saturation. I took a cue from the overall blue cast of the mountains and made sure everything else in the picture had a slight blue or blue-green cast to it, rather than an overpowering warm look.

- **Brightness/Contrast.** Objects should be plausibly close in contrast. Objects in the distance can be lower in contrast because they are masked by haze, but your foreground objects should all display the same contrast you'd expect from objects lit by the same illumination.

- **Texture/Sharpness.** It's difficult to make a good composite if one or more objects is decidedly sharper or has a different texture than the other objects in the image. For this project, most of the items dropped into the picture were close enough in sharpness to make a good match. The mountains, because they were off in the distance, didn't need to be as sharp as the components in the foreground. When you're creating your own composites, you may need to use Photoshop's Gaussian Blur or Add Noise filters to blend items carefully. Adjust contrast after blurring, if necessary, to keep your objects matched. Although you can sharpen a soft component to match the rest of an image, Photoshop's Sharpen filters add contrast that's difficult to compensate for.

- **Scale.** Unless you're creating a complete fantasy image, you'll want composited components to be realistically scaled in relation to their surrounding objects. Remember that things closer to us appear larger, so as you move an object farther back in your composition, you'll need to reduce its size.

- **Relationships.** Objects in a composited picture must relate in ways that we'd expect in real life. An object placed between a light source and another object should cast a shadow on the second object. Objects located next to water or a shiny surface should have a reflection. Two objects of known size should be proportionate not only to the rest of the image, but to each other. If there are two moving objects in an image and one of them has motion blur, the other one should, too.

- **Transitions.** The transition between one object and another should be smooth, or, at least, as we expect from an image of that sort.

- **Viewing Angle.** If your angle is high above most of the objects in the composite, you shouldn't include an object shot from down low. Viewers may not notice the discrepancy at first, but the picture won't "look" right.

Keep these things in mind as you work in the next project. You can break a few of the rules I just outlined, but not too many. Start by loading the Mountain photo from the website.

Adding Clouds

The first step is to select the sky area so substitute clouds can be dropped in. Luckily, the sky in this photo is a fairly uniform blue, so the Magic Wand is a good tool for selecting it.

1. Use the Magic Wand with Tolerance set to 20 and click in the center of the sky. This will grab most of the sky, as shown in Figure 5.33.

Figure 5.33 Grab most of the sky using the Magic Wand.

2. Use Select > Similar to capture virtually all of the rest of the sky. If you see any non-selected areas (they will "sparkle" with the selection border around them), press Q to jump to Quick Mask mode and paint in the small dots that remain unselected.

3. Choose Selection > Save Selection to save your sky mask.

4. Next, load the Sky photo from the website. Copy the image by pressing Ctrl + V, and, with your sky selection in the Mountain photo still active, choose Edit > Paste Into (or press Shift + Ctrl/Command + V) to insert the new clouds into the photo.

5. Use Edit > Transform > Scale and resize the clouds so they fit in the available area. Notice that you don't have to resize the image proportionately. You can stretch in one direction or another to make the clouds fit. The "distortion" isn't apparent because clouds are just clouds and have no natural proportions.

6. Next, adjust the opacity of the new cloud layer in the Layer Palette. One key to making composites is not having one object stick out because it is overly bright, overly sharp, or overly dramatic. By reducing the opacity of the cloud layer, the clouds will blend in with the plain blue sky underneath. I reduced the clouds to 44 percent opacity, and they blended in just fine.

7. You may make one final modification. I returned to the original mountain layer, loaded the sky selection, then inverted it (press Shift + Ctrl/Command + I) to select the mountains and foreground. I then copied that selection and pasted it down on a new layer above the clouds. Then, I used the Smudge tool to lightly smudge the edges of the mountains, removing any sharp line between the mountains and the sky. The image so far is shown in Figure 5.34.

Figure 5.34 Once the sky has been merged, the image will look like this.

Bringing the Seashore Inland

Next, we'll add an interesting shoreline to the photo, neatly covering up those houses and electric poles. Use the Inlet picture from the website. The original photo is shown in Figure 5.35.

1. Simply select the whole thing, and paste it down in the mountain photo.

2. Make all the background layers transparent by adjusting the Opacity sliders for those layers. This will let you see the seashore layer more clearly, as shown in Figure 5.36.

3. With the shore layer active, use a soft eraser brush to remove the portion of the inlet that obscures the mountains and part of the valley on the left. The image will look like Figure 5.37.

Figure 5.35 This seashore can be transplanted a few hundred miles inland.

Figure 5.36 Make the background layers transparent so you can see to edit the seashore layer.

Figure 5.37 Remove parts of the seashore to reveal the mountains and valley.

Adding a Castle

Next, take the Alcazar photo from the website, shown in Figure 5.38. The image happens to be a famous fortress almost completely destroyed during the Spanish Civil War, and then later rebuilt.

Figure 5.38 This rebuilt castle can add some interest.

1. Select only the castle using your favorite method. The Magnetic Lasso, used in Figure 5.39, works well for selecting the towers, which are clearly differentiated from the background, but the Polygonal Lasso can also be used.

2. Once you've isolated the castle, copy it and paste into the landscape, as shown in Figure 5.40. I've made the underlying layers partially transparent so you can see clearly how the Alcazar fits in.

3. The transition between the castle and the surrounding countryside isn't smooth. I fixed this by copying the rock that juts up from the right side of the inlet, pasting it down into a layer of its own, and reversing it left to right.

4. Next, use Edit > Transform > Scale to widen it slightly to fit and make it look a little different from its twin. A touch of the Clone Stamp tool to copy some texture from one place on the rock to another also differentiates the two.

Figure 5.39 Use the Magnetic Lasso to select the towers.

The finished image is shown in Figure 5.41.

Figure 5.40 Paste the castle onto the landscape.

Figure 5.41 The finished version will look like this.

Compositing Close Up

It's one thing to create a composite image of distant objects with edges that can be blurred, as we did with the fantasy landscape. Assembling a collage of images that are closer to the camera, sharper, and easier to examine closely is more of a challenge. For this next project, we'll move a kitten from a deck railing to a Chinese desk, and do all we can to make the combination look realistic. Start with the Kitten image from the website, shown in Figure 5.42, and follow along with these steps. As with the last project, I'm not going to describe every single procedure in exhausting detail, except when we work with a new feature, such as the Extract command in the next section.

Figure 5.42 Crouching kitten, hidden background.

Extracting the Kitten

Photoshop includes several tools specifically designed to help you isolate parts of images from their backgrounds. These include the Background Eraser and the Extract command. The Background Eraser is the simpler of the two: It's nothing more than an eraser with a circular cursor, similar to that used by the Magnetic Lasso discussed earlier in this chapter. Set a Tolerance level in the Option bar, choose a size for the eraser, and use the Background Eraser to remove pixels that don't closely match the pixels in your main subject. This tool is useful for objects that have a fairly hard edge and a distinct background and, in such situations, offers little advantage over selection tools, such as the Magic Wand.

The Extract command, moved from the Image menu to the Filter menu in Photoshop 7 and later versions, provides much more sophisticated removal of surrounding areas. You can carefully paint a mask around the edges of your object, adjust the borders, and preview your result before extracting the object. Extract works very well with wispy or hairy objects. Follow these steps.

1. The Extract command works best with images that are sharp, so the first thing to do is sharpen the kitten image using Filter > Sharpen > Unsharp Mask. Use a setting of 100 percent or more to make every hair on the kitten's body stand out.

2. Activate the Extract command by choosing Filter > Extract, or by pressing Alt/Option + Ctrl/Command + X. The dialog box shown in Figure 5.43 will appear.

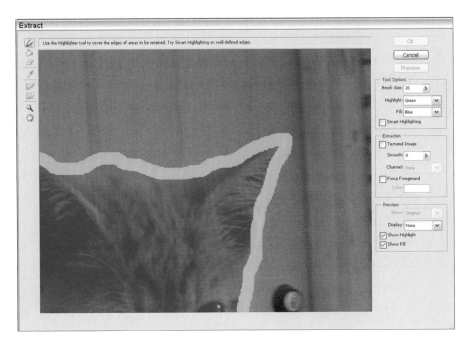

Figure 5.43 The Extract command lets you remove objects from their backgrounds.

3. Zoom in on the portion of the image you want to extract. In this case, focus on the upper edge of the kitten. Zooming within the Extract dialog box is done in exactly the same way as within Photoshop. Use the Zoom tool (available from the dialog box's Tool Palette at the left edge) or simply press Ctrl/Command + space to zoom in or Alt/Option + space to zoom out.

4. Click the edge highlighter/marker tool at the top of the Tool Palette. Choose a brush size of 20 from the Tool Options area on the right side of the dialog box.

5. Paint the edges of the kitten with the marker. Use the Eraser tool to remove markings you may have applied by mistake, or press Ctrl/Command + Z to undo any highlighting you've drawn since you last clicked the mouse. The Hand tool can be used to slide the image area within the Preview window.

6. When you've finished outlining the kitten, click the Paint Bucket tool and fill the area you want to preserve.

7. Click the Preview button to see what the kitten will look like when extracted, as shown in Figure 5.44.

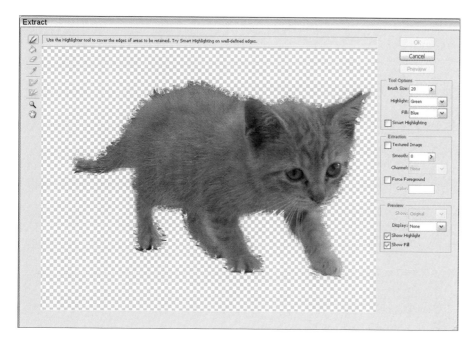

Figure 5.44 Preview your extraction before applying the effect.

8. If necessary, use the Cleanup tool (press C to activate it) to subtract opacity from any areas you may have erased too enthusiastically. This will return some of the texture of the kitten's fur along the edge. Hold down the Alt/Option key while using the Cleanup tool to make an area more opaque.

9. Use the Edge Touchup tool (press T to activate it) to sharpen edges.

10. Click on the OK button when satisfied to apply the extraction to the kitten.

Kitten on a Desktop

Load the Chinese Desk image, shown in Figure 5.45, from the website as we begin to give the kitten a new home. Follow these steps to deposit her on the shiny black surface.

1. Select the kitten from the original image, and paste her down into the Chinese Desk photo. Use Edit > Transform > Scale to adjust her size to one that's realistic for the desktop.

2. Use Image > Adjustments > Brightness/Contrast to boost the contrast of the kitten to match the harder lighting of the desk surface.

3. Press Q to enter Quick Mask mode, and using a fairly large soft-edged brush, paint the undersides of the kitten's feet, body, and tail. Press Q again to exit Quick Mask mode and use the Brightness/Contrast controls again to darken these under-surfaces.

Figure 5.45 This Chinese desk will make an interesting background for our crouching tiger kitten.

4. Press Ctrl/Command + D to deselect everything in the image, then use Quick Mask mode to paint a selection that encompasses the kitten's eyes. Exit Quick Mask mode and use Brightness/Contrast to lighten the eyes dramatically and give them much more contrast. Your image will now look like the one shown in Figure 5.46.

Figure 5.46 Darken the underside of the kitten, and lighten her eyes.

Creating a Reflection

Notice that parts of the desk are reflected in the shiny black surface. The kitten needs a realistic reflection of her own. Here's how to do it.

1. Choose Layer > Duplicate to duplicate the kitten layer.

2. Select Edit > Transform > Flip Vertical to produce a mirror image of the kitten.

3. Use Edit > Transform > Rotate to rotate the mirror image counterclockwise so it will appear at the side of the kitten, rather than in front of it.

4. Reduce the opacity of the reflection to about 30 percent, using the slider in the Layers Palette.

5. Here's the sneaky part: adjust the way the reflection merges with the shiny desktop by selecting Difference as the merging mode in the Layers Palette. This will ensure that darker parts of the reflection merge with the desktop, while letting the lighter parts show through. This produces a more realistic reflection than one in which the reflection layer completely overlays the desktop layer.

6. You can optionally apply some Gaussian Blur to the reflection to soften it, or leave the reflection sharp to give the desktop a shinier appearance. I didn't use Blur in the image shown in Figure 5.47, but you might want to.

7. Create a new transparent layer, and, using a two-pixel white brush, paint in some whiskers on the right side of the kitten. The whiskers typically are too wispy to extract well, so I usually allow them to be erased and then replace them later.

8. Set the opacity of the whiskers layer to about 60% and apply Gaussian Blur to them until they match the kitten's other whiskers fairly well.

Figure 5.47 Add a reflection and some whiskers.

More than One Way to Skin a Cat

You can colorize the kitten (or any other object you care to) in a realistic way using the following trick. I wanted to make this cat a little more tiger-like, so I enhanced its coloring a little with some bright orange-yellow. That's not as simple as you might think. If you color the cat using the Hue/Saturation controls, you'll apply color to all of it, losing some of the subtle color in its eyes. Follow these steps, instead:

1. Duplicate the kitten's layer using Layer > Duplicate.

2. Choose Image > Adjustments > Hue/Saturation, and move the Hue and Saturation controls until you get the color you want. Click on OK to apply the modification to the duplicate of the kitten layer.

3. Choose the Overlay Merging mode in the Layers Palette to merge the colorized layer with the original kitten in the layer underneath. This technique will let other colors show through, smoothly merging the new color with the original image.

4. Use the Brightness/Contrast controls on the colorized layer to get the color exactly the way you like. Usually, it's best to reduce the contrast a little and add some brightness, as I did for the final image, shown in Figure 5.48.

Figure 5.48 A slick colorizing trick gives the kitten a tiger's pelt.

Compositing Possibilities

Here's a quick summary of some of the other things you can do with compositing. You'll want to try your hand at all of these as you become a Photoshop master.

- **Remove large objects.** You can't retouch large objects out of a photo, but you can replace an unsightly barn, brother-in-law, or auto junkyard in the background with something else, such as trees, a mountain, or a lake.

- **Relocate things in the photo.** Compositing gives you the opportunity to correct faulty compositions, change the center of interest in a photo, or make something else a little easier to see.

- **Replace components of the photograph.** That photo of your home looks great, but you no longer own that car parked out front. Drop in a picture of your new jalopy using Photoshop CS's compositing techniques.

- **Adding new objects to a photo.** Could your beach scene use some palm trees? Would you like to see J-Lo standing in the middle of your class reunion photo? Do you hope to work for a tabloid newspaper some day? Experiment with adding objects using compositing.

- **Squeeze things together, or stretch them apart.** If you have a picture that is too wide for your intended use, you can often take the left and right halves, overlap them, disguise the seam, and end up with a narrower photo that fits, but doesn't look distorted.

Combining Compositing and Retouching

Do you remember those photos taken at your wedding reception, in which your new brother-in-law managed to intrude on every photo? Do you have a great-looking group shot of everybody in your department at work—including Elmo, who was fired last month? Wouldn't it be great if you could just paint the offenders out of a photograph with one stroke? Photoshop takes more than one stroke, but it can do the job for you. Try this project to see how easy it is. Lacking a nasty in-law, we're going to clean up a vacation photo by deleting a poorly posed subject, shown at left in Figure 5.49. Our weapons of choice for this exercise are the Clone Stamp retouching tool and a simple compositing technique. You can follow along using the kids file on the website.

The obvious solution, of course, would be to crop the kid out of the picture. However, that would snip out the interesting house on the hill in the background. Another remedy would be to copy the portion of the fence at the right of the picture and paste it down over the unwanted subject. Unfortunately, that stretch of fence and its background is very dark, and duplicating it would provide an

Figure 5.49 We can remove the kid at left painlessly.

unattractive dark area at the lower-right corner of the picture. Cloning lets us preserve the background area that's already there, deleting only the boy. Here's how to do it.

1. Press S to choose the Clone Stamp tool, and select a medium-sized (say, 35-pixel) soft-edged brush.

2. Hold down the Alt/Option key and click in the foliage between the fence railings to select that area as the source for cloning.

3. Carefully clone over the boy, a little bit at a time. Resample the foliage by Alt/Option + clicking frequently. If your clone "source" (represented by a cross-hair that appears briefly to one side of your brush icon each time you click) moves into an area that has already been cloned, you'll get a repeating fish-scale effect like the one shown in Figure 5.50.

4. Continue cloning to paint over the boy completely. Don't worry about the fence railing at this time; we'll fix that later. The important thing is to reproduce a realistic background as it would appear behind the subject if he weren't there. After a while, your image should begin to look like the examples shown in Figure 5.51.

5. Copy a horizontal section of the railing from the far-left side of the fence, using the Rectangular marquee tool. You should be able to use this tool to select only the fence railing, and none of the background area.

Figure 5.50 Avoid the fish-scale look that comes from cloning from an area that already has been cloned.

Figure 5.51 The kid is gradually cloned away.

6. Paste the horizontal section into the image over a portion of the rail that has been obscured by cloning.

7. Repeat steps 5 and 6 until all the horizontal railings have been "patched." Then do the same for the vertical railings. Merge all the transparent layers containing the railings (make all the layers except those containing railings visible, and with the top rail layer selected, press Shift + Ctrl/Command + E [Merge Visible]). You'll end up with an image that looks like Figure 5.52. (I've left the selection boundaries visible so you can see the duplicated portion of the fence.)

Figure 5.52 Add railings from the other side of the picture.

8. The remaining boy is still a bit too much taller than the girls in the photo, so you can copy him, paste his image into the picture, and move him down a bit. Use the Clone Stamp tool, as necessary, to blend in the background.

9. Finally, use the Burn toning tool to darken the background and the girls at left. The finished picture looks like Figure 5.53.

Figure 5.53 The finished image looks like this.

Next Up

Color correction is another important image editing technique you'll want to master as you learn to enhance your photos. In the next chapter, I'm going to show you at least four ways to improve colors of any image, or modify them to create some special effects.

6

Correcting Your Colors

Color is cool. Color is hot. Photographers know that color is a powerful tool that can grab the eye, lead our attention to specific areas of an image, and, through some unknown process, generate feelings that run the emotional color gamut from ardor to anger.

Conversely, *bad* color can ruin an image. It's a fact of life that a well-composed image that might look sensational in black and white can be utterly ruined simply by presenting it in color with inappropriate hues or saturation. Bad color can override every other aspect of a photograph, turning wheat into chaff. But what, exactly, is bad color?

The most interesting thing about color is that the concept of good and bad can vary by the image, the photographer's intent, and the purpose of the finished photograph. The weird colors of a cross-processed image are very bad if they show up in your vacation pictures, but wonderfully evocative in a fashion shoot. A photo that has a vivid red cast may look terrible as a straight portrait, but interesting when part of a glamour shot taken by the glowing embers of a fireplace. A picture of a human with even the tiniest bit of a blue tinge looks ghastly, but might add the desired degree of chill to a snowy winter scene.

Strictly speaking, you don't have to understand how color works to use it to make corrections or generate striking effects. It's entirely possible to use trial-and-error experimentation to arrive at the results you want. However, just because you don't need an electrical engineering degree to operate a toaster, it's good to know a little something about electricity before you go poking around inside with a fork.

This chapter provides a gentle introduction to the color theories that photographers work with everyday, and which become even more useful when you begin working with Photoshop. You'll learn more about the most frequently used color models and the differences between the way color is viewed in the real world, captured by a film or digital camera, displayed on your monitor, and output by your printer. I'll spare you the hypertechnical details of working with color curves. If you need to fine-tune color that precisely, you need a prepress guide like Dan Margulis' *Professional Photoshop.*

All the color correction tools in this chapter will be easy to use. Even so, you'll be able to work with them effectively because, before we ever touch a slider, I'm going to give you enough background in color that correction will be almost second nature to you.

Wonderful World of Color

In a sense, color is an optical illusion. Human perception of color is a strange and wonderful thing, created in our brains from the variation of the wavelengths of light that reach our eyes. If you remained awake during high-school science class, you'll recall that the retina of the eye contains rod cells (which are used for detail and black-and-white vision when there is not much light) and three types of cone cells, which respond to a different wavelength of light, all in the 400 nanometer (violet) to 700 nanometer (red) range of what we call the color spectrum.

All the colors we could see (if our eyes were constructed that way) would reside in that continuous color spectrum, like the one shown in Figure 6.1. However, we can't directly sense each of those individual colors. Instead, each of the three kinds of cone cells in our eyes "see" a different set of frequencies, which happen to correspond to what we call red, green, and blue (RGB). Our brains process this RGB information and translate it into a distinct color that we perceive.

Figure 6.1 Our eyes don't perceive the full spectrum of color, but capture hues through three different kinds of cone cells in the retina.

Color films use a minimum of three different layers of photosensitive emulsion, each sensitive to red, green, and blue light. Digital cameras have three sets of color sensors, and scanners use three light sources, three arrays of sensors, or filters to capture red, green, and blue information. Finally, when digital information is seen on computer monitors, the same three colors (in the form of LCD pixels or CRT phosphors) complete the circle by displaying the color information for our eyes to view again.

Digital cameras work something like color film, responding to red, green, and blue light. However, except for some alternative technologies, such as the Foveon sensor currently used only in the Sigma SD9 and SD10 digital SLR cameras, and the seldom seen Polaroid X530 point-and-shoot model, camera sensors do *not* have separate red/green/blue layers. Instead, each pixel in a digital camera image is sensitive to only one color, and interpolation is used to calculate the correct color for a particular photosite if something other than the color it's been assigned falls on that pixel.

The various capture and display processes are significant for an important reason. *None* of the systems used to grab or view color respond to red, green, and blue light in exactly the same way. Some are particularly sensitive to green light; indeed, digital cameras are designed with twice as many green-sensitive sensors than red or blue. Most systems don't respond to all the colors in a perfectly linear way, either, so that a hue that is twice as intense may register slightly less or a bit more intense.

And it gets worse: The models used to represent those colors in the computer also treat colors in different ways. That's why an image you see in real life may not look exactly the same in a color slide, a color print, a scanned image, on your screen, or when reproduced by a color printer or printing press. Simply converting an image from RGB to CMYK (more on that later) can change the colors significantly. The concept of the range and type of colors that can be captured, manipulated, and reproduced by a given device or system—its color gamut—is an important one for photographers working in Photoshop.

Color Models

Artificial color systems, which include computer scanners, monitors, printers, and other peripherals, attempt to reproduce, or model, the colors that we see, using various sets of components of color. If the model is a good one, all the colors we are capable of detecting are defined by the parameters of the model. The colors within the definition of each model are termed its *color space*. Because nearly all color spaces use three different parameters such as colors (red, green, and blue, for example) or qualities (such as hue, saturation, and brightness), we can plot them as x, y, and z coordinates to produce a three-dimensional shape that represents the color gamut of the model.

The international standard for specifying color was defined in 1931 by the Commission Internationale L'Eclairage (CIE); it is a scientific color model that can be used to define all the colors that humans can see. However, computer color systems are based on one of three or four other color models, which are more practical because they are derived from the actual hardware systems used to reproduce those colors.

None of these systems can generate all the colors in the full range of human perception, but they are the models with which we must work. There have been some efforts to define new color working spaces, such as sRGB, but so far nothing has appeared that will completely take over the photography and computer graphics industries. Indeed, learning to work with Photoshop's sRGB setting was one of the most popular topics among puzzled users when Photoshop 6 was introduced. The topic has been renewed with the popularity of digital cameras, because some of them, like my own Nikon D70, can use several slight variations of color models, including sRGB and what is called Adobe RGB. Your best bet is to learn something about all color working spaces, since image editors like Photoshop support several different color models.

Of the three most common models, the ones based on the hue-lightness-saturation (HLS) and hue-saturation-value (HSV) of colors are the most natural for us to visualize, because they deal with a continuous range of colors that may vary in brightness or richness. You use this type of model when you adjust colors with the Hue/Saturation dialog boxes.

Two other models, called additive color and subtractive color, are easier for computers to handle, because the individual components are nothing more than three basic colors of light. Throughout this book, I've referred to these models as RGB and CMY (or CMYK, for cyan, magenta, yellow, and black).

Additive color is commonly used for image capture by cameras and scanners, and in computer display monitors, while subtractive color is used for output devices such as printers. Since you need to understand how color works with these peripherals, I'll explain the additive and subtractive models first.

Additive Color

Computer monitors produce color by aiming three electronic guns at sets of red, green, and blue phosphors (compounds which give off photons when struck by beams of electrons), coated on the screen of your display. LCD and LED monitors use sets of red, green, and blue pixels to represent each picture element of an image that are switched on or off, as required. If none of the colors are displayed, we see a black pixel. If all three glow in equal proportions, we see a neutral color—gray or white, depending on the intensity.

Such a color system uses the additive color model—so called because the colors are added together, as you can see in Figure 6.2. A huge selection of colors can be produced by varying the combinations of light. In addition to pure red, green, and blue, we can also produce cyan (green and blue together), magenta (red and blue), yellow (red and green), and all the colors in between. As with

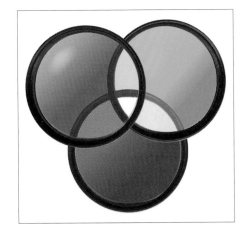

Figure 6.2 The additive color system uses beams of light in red, green, and blue hues.

grayscale data, the number of bits used to store color information determines the number of different tones that can be reproduced.

Figure 6.2 shows one way of thinking about additive color, in a two-dimensional color space. The largest circles represent beams of light in red, green, and blue. Where the beams overlap, they produce other colors. For example, red and green combine to produce yellow. Red and blue add up to magenta, and green and blue produce cyan. The center portion, in which all three colors overlap, is white. If the idea that overlapping produces *no* color, rather than some combined color seems confusing, remember that the illumination is being added together, and combining all three of the component colors of light produces a neutral white with equal amounts of each.

However, if you look at the figure, you'll see that it shows overlapping circles that are each more or less the same intensity of a single color (allowing some artistic license for the 3D "shading" effect added to keep the individual circles distinct). For that reason, this two-dimensional model doesn't account for the lightness or darkness of a color—the amount of white or black. That added dimension is dealt with by, literally, adding a dimension, as you can see in the mock 3D model shown in Figure 6.3.

The figure shows red, green, and blue colors positioned at opposite corners of the cube, with their complementary colors arranged between them. White and black are located opposite one another, as well. Any shade that can be produced by adding red, green, and blue together can be represented by a position within the cube.

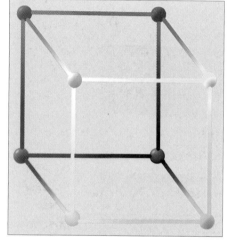

Figure 6.3 The RGB color space can be better represented by a three-dimensional cube, simplified to corners and edges in this illustration.

No widely used display device available today produces pure red, green, or blue light. Only lasers, which output at one single frequency of light, generate absolutely pure colors, and they aren't used for display devices. We see images through the glow of phosphors, LEDs, or LCD pixels, and the ability of these to generate absolutely pure colors is limited. Color representations on a display differ from brand to brand and even from one display to another within the same brand.

Moreover, the characteristics of a given display can change as the monitor ages and the color-producing elements wear out. Some phosphors, particularly blue ones, change in intensity as they age, at a different rate than other phosphors. So, identical signals rarely produce identical images on displays, regardless of how closely the devices are matched in type, age, and other factors.

In practice, most displays show far fewer colors than the total of which they are theoretically capable. Actually, the number of different colors a display can show at one time is limited to the number of individual pixels. At 1024 × 768 resolution, there are only 786,432 different pixels. Even if each one were a different color, you'd view, at most, only around three-quarters of a million colors at once. The reason your digital camera, scanner, display, and Photoshop itself need to be 24-bit compatible is so the *right* 786,432 pixels (or whichever number is actually required) can be selected from the available colors that can be reproduced by a particular color model's gamut. In practice, both scanners and digital cameras capture more than 24 bits worth of color, to allow for the inevitable information lost in translating a full-spectrum image to digital form. To understand why, you need to understand a concept called *bit depth*.

As you know from working with Photoshop, the number of theoretical colors that can be represented is measured using that bit depth yardstick. For example, "4-bit" color can represent the total number of colors possible using four bits of binary information (0000 to 1111), or 16 colors. Similarly, 8-bit color can represent 256 different colors or grayscale tones, while "high color" 15- or 16-bit displays can represent 32,767 or 65,535 colors. You'll sometimes encounter high color images when you're displaying at very high resolutions using video cards which don't have enough memory for 24-bit color at that resolution.

For example, perhaps you own a 21-inch or larger monitor capable of displaying images at 2048 × 1536 pixels of resolution, and you are working with an older video card that can display only 65,535 colors at that resolution. This example is

WHEN ARE 32 BITS ACTUALLY 24 BITS? AND WHEN IS 32 MORE THAN 32?

In the past, when you used Photoshop with so-called 32-bit color images, you were actually working with ordinary 24-bit images, plus an extra 8 bits used to store grayscale alpha channel information. The image itself was usually a normal 24-bit image. In this case, the extra 8 bits store your selections, layer masks, and so forth. On the other hand, in Photoshop CS 2.0 terminology, "16-bit color" usually doesn't refer to those "high-color," 65,535-hue images, either. Within Photoshop "16-bit color" means 16 bits *per color channel*, so the image is actually a 48-bit (16 bits × 3 channels) representation. Photoshop 2.0 added an extra dimension—that of high-dynamic range color. HDR color also uses 16-bits of information to store information about each channel. However, there is a difference, one that can be confusing until you wrap your mind around it. Those 16 bits of information are stored as *floating decimal point* numbers, which are inherently a lot more accurate. If it's been as long for you as it has for me since math class, the easiest way to understand the difference is to think of expressing the idea of one-third only with integers (33 percent) or with a floating point number like 33.3333333333333333 percent. Less information is lost to rounding errors, etc. HDR uses 32-point floating point numbers to help preserve the dynamic range of your color images. You'll learn more about this later in the chapter.

a bit farfetched, because most video cards today have enough memory to display at least 16.8 million colors at whatever their maximum resolution is. You will, however, sometimes encounter a card that must step down to a lower color depth to display its absolute top resolution.

For most applications, 16-bit color is as good as 24-bit color. Image editing with Photoshop CS 2.0 is not one of them. It actually has robust high dynamic range (HDR) capabilities that extend even *beyond* 24 bit color. So, 24-bit color is, at best, the minimum you should work with. Happily, the standard today is that video cards generally have 64MB or more of memory, and are fully capable of displaying 24-bit full color at any supported resolution, and 16.8 million different hues. Scanners and some high-end digital cameras can even capture 36 bits or 48 bits of color, for a staggering billions and billions of hues. The extra colors are useful to provide detail in the darkest areas of an image, especially when you consider that many bits of information are lost during the conversion from an analog signal (the captured light) to digital (the image file stored on your computer).

Subtractive Color

There is a second way of producing color that is familiar to computer users—one that is put to work whenever we output our Photoshop images as hard copies using a color printer. This kind of color also has a color model that represents a particular color gamut. The reason a different kind of color model is necessary is simple: When we represent colors in hardcopy form, the light source we view by comes not from the image itself, as it does with a computer display. Instead, hard copies are viewed by light that strikes the paper or other substrate and then is filtered by the image on the paper, then reflected back to our eyes.

This light starts out with (more or less) equal quantities of red, green, and blue light and looks white to our eyes. The pigments the light passes through before bouncing off the substrate absorb part of this light, subtracting it from the spectrum. The components of light that remain reach our eyes and are interpreted as color. Because various parts of the illumination are subtracted from white to produce color, this color model is known as the *subtractive* system.

The three primary subtractive colors are cyan, magenta, and yellow, and the model is sometimes known as the CMY model. Usually, however, black is included in the mix, for reasons that will become clear shortly. When black is added, this color system becomes the CMYK model (black is represented by its terminal character, *k*, rather than *b* to avoid confusion with the additive primary blue). Figure 6.4 shows the subtractive color model in a fanciful representation, retaining the color filter motif I started out with in

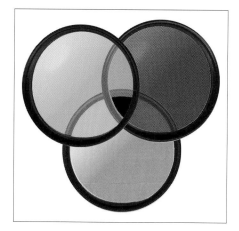

Figure 6.4 The subtractive color system uses cyan, magenta, and yellow colors.

describing the additive color system. (You couldn't overlap filters to produce the colors shown, although you could print with inks to create them.)

In subtractive output devices such as color printers or printing presses, cyan, magenta, yellow, and, usually, black pigments (for detail) are used to represent a gamut of colors. It's obvious why additive colors won't work for hard copies: It is possible to produce red, green, and blue pigments, of course, and we could print red, green, and blue colors that way (that's exactly what is done for spot color). However, there would be no way to produce any of the other colors with the additive primaries. Red pigment reflects only red light; green pigment reflects only green. When they overlap, the red pigment absorbs the green, and the green absorbs the red, so no light is reflected and we see black.

Cyan pigment, on the other hand, absorbs only red light (well, it is *supposed* to). It reflects both blue and green (theoretically), producing the blue-green shade we see as cyan. Yellow pigment absorbs only blue light, reflecting red and green, while magenta pigment absorbs only green, reflecting red and blue. When we overlap two of the subtractive primaries, some of at least one color still reflects. Magenta (red-blue) and yellow (red-green) together produce red, because the magenta pigment absorbs green and the yellow pigment absorbs blue. Their common color, red, is the only one remaining. Of course, each of the subtractive primaries can be present in various intensities or percentages, from 0 to 100%. The remainder is represented by white, which reflects all colors in equal amounts.

So, in our example above, if the magenta pigment was only 50% present and the yellow represented at 100%, only half of the green would be absorbed, while 100% of the blue would be soaked up. Our red would appear to be an intermediate color, orange. By varying the percentages of the subtractive primaries, we can produce a full range of colors.

Well, theoretically we could. You'll recall that RGB displays aren't perfect because the colors aren't pure. So, too, it is impossible to design pigments that reflect absolutely pure colors. Equal amounts of cyan, magenta, and yellow pigment *should* produce black. More often, what you'll get is a muddy brown. When daily newspapers first began their changeover to color printing in the 1970s, many of them used this three-color system, with mixed results.

However, better results can be obtained by adding black as a fourth color. Black can fill in areas that are supposed to be black and add detail to other areas of an image. While the fourth color does complicate the process a bit, the actual cost in applications like offset printing is minimal. Black ink is used to print text anyway, so there is no additional press run for black. Moreover, black ink is cheaper than critical process color inks, so it's possible to save money by using black instead of laying on three subtractive primaries extra thick. A typical image separated into its component colors for printing is shown in Figure 6.5.

Figure 6.5 Full-color images are separated into cyan, magenta, yellow, and black components for printing.

The output systems you use to print hard copies of color images use the subtractive color system in one way or another. Most of them are unable to print varying percentages of each of the primary colors. Inkjet printers, color laser printers, and thermal wax transfer printers are examples of these. All these systems must simulate other colors by dithering, which is similar to the halftoning system discussed earlier. A few printers can vary the amount of pigment laid down over a broader range. Thermal dye sublimation printers are an example of this type. These printers can print a full range of tones, up to the 16.8 million colors possible with 24-bit systems.

The subtractive color system can also be represented in three dimensions, as I've done in Figure 6.6. In this illustration, the positions of the red, green, and blue colors have been replaced by cyan, magenta, and yellow, and the other hues rearranged accordingly. In fact, if you mentally rotate and reverse this figure, you'll see that it is otherwise identical to the one in Figure 6.3; RGB and CMYK are in this sense two sides of the same coin. However, don't make the mistake of thinking their color spaces are identical. There are colors that can be displayed in RGB that can't be printed using CMYK.

When you view color images on your display during image editing with Photoshop, the colors in the image file are always converted to additive (RGB) colors for display—regardless of the color model

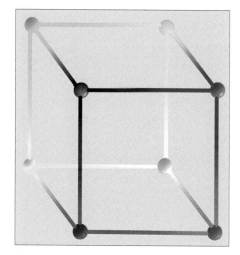

Figure 6.6 The subtractive color model can also be represented by a 3D cube.

used to represent the actual image. However—and this is important—the color model used for the actual file remains the same, unless you change modes and then save the file. In truth, Photoshop uses another color model, called Lab (discussed below), as an intermediate when converting from one color to another.

For example, if you load a file that has been saved using the CMYK color model, a program like Photoshop will let you work on it in CMYK mode, even though the colors must be converted to RGB for viewing. In general, CMYK colors will seem less saturated and duller than RGB colors. That's because RGB colors can be made brighter by pumping more light through the device you're using to view them. CMYK colors are limited by the brightness of the substrate (a "whiter" paper will reflect more light and brighter colors) and the amount of ink used.

Within Photoshop, you don't actually lose any colors unless you physically convert the file from one mode to the other. If you do convert from CMYK to RGB mode and back again, because CMYK can represent some colors that are outside the RGB gamut—and vice versa—you will lose some hues each time. Stick with CMYK if that's the mode your file was created in, especially if you will be outputting to a printer or color separation system that expects to work with CMYK colors. That way, you'll avoid creating RGB colors which cannot be reproduced by the CMYK output system. Photoshop will handle your file in Lab mode, and protect your colors.

Lab color was developed by the CIE as a device-independent international standard. Lab consists of three components, a luminance channel, plus a* and b* channels that represent green to magenta and blue to yellow, respectively. Because CIELab can represent all the colors found in both RGB and CMYK, it serves as a perfect intermediate format for Photoshop. There are some highly technical operations that can be carried out in Lab mode. In addition, Lab colors more closely reflect how humans perceive color, so if there is a difference in color in CIELab mode, humans will probably perceive a difference, too. That's not always the case with RGB and CMYK modes.

Other Color Models

The hue-saturation-brightness color model, also known as HSB or HLS (for hue-lightness-saturation), is a convenient way to manage color for some operations. For example, if you want to adjust the saturation of a color without modifying its hue or brightness, HSB mode (using Image > Adjustments > Hue/Saturation) is the way to go. In this model, individual colors, called hues, are represented as they are in a rainbow, as a continuous spectrum, arranged in a hexagon like that shown in Figure 6.7. The full color space is represented as a double hexcone that extends upwards and downwards from the hexagon, as shown in Figure 6.8. The top of the axis drawn through the center of the cones represents pure white, while the

Figure 6.7 The hue/saturation/brightness color model starts with a color circle or hexagon like this one.

bottom point represents black. Moving higher in the cone produces lighter colors; moving lower in the bottom cone produces darker colors. Saturation is represented by movement in a third direction, outward from the center axis. The center represents a desaturated color and the outer edges represent fully saturated hues.

All colors can be represented by three parameters in this model. The hue is the particular position of a color in the color wheel. Hues are often represented by angles, beginning with red at 0° and progressing around in a counterclockwise direction to magenta at 60°, blue at 120°, and so forth. The saturation of the color is the degree to which that color is diluted with white. A hue with a great deal of white is muted; a red becomes a pink, for example. A hue with very little or no white is vivid and saturated. Brightness can be thought of as the degree to which a color is diluted with black. Add black to our desaturated red (pink), and you'll get a very dark pink. Various combinations of hue, saturation, and brightness can be used to produce just about any color we can see. Individual hues can be found along the edges of the hexagon. Moving from that edge toward the center within the same plane indicates a color that is less saturated. The center of the hexagon represents zero saturation. The axis extending through the center of the hexcones represents lightness and darkness, with white at the top and black at the bottom of the line.

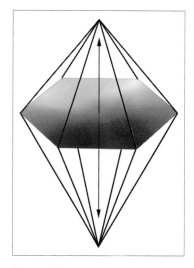

Figure 6.8 The full color space is represented by two hexagonal cones. Moving from the center outward produces more saturated colors, while moving up or down the axis of the cones darkens or lightens the color.

Capturing Color Images

Today we have several options for capturing images for manipulation in Photoshop. Color scanners have been around the longest, for around 50 years, in fact. The first ones I saw early in my career cost more than a million dollars when you included the computer equipment needed to drive them, and they were intended only for professional graphics applications at service bureaus and large publications. Today, color scanners, like the one shown in Figure 6.9, can cost less than $100.

Color scanners are nothing more than a system for capturing the proper amount of each of the primary colors of light in a given image. So, these scanners use three different light sources—one each of red, green, and blue—to scan a color image. To do so, some older scanners actually made three passes over the image— once for each color. More recent scanners use multiple

Figure 6.9 Modern color scanners can cost $100 or less.

light sources, or "rotate" their illumination, using red/green/blue light in succession to capture an image in a single pass.

The amount of light reflected by the artwork for each color varies according to the color of the pigments in the original. Cyan pigment, for example, absorbs red light and reflects blue and green. So, when a cyan area is illuminated by the red fluorescent light in a scanner, relatively little light is reflected. Most of the light produced by the blue and green fluorescents is reflected. Your scanner software records that area of the original as cyan. A similar process captures the other colors in your subject during the scan. Even if you don't use a scanner yourself, you may work with scanned images that are captured by your photofinisher when converting your color slides or prints to digital form for distribution online or as a PhotoCD or Picture CD.

Digital cameras cut out the middle step by creating color images directly. Where scanners use a linear array that grabs an image one line at a time, digital cameras use a two-dimensional array that grabs a complete bitmap in one instant. Today, digital cameras with 3.3 to 6 megapixels (or more) of resolution can capture images that are virtually indistinguishable from those grabbed on film when reproduced or enlarged to 8 × 10 inches or less.

You'll find more information about color scanners in my book *Mastering Digital Scanning with Slides, Film, and Transparencies* (ISBN: 1-59200-141-6) and lots more nuts-and-bolts on digital cameras in *Mastering Digital Photography* (ISBN: 1-59200-114-9). If you want to learn how digital cameras capture color, check out *Mastering Digital Photography* or *Mastering Digital SLR Photography*. All three books are available from Course Technology, and you can find more information about them at my website, **www.dbusch.com.**

Color Calibration and Gamma Curves

Conventional film is well-known for having color reproduction characteristics that vary over a considerable range. Some films are prized for their vivid, saturated colors and are used to make product shots exciting or to brighten an overcast day. Other films are chosen for their neutrality or realistic flesh tones. Digital color offers new capabilities, but carries with it the same color reproduction concerns that film has long displayed. Whether you're shooting film or pixels, in most cases, you'll want your image to closely approximate the original. Neither color display systems nor color hardcopy output devices are consistent or particularly accurate. The best you can do is calibrate your peripherals so that there is a relationship between the colors in the original, what you see, and what you get as output.

The process is complicated by two facts. First, the response of any color system is rarely linear. And, to make things worse, it's difficult to describe a color in such a way that it means exactly the same thing to everyone. Assume for a moment a

24-bit system with 256 different tones of each color. A value of 0 for a particular color should represent no color; a value of 255 should represent the maximum intensity of that color. On a linear scale, 64 would represent about 25% intensity, 128 would be 50%, and so on. Yet, in real applications, an intensity of 64 is not half that of 128. It corresponds to some other percentage, depending on the characteristics of the device being used. The relationship of the actual representation to the ideal is known as a gamma curve.

Scanners do happen to conform to the ideal rather closely, but computer displays and printers tend to vary greatly. If you know the gamma curve of a particular device, however, you can correct it. For example, if you know that, with a certain device, a value of 64 produces an intensity that is only 90% of what it should be to be linear, you can boost that value by an appropriate amount whenever it occurs.

This is done by building a gamma correction table using the tools supplied by your scanner vendor. The table will include a value for each of the levels used in a system. The correction values can be substituted automatically by your software for the default values, theoretically producing a perfect, 45° gamma curve. Many vendors provide device characterization files for their products. If you're using Windows, you can follow the instructions at the end of this chapter for using the Adobe Gamma application to profile your monitor. Mac OS X users can use their operating system's built-in gamma correction tools instead.

Color Correction

Sometimes a horrid-looking image may have nothing more wrong with it than the balance of colors used to represent the image. Other times, the balance may be okay, but you'd like to make the colors look horrid in order to produce a desired special effect in your image.

Color balance is the relationship between the three colors used to produce your image, most often red, green, and blue. You need to worry only about three different factors.

- **Amount of Red, Green, and Blue.** If you have too much red, the image will appear too red. If you have too much green, it will look too green. Extra blue will make an image look as if it just came out of the deep freeze. Other color casts are produced by too much of two of the primary colors when compared to the remaining hue. That is, too much red and green produce a yellowish cast; red and blue tilt things toward magenta, and blue and green create a cyan bias. Figure 6.10 shows the same image with red, green, and blue color casts.

- **Saturation.** That is, how much of the hue is composed of the pure color itself, and how much is diluted by a neutral color, such as white or black. Figure 6.11 shows the image with low, normal, and high saturation.

■ **Brightness/contrast.** Brightness and contrast refer to the relative light-ness/darkness of each color channel and the number of different tones avail-able. If, say, there are only 12 different red tones in an image, ranging from very light to very dark, with only a few tones in between, then the red por-tion of the image can be said to have a high contrast. The brightness is deter-mined by whether the available tones are clustered at the denser or lighter areas of the image. Pros use something called histograms to represent these relationships, but you don't need to bother with those for now. Figure 6.12 shows the image with the contrast and brightness set low, normally, and high.

Figure 6.10 Left to right you'll find reddish, greenish, and bluish color casts.

Figure 6.11 The image has low saturation (left), normal saturation (middle), and high color saturation (right).

Figure 6.12 Brightness and contrast have been set low at left, normally in the middle, and high at right.

You may wonder what causes bad color in the first place. Indeed, knowing the sources of bad color can help you avoid the need for much color correction. Unfortunately, there are many culprits, whether you're using color negative film or slides, a scanner, or a digital camera. Here are the major sources of bad color.

Problem: Wrong Light Source

Reason: All color films are standardized, or balanced, for a particular "color" of light, and digital cameras default to a particular "white balance." Both are measured using a scale called *color temperature*. Color temperatures were assigned by heating a mythical "black body radiator" and recording the spectrum of light it emitted at a given temperature in degrees Kelvin. So, daylight at noon has a color temperature in the 5500° to 6000° range. Indoor illumination is around 3400°. Hotter temperatures produce bluer images (think blue-white hot) while cooler temperatures produce redder images (think of a dull-red glowing ember). Because of human nature, though, bluer images are called "cool" and redder images are called "warm," even though their color temperatures are actually reversed.

If a photograph is exposed indoors under warm illumination using film or a digital camera sensor balanced for cooler daylight, the image will appear much too reddish. If you were using a slide film, you'd get reddish slides. The photoprocessing lab can add some blue while making prints from "daylight balanced" color negatives exposed under this warm light, though, giving you reasonably well-balanced prints. Some professional films are balanced for interior ("tungsten") illumination. If one of these is exposed under daylight, it will appear too blue. Again, prints made from tungsten-balanced color negatives can be corrected at the lab.

At the same time, your digital camera expects to see illumination of a certain color temperature by default. Under bright lighting conditions it may assume the light source is daylight and balance the picture accordingly. In dimmer light, the camera's electronics may assume that the illumination is tungsten, and color balance for that. This may be what happens when your digital camera's white balance control is set to Auto. Of course, digital cameras, being the sophisticated beasts they are, can often detect white balance fairly accurately with no input by you. Some electronic flash units can even report to the camera the particular white balance which they are outputting, since a flash's color temperature can vary depending on how brief the flash exposure is. Figure 6.13 shows an image exposed under tungsten illumination with a daylight white balance.

Figure 6.13 Exposing daylight film under tungsten illumination, or taking a digital picture with a daylight white-balance setting produces a reddish image.

Solution: You can often make corrections for this type of defect digitally in Photoshop. However, to avoid the need entirely, use the right white balance setting with your camera, or purchase the correct film, or use a filter over the camera lens to compensate for the incorrect light source. You may not need to bother with color negative films because they can be corrected during the printing step, but will certainly want to do something in the case of slide films, because what you shoot is what you get. Note: the light a filter removes must be compensated for by increasing the exposure in the camera.

With a digital camera, set the white balance manually using your camera's controls. Your camera probably has a setting that allows you to point the lens at a white object and let it use that as its white point. Or, your camera may have some built-in white-balance settings for tungsten, fluorescents, daylight, and other sources.

Problem: Fluorescent Light Source

Reason: The chief difference between tungsten and daylight sources is nothing more than the proportion of red and blue light. The spectrum of colors is continuous, but is biased toward one end or the other. However, some types of fluorescent lights produce illumination that has a severe deficit in certain colors, such as only particular shades of red. If you looked at the spectrum or rainbow of colors encompassed by such a light source, it would have black bands in it, representing particular wavelengths of light. You can't compensate for this deficiency by adding all tones of red, either digitally or with a filter that is not designed specifically for that type of fluorescent light. Figure 6.14 shows an image that was exposed under fluorescent lights using a tungsten light balance.

Figure 6.14 Some fluorescent lights can produce a greenish image.

Solution: Use the Fluorescent setting of your digital camera. If working with film, your camera retailer can provide you with color filters recommended for particular kinds of fluorescent lamps. These filters are designed to add only the amounts and types of colors needed. Since it's difficult to correct for fluorescent lights digitally, you'll want to investigate this option if you shoot many pictures under fluorescents and are getting "greenish" results. You can also shoot in the RAW format if your digital camera has that feature, and correct the color as you convert in Photoshop.

Problem: Incorrect Photofinishing

Reason: Here's one that digital photographers don't have to worry about. Equipment that makes prints from color negatives is highly automated, and usually can differentiate between indoor and outdoor pictures, or those that have a large amount of one color. Sometimes the sensors are fooled and you end up with off-color prints, or those that are too light or dark. The processing of color slides won't usually have any effect on the color balance or density of the transparencies, unless something is way out of whack, so you'll usually be concerned only about the color balance of prints.

Solution: Change finishers if it happens often. Ask that your prints be reprinted. If you'd rather not bother, you can often make corrections digitally after you've scanned the prints.

Problem: Mistreatment of Original Film

Reason: Your digital film cards won't deteriorate if you expose them to harsh environments briefly, but the same is not true for film. If you regularly store a camera in the hot glove compartment of your car, or take a year or more to finish a roll of film, you can end up with color prints that are off-color, sometimes by quite a bit. If your prints have a nasty purple cast, or even some rainbow-hued flares in them, your negatives probably suffered this indignity. X-rays can also damage film by fogging it.

Solution: Usually, film that has been "fogged" by X-rays, heat, or latent image-keeping effects cannot be corrected. If it hurts when you do that, don't do that. Figure 6.15 shows an image faded by heat and light.

Problem: Mixed Light Sources

Reason: You bounced your flash off a surface such as a colored wall or ceiling, and the pictures picked up the color of that surface. Or, you took an indoor picture with plenty of tungsten light, but the subject is near a window and is partially illuminated by daylight. Mixed lighting also occurs when strobe shots are influenced by room lighting or fluorescents.

Figure 6.15 Leave your camera in the trunk for too long, and you may end up with a fogged image like this one.

Solution: Avoid these situations. If some of your image is illuminated by the colored bounce flash, or daylight streaming in through a window, and other portions by another light source, you'll find it very difficult to make corrections. Investigate turning that picture into an "arty" shot.

Problem: Faded Colors

Reason: The dyes in color prints and slides are not stable, and will change when exposed to strong light or heat for long periods (one to five years), or with no further impetus even if kept in the dark for much longer periods (five to twenty years, and up).

Solution: In the case of color prints, you can sometimes make a new print from the original negative if you can find the negative and it was kept in a cool, dark place, or from the original digital file. Faded color prints and original slides can often be corrected digitally after scanning, because the color changes tend to take place faster in one color layer than another. You may be able to "add" missing colors by reducing the amount of the other colors in the photograph. There are a variety of Photoshop plug-ins that can help save faded images, too.

Problem: Unexpected Blue Cast in Flash Photographs

Reason: Certain fabrics, particularly whites, reflect a huge amount of ultraviolet light, making that neutral white garment turn a horrid blue. Because our eyes can't perceive ultraviolet light (except in the form of a brighter, whiter wash), but film can, we don't see this bluish cast as dramatically as the film does. Wedding photographers in particular have to cope with this. Certain flowers also reflect light that we can't see, too.

Solution: Warming filters can cope with this, but you can often fix the problem in Photoshop by adding a little red to your photo. Human faces tend to accommodate a bit of extra warmth, as you can see in Figure 6.16.

There are other reasons why you can end up with poorly balanced images, but this section has covered the ones you can do something about. Now, let's look at four different ways to color correct these images.

Figure 6.16 Extra ultraviolet reflection from white fabrics can produce bluish pictures like the one at top. Fortunately, Photoshop can correct for this error.

Color Correction Made Easy

Entire books have been written on sophisticated color correction techniques, but I'm going to make the process fairly easy. I'll start out with several traditional ways to correct color in images, and move on to some newer, easier alternatives. You can select the method you're most comfortable with: hands-on, seat-of-the-pants correction, or the simple, automated alternatives provided by Photoshop.

Just keep in mind as you try to improve the color balance, brightness/contrast, and other attributes of photographs, that none of the following methods can add detail or color that isn't there. All techniques work well with photographs that have, say, all the colors somewhere, but with too much of one hue or another. The extra color can be removed, leaving a well-balanced picture behind. Or, you can beef up the other colors, so they are in balance once again. Photoshop can do that by changing some pixels that are relatively close to the color you want to increase to that exact color.

But remember that removing one color, or changing some colors to another color doesn't add any color to your image: Either way, you're taking color out. So, if you have a photograph that is hopelessly and overpoweringly green, you're out of luck. When you remove all the green, there may be no color left behind. Or, you can add magenta until your subject's face turns purple, and all you'll end up with is a darker photo. You must start with a reasonable image; color correction is better suited for fine-tuning than major overhaul.

We're going to start out with some easy tools built into Photoshop CS 2.0 as well as earlier versions, then show you some tricks you can do with the latest Photoshop color correction tools.

Using Color Balance Controls

The first way we'll color correct an image is using the color balance controls that virtually every image editing program has. This method is oriented most towards brute force, and may be a little complicated for the neophyte. Stick with me, though. I have alternatives for you later in the chapter that are a breeze to master. This section lays down some principles you can use to create wild color effects, even if you decide to perform normal color corrections by one of the other methods.

In Photoshop, you'll find the color balance controls under Image > Adjustments > Color Balance, or just press Ctrl/Command + B if you're in a hurry. The dialog box looks like Figure 6.17. Note that Photoshop lets you set color balance separately for shadows, midtones, and highlights. What we're interested in at this point are the color sliders.

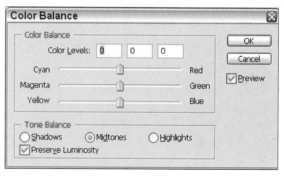

Figure 6.17 Photoshop's Color Balance controls let you increase or decrease any color.

These let you adjust the proportions of a particular color, from 0 percent to 100 percent. You can either add one color or subtract its two component colors. For example, moving the Cyan/Red slider to +20 (sliding it toward the red end) has the exact same effect as moving the Magenta/Green and Yellow/Red sliders both to the −20 position (toward the left).

Which should you choose? If you want to add pure red (or green, or blue), you can move the relevant control to the right. If your needs lean a little more toward one of the component colors than the other, move those sliders to the left, instead. The following example will show what I mean.

Figure 6.18 shows a scenic photo of a mountain view. Unfortunately, the original print was over 20 years old, and took on a strong reddish cast as it faded. I could have removed this red tone by simply sliding the Cyan/Red control towards the

Figure 6.18 This photo has a distinct reddish cast.

Cyan, which is the opposite, or complementary color of red. Because Photoshop lets you preview the results, it would have been just a matter of subtracting red (adding cyan) until the picture "looked" right. In this case, a value of −36 applied only to the middle tones of the photo (those other than the highlights or shadows) would have been about perfect. In most cases, that's all you'll need to do to get the result shown in Figure 6.19.

So, you can see that it is possible to remove red in one of two ways:

- Add cyan (thereby subtracting red)
- Add green and blue (thereby subtracting magenta and yellow)

I know it's a little confusing without looking at the color wheel, but the basic rules are simple. Reduce a color cast by:

- Adding the color opposite it on the color wheel
- Subtracting the color itself
- Subtracting equal amounts of the adjacent colors on the color wheel
- Adding equal amounts of the other two colors on its color wheel triangle

If you keep the color wheel in mind, you won't find it difficult to know how to add or subtract one color from an image, whether you are working with red, green, blue or cyan, magenta, yellow color models.

Figure 6.19 Adding cyan removes the cast.

The biggest challenge is deciding in exactly which direction you need to add/subtract color. Magenta may look a lot like red, and it's difficult to tell cyan from green. You may need some correction of both red and magenta, or be working with a slightly cyanish-green. Your photo retailer has color printing guide books published by Kodak and others which contain red, green, blue, cyan, magenta, and yellow viewing filters. Use them to view your image until you find the right combination of colors.

Adjusting Hue/Saturation/Brightness

You may encounter images that can be improved by changing the hue, saturation, or brightness of one color only. Photoshop lets you work with the HSB color model through the Image > Adjustments > Hue/Saturation dialog box, shown in Figure 6.20. This control lets you adjust these individual values for each color channel.

For example, you might have a holiday picture that needs to have its reds and greens enriched, but with muted blues. Perhaps the green grass and foliage in another color have picked up an undesirable color cast and you want to shift all the green values one way or another to improve the color. Or, you may want to darken or lighten just one color in an image (rather than all of them, which is done through the

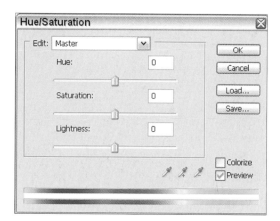

Figure 6.20 Photoshop's Hue/Saturation dialog box lets you work with hue, saturation, and brightness (or lightness) components separately.

conventional Lighten/Darken controls). Any of these are possible with the Hue/Saturation dialog box. Just select the color channel you want to work with, and move the sliders to get the effects you want. Figure 6.21 shows an Irish landscape that has been made considerably greener using this dialog box.

Figure 6.21 Photoshop's Hue/Saturation control brightened the foliage in this picture.

Using Color Ring Arounds and Variations

Color labs that deal primarily with professional photographers charge a lot more for the same size print as, say, an amateur-oriented photofinisher. Instead of a dollar or two for a photofinisher's 8 × 10-inch print, you can pay $10.00 to $20.00 and up (way up) for the same size print from a professional lab. Why the difference?

Both amateur and pro labs can produce automated (or machine) prints, although the equipment may be very different. The pro lab also offers handmade, or custom prints, produced one at a time with an enlarger and painstaking manual techniques. The exact color balance of a custom print is often crucial, so a pro lab may produce five or six variations and let the client choose the preferred example. That's why custom prints are worth the extra money: You're paying not only for the handwork, but for the ability to choose from among several different prints. It's faster and more efficient for the lab to produce the variations all at once than to go back and make tiny corrections over and over until the exact version you want is produced.

The same logic holds true in the digital world. You can play with the color balance of an image for hours at a time, never quite achieving what you are looking for. After a lot of work, you might decide that an earlier version really did look better after all.

Photoshop was one of the first image editors to jump on the "color ring around" or "variations" bandwagon. In this mode, the software itself generates several versions of an image, arranged in a circle or other array so you can view a small copy of each one and compare them. Photoshop's Variations mode is especially useful, so I'll use it to illustrate a third way to color correct problem photos.

Working with Photoshop's Variations Option

For this exercise, we're going to use a typical color portrait that has been goofed up big time. It's been printed quite a bit too dark, with plenty of extra red. Yet, hiding underneath this disaster is a good photo. We can use Photoshop's Variations to fix this image. Just follow these steps:

1. If you want to follow along, you can load the Close-up image from the Course website (**www.courseptr.com/downloads**). Otherwise, experiment with a photo image of your own. The principles are exactly the same.

2. With Photoshop, you can generate a color ring around by choosing Image > Adjustments > Variations. The Variations dialog box is shown in Figure 6.22.

   There are several components in this window:

   ■ In the upper-left corner, you'll find thumbnail images of your original image paired with a preview with the changes you've made applied. As you apply corrections, the Current Pick thumbnail will change.

   ■ Immediately underneath is another panel with the current pick surrounded by six different versions, each biased toward a different color: green, yellow, red, magenta, blue, and cyan. These show what your current pick would look like with that type of

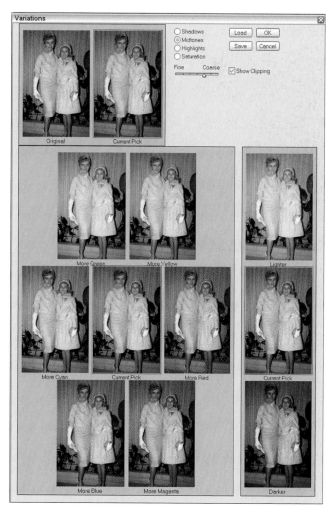

Figure 6.22 Photoshop's Variations dialog lets you compare alternate versions of an image.

correction added. You can click on any of them to apply that correction to the current pick.

■ To the right of this ring around is a panel with three sample images: the current pick in the center with a lighter version above and a darker version below.

■ In the upper-right corner of this window is a group of controls that modify how the other samples are displayed. I'll describe these controls shortly.

3. If the Midtone button is not depressed, click on it. You also want the pointer in the Fine…Coarse scale to be in the middle, and the Show Clipping button checked. The purpose of each of these controls is as follows:

■ The radio buttons determine whether the correction options are applied to the shadows, midtones, or highlights of the image, or only to saturation characteristics. You may make adjustments for each of these separately.

■ The Fine…Coarse scale determines the increment used for each of the variations displayed in the two lower panels. If you select a finer increment, the differences between the current pick and each of the options will be much smaller. A coarser increment will provide much grosser changes with each variation. You may need these to correct an original that is badly off-color. Since fine increments are difficult to detect on-screen, and coarse increments are often too drastic for tight control, I recommend keeping the pointer in the center of the scale.

■ The Show Clipping box tells the program to show you in neon colors which areas will be converted to pure white or pure black if you apply a particular adjustment to highlight or shadow areas (midtones aren't clipped).

■ You may load or save the adjustments you've made in a session so they can be applied to the image at any later time. You can use this option to create a file of settings that can be used with several similarly balanced images, thereby correcting all of them efficiently.

4. Our image is too cyan so the More Red thumbnail will look better. Click on it to apply that correction to the current pick. In fact, we needed to click twice, since the original image is very cyan.

5. The image is also too light. Click on the Darker thumbnail.

6. Click on the OK button in the upper right of the dialog box when finished.

In this example, we worked only with the midtones. In most cases, the shadows, midtones, and highlights will need roughly the same amount of correction. In others, though, the shadows or highlights may have picked up a color cast of their own (say, reflected from an object off-camera). Variations lets you correct these separately if you need to.

More often, though, you'll use the Shadow-Midtone-Highlights option to improve the appearance of images that have too-dark shadows or washed-out highlights. Where any image editor's Brightness/Contrast controls generally affect all the colors equally, this procedure lets you lighten shadows (bringing out more detail) or darken highlights (keeping them from becoming washed out) without affecting other portions of the image. The technique also lets you avoid nasty histograms and gamma curves.

Image Correction Made Easier With Photoshop CS 2.0

The techniques I've just described have been available with all recent versions of Photoshop. Once you've learned to use them, you'll want to explore some of the more advanced tools introduced or perfected with Photoshop CS 2.0.

Using Exposure Controls

Photoshop's Shadow/Highlight dialog box does what the Brightness/Contrast controls should have done in the first place. As you'll recall, the Brightness/Contrast sliders darken/lighten and adjust the contrast of *all* the pixels in an image. So, when you have a dark area that needs a bit of brightening, adjusting the Brightness slider provides a lighter tone in the dark area, but also makes highlight areas that were probably just fine brighter, too.

The Shadow/Highlight command offers separate lightening/darkening controls for dark areas and light areas. It's a great tool for making adjustments in images that need fixing in one area or the other, or different amounts of compensation in each area. Figure 6.23 is an example of such a photo, a rural church that is heavily backlit. By selecting Image > Adjustments > Shadow/Highlights, the dialog box shown in Figure 6.24 appears. Photoshop's controls for this dialog box default to a setting suitable for most backlit pictures, with the Shadow slider set to 50 percent and the Highlight slider set to 0 percent. For this (exaggerated) example, I've

Figure 6.23 This sort of backlit photo is perfect for Photoshop CS's new Shadow/Highlight command.

brightened the shadows even more (to 55 percent) and darkened the highlights (to 40 percent), creating the version shown in Figure 6.25.

You can achieve more sophisticated results by clicking the Show More Options box to reveal some additional controls, shown in Figure 6.26. As you can see, both the Shadows and Highlights sliders have been augmented by two new sliders, labeled Tonal Width and Radius.

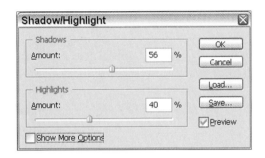

Figure 6.24 The basic version of the dialog box can make simple changes.

Figure 6.25 For this example, the highlights have been darkened and the shadows lightened, both independently of each other.

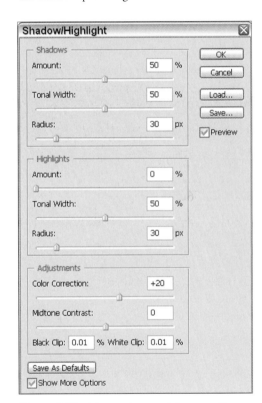

Figure 6.26 Advanced controls let you adjust the number of tones being controlled and the size of the area used to determine whether a pixel is a highlight or shadow pixel.

Tonal Width

You can use the Tonal Width slider to specify the number of different tones (from 0 to 256) that will be modified. The readout is in percentages, but you can mentally calculate the tones that will be affected. For example, at the default 50 percent setting, roughly half, or 128 of the tones (in either shadows or highlights) will be modified. At 25 percent, only 64 tones are susceptible to the changes you apply.

It's important to know just where those tones reside. Smaller percentages restrict the adjustments to only the darkest tones (with the Shadow slider) or the lightest tones (with the Highlight slider). So, setting the Shadows Tonal Width slider to 25 percent means that your tonal adjustments will be applied only to the tones represented by the values 0 to 63. The same setting on the Highlights Tonal Width slider would limit changes to tones with values 192 to 256.

Using values that are too large produces a halo effect at the bright/dark boundaries, which you can see in Figure 6.27.

Figure 6.27 Setting either Tonal Width number to a value that is too high produces a halo effect at the boundaries between light and dark areas.

You can usually tell roughly how to adjust the Tonal Width sliders by looking carefully at your image. If you need to brighten the darkest shadow areas, but the lighter areas are okay, restrict the Shadow Tonal Width's coverage to a narrow range. If all the shadow areas need adjustment, use a higher number (looking carefully for those haloes). Conversely, you can independently apply adjustments to the brightest highlights, darker highlights, or all highlights, as you prefer.

Radius

The Shadow/Highlight control examines each pixel in your image and classifies it as a shadow pixel or highlight pixel (or, as a midtone if it's right smack in the middle). Ordinarily, the feature does a good job of classifying pixels, as it checks adjacent pixels and uses their relationship with the pixel being processed to make its assessment. However, you can enlarge or contract the size of the pixel's "neighborhood" using the Radius slider. The ideal radius varies from image to image and the only way to determine the optimum setting is to monitor your image. A radius that is too large will brighten shadows too much, or excessively darken highlights.

You'll need to play with this control to get exactly the right effect.

Color Correction

Adjusting the highlights and shadows areas of images almost invariably causes color shifts in the area modified. Tones that are too dark or too light tend to mask the true color of a pixel, because the hue is no longer visible once a portion of an image becomes excessively dark or washed out. Restoring a pleasing tone often makes these colors visible again.

Figure 6.28 shows a tightly cropped version of another shot of the country church's tower. This one exhibits a lot of lens flare, which shows up as blotchy areas. (These can be fixed with retouching, discussed in Chapter 4.) However, this less-than-perfect image is just about perfect for showing how and why color correction is needed when you adjust shadow and highlight areas.

At top is the original image. In the middle, after shadow compensation has been applied, you can see that a color cast has been picked up that's most noticeable in the windows. At bottom, the Color Correction slider has been moved to the left to eliminate the color cast by reducing the amount of color saturation. The photo ends up with a neutral shadow area with no strong color cast of its own. If your image has strong color casts that are beyond the capabilities of this control, try using Image > Adjustments > Hue/Saturation to complete the job.

Brightness

This control is an additional slider (not shown in Figure 6.26) which appears only when you're editing grayscale images. Use it to provide slight adjustments to the brightness, if necessary.

Midtone Contrast

So far, we've been working exclusively with the darkest, shadow tones and brightest, highlight tones. The Midtone Contrast slider gives you a way of adjusting the contrast of the middle tones slightly to fine-tune your image.

Black-and-White Clipping

Some images may benefit from dropping the very lightest and darkest tones entirely, changing white areas with little detail to

Figure 6.28 At top, the original image; middle: a color cast appears in the windows after shadow compensation has been applied; bottom: color correction applied to the shadows.

pure white, and dark areas with not much detail to complete black. This has the effect of increasing the contrast of the image. If you're trying to edit an image with extraneous detail in the light or dark areas, and you'd prefer those areas to appear as white or black, enter a value into the Black Clip and White Clip boxes.

Using Live Histograms

As you learned from working with the Levels command, histograms are a useful tool for displaying information about the number of tones present in an image at each brightness level. A histogram consists of a series of up to 256 different vertical lines in a graph, arranged horizontally with the black tones represented on the left side of the graph, the white tones at the right side, and the middle tones located (you guessed it) in the middle of the graph. The taller each of the lines is, the more tones that are present at that brightness level. A typical histogram has one or more peaks, and the black-and-white tones often don't extend to the theoretical limits possible for the image (0 for pure black at the left side and 255 for pure white at the right side).

Your digital camera may provide a histogram similar to the one shown in Photoshop, although they are used a little differently. With a camera, the histogram is used primarily to judge exposure and your main remedy is to increase or decrease exposure for the next picture you take under the same conditions. Within Photoshop, the histogram can actually be used to provide tonal corrections after the fact.

Figure 6.29 shows an image and its histogram. The tones are spread fairly evenly throughout the picture, and an eye with even a little experience can "read" this histogram fairly easily. For example, that little bump of tones at the far right of the histogram corresponds to the lightest tones of the image, the sky and the

Figure 6.29 The curves of the histogram tell a story about the photo's tonal values.

brightest leaves. The small number of tones at the far left correspond to the sparse distribution of very dark tones, chiefly in the shadows.

An overexposed photo might have most of the tones concentrated at the right side of the histogram, and an underexposed photo would probably have most tones concentrated at the left side. The Levels command, discussed earlier in this book, lets you make adjustments for these lopsided distributions, and includes its own histogram display.

Photoshop CS 1.0 had a brand-new Histogram Palette, which provides a lot more information to work with. You can see this palette's "live" histogram display in Figure 6.30. Several views are available; the illustration shows the expanded view with combined RGB histogram at the top, and separate red, green, and blue channel histograms arrayed at the bottom. In between are some information readouts that I'll explain shortly. You can also select an expanded view that hides the separate RGB histograms, and a basic version with no extra data, as shown in Figure 6.29.

If the Histogram Palette is not visible on your screen, you can access it by choosing Window > Histogram. The numeric display in the middle of the palette probably looks like a lot of mumbo jumbo on first glance, but as you become experienced using the Histogram Palette, you'll find this information increasingly valuable.

Among the data on display are:

- **Mean.** This represents the average intensity value of all the pixels in the image. If the number is very low, that will confirm that the image is rather dark; a high number means that the image is, on average, very bright.

- **Standard Deviation.** This is a statistical term that tells you how much the intensity values vary from each other. A low number can mean that the contrast of the image is low, while a high number can point to a high contrast image.

- **Median.** The median is the middle number in the range of intensity values; half the individual values are higher than the median, while half are lower.

- **Pixels.** This is nothing more than the number of pixels in the image.

- **Level.** This readout shows the intensity level of the pixels under the cursor.

- **Count.** This value tells you how many pixels have the same value as the pixels under the cursor. For example, if you want to know how many dark shadow pixels are in an image, move the cursor to a dark area and read the count.

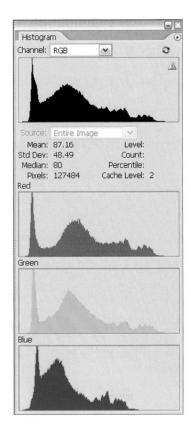

Figure 6.30 Photoshop CS' Histogram Palette shows a live, interactive view of the tonal values present in your image.

- **Percentile.** This represents the number of pixels equal to or darker than the pixels under the cursor. For example, if the Percentile reads 70, then those pixels are brighter than 70 percent of all the pixels in the image.

- **Cache Level.** Photoshop's Preferences include an option for caching histogram information so the program doesn't have to calculate it anew each time a histogram is displayed. When the tonal values of an image are changed, a new histogram is stored in the cache. If you've set the caching option (to improve performance, because Photoshop can check the cache rather than calculating a new histogram each time the histogram is displayed), this read-out shows which Cache level is being accessed. When it has a value of 1, that means the histogram for the original image is being displayed.

To really understand the Histogram Palette, you have to use it. Figure 6.31 shows it being used in tandem with the Levels command. In the illustration, I've moved the Midtone slider slightly to the left in the Levels dialog box. The Histogram Palette mirrors this movement, but shows both the original histogram (in ghost form) and the new histogram (in solid color), as well as the changes in the red, green, and blue histograms. As you gain experience, you can see how making changes in the Levels command affects the overall image as well as individual colors.

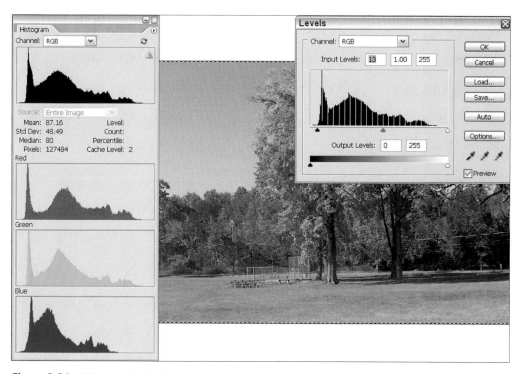

Figure 6.31 When used with the Levels command, the Histogram Palette shows the results of your modifications in a real-time display.

Matching Color

The need for color matching is one of the most common situations you'll encounter. Perhaps you took pictures of your family outdoors on a cold winter day, and more photos in the spring in late afternoon. It's unlikely that the skin tones of the two sets of pictures will match at all. Or, you might have taken some product shots and want the colors to match more closely because you'll be printing them side by side in a brochure. Photoshop CS's Match Color facility lets you select one image as a source and then apply the color palette from that image to a second image or group of images.

Another situation you'll encounter crops up when you're making composites. You've cut an element from one image, pasted it down in another, and discovered that the colors, which should be similar, vary widely. Match Color lets you fix those, too, because you can apply palettes from one layer to another layer in the same image.

This is another one of those features that can be learned very quickly just by performing a quick exercise. If you like, you can follow along using the files Teryn Outdoors 1 and Teryn Outdoors 2 on the website. You can see the original images in Figure 6.32. The image at left was taken outdoors in open shade on a bright, sunny day. The image at right was taken in roughly the same spot, but on an overcast day. The second photo is much bluer than the first, and it would be nice to match the colors more closely without jumping through Photoshop's usual color-adjustment hoops. Follow these steps to see how easy it can be.

1. Select the girl's face in the sunny day picture using the Lasso tool. Match Color can work from the image's full palette, if you want, but often produces better results if you tell it exactly which colors you'd like to match.

Figure 6.32 Match Color can be used to provide consistent color between these two very different images.

2. Choose Image > Adjustments > Match Color to produce the dialog box shown in Figure 6.33.

3. From the Source drop-down list, choose the image containing the color palette you want to apply to your current picture.

4. If you've zeroed in on a selection, mark the Use Selection in Target to Calculate Adjustment box in the lower half of the dialog box.

5. If you're using a layer other than the default background layer, select that layer from the Layer drop-down list.

6. Click the Neutralize button if the target image has a color cast. You can make further changes in the brightness (Luminance), saturation (Color Intensity), and amount of color change to apply (Fade) using the sliders in the Image Options area. Adjust these controls until your target image looks like you want.

7. Click on OK to apply the new color palette to your target image.

8. Apply any final changes using the Levels command or other Photoshop controls until the images match closely. You'll sometimes need to make a few touch-ups after the Match Color command has done its stuff.

Your final results will look something like Figure 6.34.

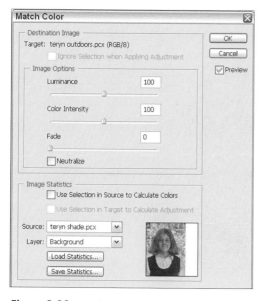

Figure 6.33 Work with the Match Color dialog box.

Figure 6.34 With the colors matched, this image more closely resembles the original shot.

Replacing Color

Don't care for a particular color in your image? Perhaps your model was wearing a red dress and you'd prefer to see her in blue. Photoshop's great Replace Color command can come to your rescue. I ended up using this feature a lot for my last digital photography book. A fuss-budgety technical editor complained that all my product photographs were taken using the same background material. It took about five minutes with Photoshop's Replace Color facility to change several of the illustrations to a new background color, without affecting the other colors in the image, as you can see in Figure 6.35.

Figure 6.35 Presto change-o, the purple background has magically been transformed into a brown one.

The command is ridiculously easy to use. Follow these steps with your own image:

1. Choose Image > Adjustments > Replace Color to produce the dialog box you see in Figure 6.35.

2. Click the Image box underneath the preview to see the original color image.

3. Use the Eyedropper tool to click in the color you'd like to change. Use the Add or Subtract eyedropper tools to expand or contract the colors selected.

4. Use the Fuzziness slider to allow Photoshop to replace additional colors that are close to the ones you've selected. Because this image had few color tones other than the background, I used a high fuzziness level to select virtually everything in the background.

5. Use the Hue, Saturation, and Lightness sliders to change the color, richness, and brightness of the replacement color. You can view the results as a preview in your original image if the Preview box is marked.

6. Click on OK to apply the replaced color to your image.

The Color Replacement Tool

Photoshop CS's Color Replacement tool is quick and easy to use, and a good complement to the Replace Color command. You can deploy this tool to "paint over" one color with another, retaining the brightness and contrast of the original image as you replace one color with another. It makes a good tool for changing red-eye effects to a more conventional pupil color, or for transforming any particular color into another one in a painting mode.

This tool operates like any other brush tool, using brush tips and other accouterments. You'll find it on the Tools Palette hidden within the same icon as the Healing Brush and Patch tools in Photoshop CS 1.0. For Version 2.0, it has been moved to the Brush Tool and Pencil Tool icon. The steps needed to use this useful tool are as follows.

1. Select the Color Replacement tool.

2. Choose a Brush tip in the Options bar.

3. Choose the Color blending mode.

4. Select a Sampling mode. Your choices include:

   ■ **Continuous.** This samples colors to be replaced continuously as you paint. As you move the brush, Photoshop will detect the colors the cursor passes over and define those colors as those that will be replaced with the foreground color.

   ■ **Once.** This option chooses a color at the point where you first click. Only colors that are similar to the color you first click on will be replaced.

   ■ **Background Swatch.** This option replaces color only in areas that contain the current background color. Use this option when you want to replace only a specific color with another.

5. Choose a Limits option to determine which pixels will be snared during the replacement process. Your choices include:

   ■ **Discontiguous.** This replaces the sampled color when the brush passes over it.

   ■ **Contiguous.** Use this option to replace similar colors that are touching those sampled.

■ **Find Edges.** This replaces connected areas while preserving edges in your image, extending your painting into contiguous areas, but stopping when Photoshop detects an edge.

6. Set the Tolerance level to a percentage, in order to define how similar a color must be to the sampled color to be eligible for replacement. Low numbers tell the Color Replacement brush to replace *only* colors very similar to the pixels you sample, while higher numbers spread the replacement over a larger range of colors.

7. Select the foreground color you want to use to replace the colors you paint over.

8. Click in the color you want to replace.

9. Paint over the color to be replaced.

An example of an image that has undergone color replacement is shown in Figure 6.36.

Figure 6.36 Martian peppers? No, just Photoshop CS's Color Replacement tool at work.

Using Exposuremerge

Adobe has applied its new-found High Dynamic Range color capabilities to the new Exposuremerge tool. This feature is a way of producing images with a full, rich dynamic range that includes a level of detail in the highlights and shadows that is almost impossible to achieve with digital cameras, which have a tendency to blow out highlights when you expose for the shadows or midtones. While not, strictly speaking, a color correction tool (it's more of a tonal fixer upper), Exposuremerge is an advanced capability that belongs in this more technical chapter.

Suppose you wanted to photograph a dimly-lit room that had a bright window showing an outdoors scene. Proper exposure for the room might be on the order of 1/60th second at f2.8 at ISO 200, while the outdoors scene probably would require f11 at 1/400th second. That's almost a 7 EV step difference (approximately 7 f-stops) and well beyond the dynamic range of any digital camera.

When you're using Exposuremerge, you'd take two to three pictures, one for the shadows, one for the highlights, and perhaps one for the midtones. Then, you'd use the Exposuremerge command to combine all of the images into one HDR image that integrates the well-exposed sections of each version. You can understand how the process works by examining Figures 6.37, 6.38, and 6.40. Here are the steps followed to get the final result.

1. Set your camera up on a tripod to hold it steady for the individual shots. The photos must be as close to identical—other than exposure—as possible.

2. Prepare to take two or three photos at different exposure times. You should vary the shutter speed, rather than the lens opening, because changing the aperture will modify the depth-of-field and may change the apparent size of some components of the photo, such as points of light. If your camera has a bracketing command, you can use that to change the shutter speed between shots *only* if your camera allows relatively large exposure increments, such as 1 EV between bracketed shots. Generally, most cameras bracket using smaller 1/2 or 1/3 EV steps that are not suitable for Exposuremerge.

3. Make the individual photos at least one or two EV steps apart, such as 1/60th second for the first and 1/250th second for the next, and perhaps 1/15th second for the third. Smaller increments will provide little extra information for Exposuremerge to work with; larger increments may create photo sets that are so far apart in exposure that there is not sufficient overlap to produce a smooth tonal range.

4. Save in RAW or TIFF format in your camera so you'll get full-range, 16-bit/channel images, rather than the 8-bit/channel images created by JPEG. However, if Exposuremerge works with 8-bit/channel images, it will combine them into one new 16-bit/channel image using the HDR capabilities.

5. If you use an application to transfer the files to your computer, make sure it does not make any adjustments to brightness, contrast, or exposure. You want the real raw information for Exposuremerge to work with. You'll end up with two photos like the ones shown in Figures 6.37 and 6.38.

Figure 6.37 Make one exposure for the shadow areas.

Figure 6.38 Make a second exposure for the highlights, such as the sky.

6. Activate Exposuremerge by choosing File > Automate > Merge to HDR.

7. Select the photos to be merged, as shown in Figure 6.39.

6. Once Exposure merge has done its thing, you must save in .PSD, .PFM, .TIFF, or .EXR formats to retain the floating point data, in case you want to work with the HDR image later on. Otherwise, you can convert to a normal 24-bit file and save in any compatible format.

If you do everything correctly, you'll end up with a photo like the one shown in Figure 6.40, which has the properly exposed foreground of the first shot, and the well-exposed sky of the second image. Note that, ideally, nothing should move between shots. In the example pictures, the river is moving, but the exposures were made so close together that, after the merger, you can't really tell.

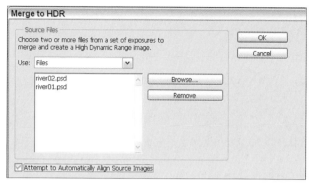

Figure 6.39 Use the Merge to HDR command to combine the two images.

Figure 6.40 You'll end up with an extended dynamic range photo like this one.

Calibrating Your Monitor

While color corrections are something you're likely to do every day, setting up your computer for color management is something you are likely to do when you first install Photoshop, and then at intervals later on as your needs or equipment change. This section outlines the use of the Adobe Gamma control for your monitor. Adobe Gamma works with both the Windows and Macintosh OS's own internal color management systems to create an ICC profile for your display. Just follow these steps to get set up.

1. Open the Adobe Gamma application. In Windows, you can access it from the Windows Control Panels panel (Start > Settings > Control Panel). Under Mac OS 9.x only, you'll find the Adobe Gamma application in your System folder in the Control Panels folder. The first window you see looks like Figure 6.41.

> **NOTE**
>
> Adobe Gamma exists along with Mac's ColorSync calibration located in the Monitors control panel in OS 9.x. However, if you are using Adobe Gamma with Mac OS 9.x, you should disable ColorSync. Adobe Gamma does not exist in Mac OS X. If you have a dual boot system you can create a profile in OS 9.x and copy it over to OS X. There is a monitor calibration feature in the monitor preferences panel that uses ColorSync. Also, this calibration is generally for CRT monitors. LCD monitors have fewer adjustable parameters and not all of them are suitable for image editing.

2. You'll be given a choice of using a step-by-step, wizard approach, or going directly to the control panel itself. The wizard merely presents the choices provided in the control panel one at a time. If this is the first time you've used Adobe Gamma, you'll want to work with the parameters one at a time. Click the Step by Step (Assistant) button (on the Mac) or the Step by Step (Wizard) button on the PC, and click Next. (If you have more than one monitor connected to your computer, the wizard will prompt you to drag the dialog box onto the monitor you want to calibrate.)

3. In the next dialog box, shown in Figure 6.42, you'll be invited to assign a unique name for the profile you're creating. If you've previously saved a profile and want to edit that, you can click the Load button and locate the profile on your hard disk. For example, you may have a monitor profile provided by the vendor of your particular display (if not, check their website). Click Next to move to the next dialog box.

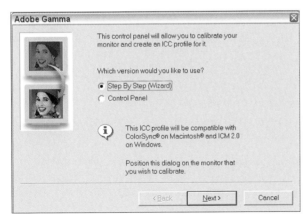

Figure 6.41 First choose whether to use the Assistant/ Wizard or work directly with the control panel.

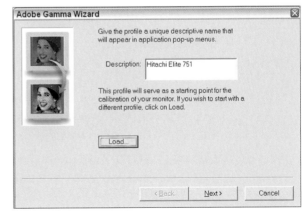

Figure 6.42 Assign a name to your new profile.

4. You should see a white box, with two darker boxes inside it (the center box may be difficult to see, as it is a very dark gray). Follow the instructions shown in the dialog box in Figure 6.43, and set your monitor's contrast control to its highest setting. Then adjust the brightness control to make the center box dark, but not totally black. Then, click Next to move to the next dialog box.

5. In the dialog box shown in Figure 6.44, you'll need to select the type of phosphors that your monitor uses. You may want to check the manual that came with your monitor to see if the phosphors indicated match anything on the list. If you're working with a profile provided by your monitor vendor, the type of phosphors will already be correct. Click the Next button to proceed.

Figure 6.43 Set your monitor's brightness to its highest setting, then adjust the brightness control until the center box is dark.

Figure 6.44 Choose the type of phosphors used in your monitor.

6. Choose the target gamma for your system from the drop-down list. Macintosh OS uses a gamma setting of 1.8, while the Windows default is 2.20. When the target is chosen, move the slider shown in Figure 6.45 until the gray center box merges with the surrounding gray frame. Then, click Next to move on.

7. Next, you should set the color temperature of your monitor. In most cases, the default value of 6500K, shown in Figure 6.46, will work fine. Change this setting only if your monitor manufacturer recommends it.

8. If you're curious, you can "measure" your monitor's color temperature visually. Turn down the ambient light in your work area and click the Measure button in the dialog box. The Adobe Gamma tool will show you three gray squares against a black screen. Click the left square to make them all cooler, or the right square to make them warmer. When you are satisfied that you have a neutral gray, click the center square or press Enter to create your

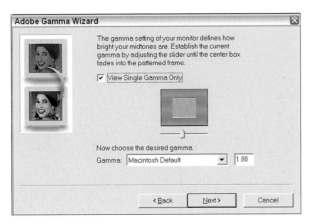

Figure 6.45 Merge the center gray box with the surrounding gray frame.

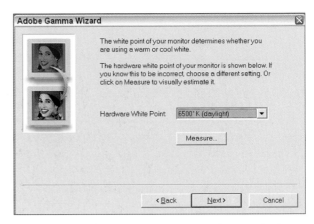

Figure 6.46 Choose a color temperature for your display.

Custom hardware white point. If you change your mind, you can still select 6500K or another color temperature from the drop-down list.

9. Click Next to proceed to the dialog box shown in Figure 6.47. There, you can choose to work at a different white point from the one you've just set for your hardware. You will rarely need to change this. Click Next again to move to the final dialog box.

10. You're done. A dialog box pops up to allow you to compare your original monitor setting with the new one. Click Finish to save the profile and exit the Adobe Gamma application.

Figure 6.47 Normally, you wouldn't make any changes in this dialog box.

Next Up

After all this work with color images, you might be ready to work with grayscale photos for a while. The next chapter shows how easy it is to convert a good color picture to a bad black-and-white rendition, and provides the tools you need to create great grayscale images instead.

7

Beyond Black and White

There's a lot more to black and white than Paul McCartney's duet with Stevie Wonder. We've all heard phrases like "The world is not black and white" (Graham Greene), "The wings of Time are black and white" (Emerson), or even "Let me explain it to you in black and white" (every frustrated parent). The concept of monochrome represents simplicity, purity, or even polar opposites.

There are lots of reasons to use black and white, even with a full-color image editor like Photoshop, and even if you have a full-color printer available to make a hard copy. This chapter will explore how photographers who value what black-and-white imagery can do can get what they need—and beyond—from our favorite image editor. You'll learn some of the reasons why you *need* to use grayscale images, how to create better conversions from color than Photoshop normally provides on its own, plus glean a few tips on reproducing some black-and-white film looks.

Why Black and White?

Most photos today are taken in color, but that wasn't always the case. While I'm fond of pointing out that daguerreotypes were actually color photos (in the sense that they had overall tones and were not true black and white), color photography was a long time in arriving after the first photographic images were made by Nicéphore Niépce in 1826 and Henry Fox Talbot in 1835. Some early attempts at color still photography were made by Scottish physicist James Clerk Maxell, who understood that red, green, and blue were the primary colors of light, and in

1861 photographed the same scene in black and white through a set of red, green, and blue filters. By projecting the three images on a screen with appropriately colored lamps, he reproduced the image of a tartan ribbon.

However, color imaging didn't really catch on until Kodachrome film was introduced in 1935 and, in 1942, Kodacolor film for prints. Black-and-white images were still favored by amateurs and professionals through the 50s and most of the 60s. Amateurs liked B/W because it was less expensive than making color prints and more convenient than showing color slides. It was only after inexpensive high-speed color photofinishing became available that color prints began to take over.

Professionals often used monochrome for a variety of reasons. Perhaps the publications they worked for didn't publish color; black-and-white photos were standard in many magazines until the late '60s. Pros also used black-and-white images for creative reasons. Color can be distracting or destroy the mood of certain kinds of photos. Professional photographers even had cost considerations when their clients were unable to pay the tariff for full color. In the early '60s, for example, a color wedding album had to be priced much, much higher than the black-and-white version (sometimes with hand-colored images) that had been the standard for decades.

Color photography began to nudge black-and-white imaging out of the picture in the '60s and '70s, when instant-loading cameras and automated processing made color prints virtually as inexpensive as black and white (or, today, even cheaper). Affordable laser scanners at newspapers and magazines made full-color photography more practical for publications. More recently, digital tools like Photoshop, desktop scanners, and Photo CDs have removed the last vestiges of barriers to color photography. It's still possible to take black-and-white photos; many digital cameras have a monochrome setting and black-and-white film is plentiful for conventional cameras. Yet, most photos today are produced in color.

So, why are we talking about black and white? There are dozens of valid reasons for working in black and white. Here are some of them:

- Your destination for the image will display it only in black and white, and you want a fairly accurate preview of what the photo will look like. For example, you may have a photo that will be printed in black and white in a magazine, or included in a laser-printed newsletter. Two hues that are distinct in color may appear to be the same in black and white, providing an undesirable merger. If you know the image will be viewed in monochrome, you'll want to work with it in that mode.

- You don't know how your photo will be used, and want to cover all the bases. I submit two or three photos a month to our local newspaper. I give them color 5 × 7 prints because they publish them in color about 25 percent of the time. But I also preview the photo in black and white to see what it will look like in that mode. Given the vagaries of reproduction on newsprint, this is a very good idea.

■ The picture you are working with originated as a black-and-white photo.

■ Color is distracting. A big red or yellow blob in the upper-right corner of a photograph may command our attention, especially when our intended subject is a muted pastel. Our eye is attracted to color first, and then to brightness. In Figure 7.1 at left, the big red whatsit at the top of the frame grabs our attention, and it's hard to look away from. In black and white, however, as at right, it becomes just a framing element that surrounds the water and shore.

Figure 7.1 The red object at the top of the frame grabs our attention, but becomes just another framing device in black and white.

- Color destroys the atmosphere. Moody pictures, high contrast photos, documentary photos with a gritty feel, and many other subjects may all look better in black and white. Would Dorothea Lange's immortal photo, "Migrant Mother" have been as effective in color? The cracked and lined face of the destitute mother of seven (who was, in fact, only 32 years old) was more powerful because it was shown in stark black and white.

- You want a historical look. A full color photo of a Civil War reenactment will be realistic, but it won't look like it could have been taken during the Civil War. Figure 7.2 wasn't really taken 150 years ago (the modern fireplace is a clue), but at least a full color image didn't tip us off.

- Color is inflammatory or disturbing. Although nearly all of Quentin Tarantino's 2003 film *Kill Bill: Vol. 1* is presented in color, one crucial fight is shown (at least in USA versions) in black and white, simply because it was felt that the gory scene would be too shocking if presented in full, living color.

- Color changes the emphasis. For example, you've probably seen figure studies in which close-ups of some body part, such as the curve of a shoulder, are made to represent something else, such as a desert landscape. The converse is also true: Edward Weston's famous still life, "Pepper #30" is said to resemble the musculature of a man kneeling (among other things). In color, it would simply be a very interesting picture of a pepper, just as the "landscape" photo would be transformed into a photo of a shoulder.

- You want to combine several color images that have widely varying color balances and have no time or inclination to make them match, or one or more of them are so off-color that you'd never be able to make them look anything other than patched together. If a color picture isn't an overriding concern, converting everything to black and white before compositing them together may be a satisfactory alternative.

Figure 7.2 Sometimes black and white can provide an historical look to an image.

Converting Color to Black and White

From time to time you'll need to convert a color picture to black-and-white, whether the original was taken on film or in pixels. Some digital cameras have a black-and-white option, perhaps augmented by a sepia option, too. You'd think they'd do a good job of creating a B/W picture because, technically, a digital camera's sensor is totally blind to color. The sensors themselves are strictly black-and-white components. They become "color sensitive" because of the color filters that are placed over each photosite on the sensor.

If there were some way to remove those color filters, then a digital camera could, theoretically produce a great-looking black-and-white image. Indeed, some vendors, such as Kodak, actually sold black-and-white-only digital cameras during the previous millennium. Because every pixel in the sensor could be used without interpolation (as is required for color digital pictures with cameras other than the Foveon-using Sigma and Polaroid cameras), a black-and-white digital shooter maximized the available resolution.

Most of the time, you'll need to convert an existing color digital or film image to monochrome. Photoshop makes it very, very easy to convert a good color photo into a bad black-and-white image. All you need to do is select Image > Mode > Grayscale from the menu bar, and presto change-o, your color image has been converted to an inaccurate black-and-white rendition. Or, perhaps, you decide to use Image > Adjustments > Desaturate, which does much the same thing, but only operates on a particular layer or selection.

Of course, images converted this way always seem to have low contrast. So, your next step probably would be to use Image > Adjustments > Brightness/Contrast to boost the contrast a bit. In a process that took only a few seconds, you've managed to convert a good color image into an excessively contrasty black-and-white photo that doesn't necessarily offer a good representation of the original. What happened? You've fallen for the same trap that has snared photographers for decades. It has long been common to increase contrast when making a black-and-white print from a color negative, and the practice has become standard operating procedure in the digital world, too.

The fallacy lies in the fact that in a black-and-white photo, the contrast, or apparent differences between objects in an image that makes them distinct, is determined solely by the relationship between the light and dark tones. This is important: In a black-and-white picture, the only way to separate various objects in a picture is through the use of the monochrome tones, the variations between them, and how they provide a three-dimensional look as they represent the lighting that illuminates the objects. There are no other visual cues to differentiate between, say, a green Granny Smith and a Red Delicious apple.

That's not true when an image is presented in color. In a color photo, *three* separate factors determine true visual contrast among objects. Those include the hue (the various colors of the image), saturation (how rich they are), and brightness (the lightness or darkness of a tone). I see this glossed over in most books about Photoshop, so I'm going to take the time to clarify the inherent problems behind color to black-and-white conversions. Understanding the problems will help you avoid them.

The following illustrations should make the situation abundantly clear. I'll use the image shown in Figure 7.3, a landscape photo of a barren dirt field with mountains and sky in the background. When converted to grayscale using Photoshop's Mode changing operation, the image looks like Figure 7.4.

Figure 7.3 The various components of this photo are easy to discern in full color.

Figure 7.4 Converted to grayscale using Photoshop's default methods tends to blend many of the colors together as similar tones.

You can see that the conversion to black and white is less than satisfactory. The browns and blues that were distinct in the original image have all turned into similar shades of gray. The typical solution is to adjust the contrast of the grayscale image, creating a result like that shown in Figure 7.5.

However, as I said, color images consist of three components: hue, saturation, and brightness. Look what happens when we can change some of the color photo's characteristics and see what Photoshop does with them.

Figure 7.5 The knee-jerk response to a low-contrast grayscale conversion is to increase the contrast and/or brightness. Bad plan, as you can see in this example.

Hue

One of the ways our eyes see contrast between objects in a photo is through the differences in color. Figure 7.6 shows the same image with the colors all skewed (I used Photoshop's Image > Adjustments/Hue/Saturation control and adjusted the Hue slider). It's easy to differentiate between the green sky and magenta field, isn't it? However, when this

Figure 7.6 Changing an image to a garish color scheme doesn't affect the grayscale conversion one whit.

Figure 7.7 Because all colors were changed equal amounts, the grayscale version looks exactly the same.

garish image is converted to grayscale, the image shown in Figure 7.7 results. It's identical to Figure 7.4. Photoshop ignores the color differences in making the conversion, as long as the colors maintain their relationships.

Moving the Hue slider rotates all the colors in an image simultaneously in one direction or another around an imaginary color wheel. That's why the Hue slider begins in a neutral middle position and can move 180 increments (degrees) positive (clockwise) to the opposite side of the color wheel, or a negative 180 degrees counterclockwise to the same position on the wheel. All the colors move equal amounts, so as far as Photoshop is concerned their relationships haven't changed and the results are the same after the image is converted to grayscale.

Saturation

Saturation is another way of creating contrast between objects in a color image. You can think of saturation as a way of measuring how pure colors are. Imagine a can of pure red paint. It would produce a color like the one shown at left in Figure 7.8. Add some white paint to the can, and you'll get a less saturated red, eventually arriving at a totally desaturated white (if you added an overwhelming amount of white paint), as shown in the squares in the top row of the figure. If you

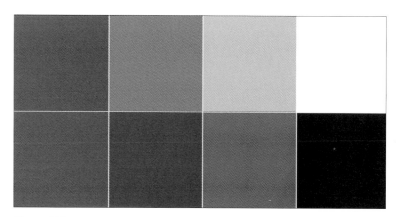

Figure 7.8 Add white or black to red, and all you get is a desaturated red that is lighter or darker than the original color.

added black paint instead, you'd end up with a darker, but also less saturated red, ending up with black, as you can see in the bottom row. This analogy doesn't precisely correspond to the way RGB colors become more or less saturated, but it's a useful way of thinking about the process.

As I said, this analogy isn't perfect, because the white paint is lighter than the red paint, and the black paint is darker, so, in terms of grayscales, the various degrees of saturation could still be told apart in a black-and-white version of the image, like the one in Figure 7.9.

However, if parts of an image were exactly the same color and brightness, and varied only in the degree of saturation, they'd look precisely the same when converted to grayscale. Figure 7.10 shows at top a gradient consisting of a single color, with the saturation carefully controlled to blend from the pure color (at the left side of the image) to the same color completely desaturated (at the right side of the image). When this saturation gradient is converted to grayscale, the completely uniform gray tone shown at the bottom of the figure results.

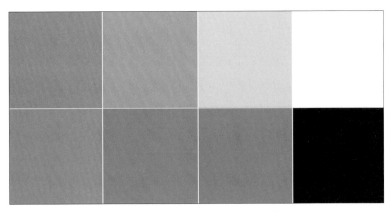

Figure 7.9 After the saturation has been adjusted, converting the colors to gray doesn't provide an accurate image.

Figure 7.10 At top is a smooth blend in which only the degree of saturation of the color changes. At bottom, you can see Photoshop has converted the blend to a uniform gray.

CREATING A SATURATION GRADIENT

Still skeptical and want to try this for yourself? Just follow these steps:

1. Fill a rectangular image or selection with a color of your choice.

2. Choose Layer > New Adjustment Layer > Hue/Saturation to create a spanking new adjustment layer that will let you modify the saturation of your color with great precision.

3. Click on OK in the New Layer box that pops up, and then click on OK in the Hue/Saturation dialog box that appears. We're not going to use the sliders to adjust the saturation just yet.

4. You'll see two thumbnails in the Hue/Saturation adjustment layer in the Layers Palette, as shown in Figure 7.11. Click the box on the right, the Layer Mask thumbnail.

5. Choose the Gradient tool from the Tool Palette, and choose the foreground/background linear gradient from the Options bar.

6. Place the cursor at the left side of the image and, with the Shift key held down (to produce a straight line), drag to the right. The gradient will be applied to the Layer mask, so that any changes to the saturation that you make will be least at the left side (where the gradient is darkest in the Layer mask) and most significant on the right side (where the Layer mask is lightest).

7. Double-click the Layer thumbnail (to the left of the Layer mask thumbnail) to produce the Hue/Saturation dialog box. Drag the Saturation slider all the way to the left. Photoshop applies the saturation gradient, as shown in Figure 7.12.

8. Convert the image to gray and watch it turn into a single strip of exactly the same shade.

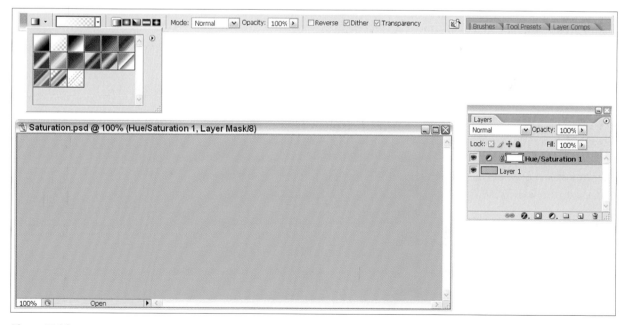

Figure 7.11 Create a layer mask to a Saturation adjustment layer to create your own blend.

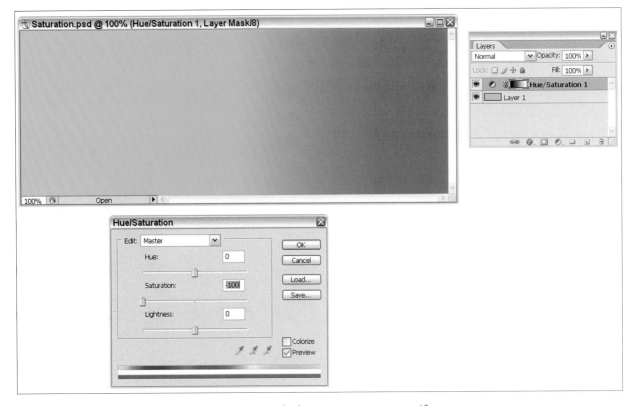

Figure 7.12 You'll end up with a blend like this one, which you can convert to a uniform gray.

In a real-world image, some colors may indeed have exactly the same brightness and color, and vary only in their degree of saturation. In such cases, we still have no difficulty differentiating the objects in the image, as you can see in the worst-case example shown in Figure 7.13. This image contains only white and "red" in various degrees of saturation, using the colors in the strip at the bottom of the figure. It's possible to make out the shapes of the objects (in this case leaves) when the only difference between them is the amount of saturation. Figure 7.14 shows the same image with all the "reds" converted to gray. It's just a big blob of gray, isn't it, just like the bottom row of Figure 7.10?

Getting back to our landscape photo, Figure 7.15 shows the image with the saturation boosted considerably. It's easy to differentiate the blue sky from the green mountains and brown field. However, converted to grayscale, it looks precisely like Figure 7.4. (Trust me, or try it yourself; we don't need yet another identical figure to prove this point.) When images that have objects that differ from others in the picture chiefly through saturation or color, that information is lost when the photo is converted to grayscale.

Figure 7.13 This is a simplified real-world image of some leaves, posterized so only four colors remain, all the same shade of red at different levels of saturation.

Figure 7.14 Converted to gray by Photoshop, all the various reds merge into a uniform gray again.

Figure 7.15 Even boosting the color saturation of the image makes no difference. The grayscale conversion looks exactly the same as Figure 7.4.

Brightness

Brightness is the third clue we use to differentiate between objects in an image. A closely related factor is contrast, which is a way of comparing the number of different tones in an image. When you adjust the brightness of an image, you're increasing (or decreasing) the lightness of every pixel in an image equally, over a range of 0 (black) to 256 (white). When you modify the contrast, you're changing the number of tones at individual brightness levels: If all 256 tones are distributed equally from black to white, the image will be relatively low in contrast. If there are only a few different tones, the image will have high contrast.

The most important thing to know is that with a grayscale image, brightness and contrast are the only tools you have left to differentiate among objects. If, in the original image, it was the color or saturation components that made elements stand out, you'll no longer have control over those factors once the image is converted to black and white. You need to make any adjustments you need to apply *before* the image is converted. That's an important point. Too often, Photoshop users blithely convert a color image to grayscale using Photoshop's default settings, and then try to adjust the brightness/contrast. At that point, you're trying to restore a distinction between objects that no longer exists.

The other important thing to keep in mind is that Photoshop does not consider hue or saturation when converting an image from color to black and white using the Mode > Grayscale or Desaturate functions. Instead, it uses an algorithm calculated to provide the best compromise, which uses approximately 60 percent of the green component of your image, 30 percent of the red, and 10 percent of the blue. However, as you've seen in the previous examples, this algorithm provides results that are often acceptable, but which are not necessarily accurate, particularly with images in which the colors or saturation provide the most important visual cues.

We can do better.

Converting to Grayscale with Channels

Let's start with an image that has lots of colors, good saturation, and plenty of contrast to work with, like the one shown in Figure 7.16 at left. It's stored on the Course website as Castle Garden. The version on the right-hand side has been converted to grayscale using Photoshop's default Image > Mode > Grayscale feature. Knowing what you've learned about how Photoshop performs this conversion, you can probably guess what's wrong, especially with the opportunity to compare them side-by-side. Notice how the red flowers, in particular, tend to blend in with the rest of the blossoms, how the green grass appears to be too light, and the sky is nowhere near as dramatic as it was in the original image.

You'll find that working in CMYK mode is the easiest way to separate all the colors you want to work with. Follow these steps to explore some of your color to grayscale conversion options.

1. Choose Image > Mode > CMYK to convert the RGB image to cyan, magenta, yellow, and black channels. These correspond to the printing plates that would be used to print this image on a press, or the colors used by your printer to produce a hard copy.

Figure 7.16 The original image is shown at left. At right, a grayscale conversion using Photoshop's default tool.

2. Switch to the Channels Palette to access each of these color layers individually, as shown in Figure 7.17.

You can examine each of the individual plates, as you can see in Figure 7.18. Sometimes you'll find that one of them provides a pleasing, although not accurate rendition. For example, the magenta channel provides a splendid rendition of the castle walls, and appears to differentiate among the individual flowers. However, the grass is much too light, and the sky not as dramatic as before.

The cyan plate shows off the sky and clouds, but most of the rest of the image is muddy. The yellow plate renders the grass as almost black and offers little detail elsewhere in the picture. The black plate is what is called a "skeleton"

Figure 7.17 Using the Channels Palette, you can view each of the cyan, magenta, yellow, and black "plates" of a CMYK image.

Figure 7.18 The top row shows the cyan and magenta color channels (left to right) while the bottom row shows the yellow and black channels (left to right).

black, reproducing nothing more than the fine detail in the shadows of the wall and darker foliage (as it's supposed to), leaving all the color information for the cyan, magenta, and yellow channels.

If you see a channel you'd like to use, continue on with these steps:

3. Choose Layer > New Adjustment Layer > Channel Mixer. Click on OK in the New Layer dialog box that pops up to create the Channel Mixer adjustment layer.

4. Click the Monochrome box in the Channel Mixer dialog box to direct your changes to a gray channel.

5. Move all the sliders to the 0 centerpoint except for the channel you want to work with. In this case, I moved the Magenta slider to the right until I got a black-and-white image I liked, as shown in Figure 7.19.

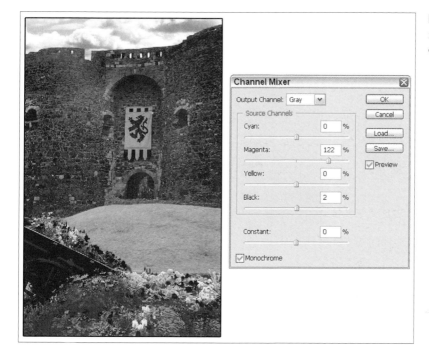

Figure 7.19 Here's a grayscale rendition using the Magenta channel.

6. Click on OK to apply the change.

7. Flatten the image (use Layer > Flatten) to create your grayscale image.

What if you want to emphasize some other tones? You can do that, too, with the Channel Mixer. Continue with these steps.

8. Chose Image > Undo to cancel the image flattening you performed in Step 7.

9. Create a duplicate of the background layer (use Layer > Duplicate Layer) and move it above the first Channel Mixer adjustment layer.

10. Select Layer > New Adjustment Layer > Channel Mixer and click on OK to create a second adjustment layer.

11. Click the Monochrome box as before in the Mixer dialog box, and then move the Yellow slider to the right while keeping the other sliders at the center point. This will emphasize the blue of the sky, as you can see in Figure 7.20.

12. Merge the two image layers with their respective adjustment layers.

Figure 7.20 Create a second layer with the sky emphasized.

Figure 7.21 The finished image will look like the one on the right. Compare it with Photoshop's default grayscale conversion on the left.

13. Use an eraser to remove everything in the sky-emphasized layer, except for the sky itself.

14. Flatten the image. Compare the results of the original, default grayscale conversion at left in Figure 7.21, with the results using channel manipulations, shown at right.

Other Grayscale Effects

Here are some other easy grayscale effects you can do. You can create an antique photo or orthochromatic look. Check out Chapter 3 if you want to see how to duplicate an infrared film image.

Antique Photograph

It's fairly easy to re-create the look of an antique photograph from the early 20th century, late 19th century, or even earlier. While the goal earlier in the chapter was to create the best possible grayscale conversion of a color image, some really bad conversions can look interesting, too. First, let's work on a fully saturated, fairly decent color image, using the original, unmodified version of our Castle Garden photo. Just follow these steps.

1. Choose Image > Calculations to access the dialog box shown in Figure 7.22. This is the Channel Calculations dialog box, which allows us to choose any channel from any layer of any image, known as the *base* channel, and merge it with a channel from any other layer, known as the *blend* channel. It's a powerful feature, indeed. This exercise will show a little of how it works.

2. In the Source 1 and Source 2 areas, make sure the Background layer from the Castle Garden photo is selected. Unless you've added layers to the image, this will be your only choice, in fact.

3. For the Channel in Source 1, select the Red channel. We'll be using it as the base channel for the merger.

4. For the Channel in Source 2, select the Green channel, making it the blend channel.

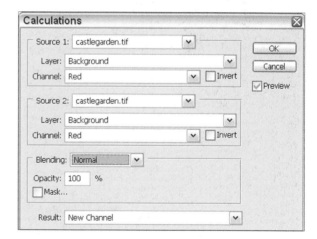

Figure 7.22 The Calculations dialog box lets you merge channels from one or more images.

5. For Blending, choose Exclusion from the drop-down list. I'll explain why shortly.

6. For Opacity, choose 50 percent. This will blend the Red and Green channels evenly, using the rules of the Exclusion blending mode.

7. In the Result box, choose New Document from the drop-down list. This will create a new image containing the blended photo.

8. Click on OK to create the new document, which should look like Figure 7.23.

9. Photoshop recognizes that the new document is simply a channel rather than a document in its own right (so far), so it's stored in Multichannel mode. You'll want to convert it to a grayscale document by choosing Image > Mode > Grayscale to create a valid document.

10. Save your file, then read on to see what happened.

You'll find the same techniques work on photos that aren't so good, too. As an experiment, I scanned a 30-year-old photo of a Roman bridge that had faded quite badly from exposure to sunlight while it was displayed on a wall. The dye layers had faded enough that I wasn't going to be able to salvage the photo in full color anyway; any corrections would have just made the image grayer. So, I applied the same Exclusion blending mode as described above. Then I added sepia toning as described in Chapter 4. The result looks like Figure 7.24.

Figure 7.23 This "antique" photo has a faded look, created by merging Red and Green channels of a full-color image.

Figure 7.24 A faded photo of an old Roman bridge was salvaged by combining channels and applying a sepia tone.

SOME EXOTIC BLENDING MODES

Photoshop's blending modes combine layers or channels in sophisticated ways, as you learned earlier in this book. In this case, we used the Exclusion mode to produce a weathered, old-timey look to the photograph, taking advantage of the way Exclusion combines pixels.

Exclusion mode is closely related to Difference mode. The latter examines the brightness information of each channel, and subtracts one from the other, depending on whichever is brighter. That sounds confusing, but it's not difficult to understand if you narrow it down to individual pixels.

Consider the following cases:

If a pixel in the Source 1 or Source 2 channel has a value of 200 and the same pixel in the other channel has a value of 100, the result will be a new pixel with a value of 100. It doesn't matter where each pixel resides; the result is always the difference between the two.

If a pixel in either channel has a value of 255 (white), the result will always be a pixel that has the opposite value of the pixel in the remaining channel. A dark pixel with a value of, say, 55 will end up as the equivalent light pixel with a value of 200 (255 minus 55). A light pixel with a value of 200 will end up as a dark pixel (255 minus 200) with a value of 55.

Conversely, if a pixel in either channel has a value of 0 (black), the composite pixel will remain exactly the same as the value of the pixel in the remaining channel. Say, the other pixel has a value of 200; the composite pixel will be 200 minus 0, or 200.

Exclusion works similarly to Difference mode, *except* that it converts any mid-toned pixels to gray, creating a lower contrast version that has the aged, faded, slightly washed out look like that in Figure 7.23.

Orthochromatic Film

It hasn't been so long ago that black-and-white films incorporated the term "pan" in their nomenclature. Tri-X Pan, Verichrome Pan, Plus-X Pan, or even Panchromatic-X were the names of films I used early in my career. The term "pan" stood for panchromatic (all colors) and was important because it meant that these black-and-white films were roughly sensitive to red, blue, and green light in equal amounts. As odd as it might seem, that wasn't always the case. In the 40s and 50s, black-and-white films were notorious for being most strongly sensitive to blue, green, and yellow light, with red showing up much darker than it ordinarily would. That explains why all the women seemed to be wearing black lipstick in black-and-white photos from that era. It also explains why red safelights can be used for developing these red-insensitive, "orthochromatic" films.

Once panchromatic films became available, ortho films lived on as a graphic arts tool, used to emphasize reds and de-emphasize other colors, and for scientific and medical applications. Ortho films aren't used for conventional photography, except as a creative tool. Here's how to approximate the effect in Photoshop.

1. Start with a photo that has plenty of reds, greens, and blues, like the one shown in Figure 7.25.

Figure 7.25 This photo has plenty of reds and other colors.

2. Choose Image > Adjustments > Channel Mixer to summon the Channel Mixer dialog box.

3. Check the Monochrome box.

4. De-emphasize all the red in the photo by moving the Red slider to the left, to approximately –76%.

5. Increase the blue and green "sensitivity" by moving the Blue and Green sliders to the right until the image has the "ortho" look you want. Don't be afraid to move past the 100% point. I used 180% and 144% for the green and blue, respectively, as shown in Figure 7.26.

6. Click on OK to apply your ortho effect.

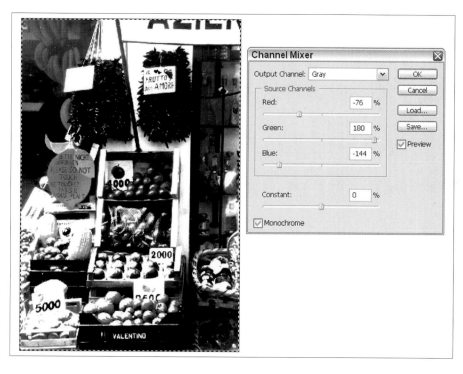

Figure 7.26 In the ortho view, all the reds have become darker, and the other colors are lighter.

Next Up

Filters have been used on conventional cameras for more than 150 years, producing effects that enhance an image or add some creative flair. Photoshop has more than 100 filters of its own built in, and there are hundreds more available from third-parties like Alien Skin, Auto FX, and Andromeda. In the next chapter, I'm going to concentrate on the filters that are most like their conventional camera counterparts. You'll learn how to re-create filter effects, and apply some that aren't even possible outside the digital realm.

8

Using Photoshop CS's Filters

For a long time, Photoshop's use of filters remained quite stagnant, with few new filters added from release to release. Indeed, many of the best filters in the Photoshop arsenal dated back to Adobe's acquisition of Aldus Corporation, and its three Gallery Effects packages almost a decade ago. These 36 filters were eventually folded into Photoshop itself, and there were only a few minor additions to Photoshop's default array for many years.

Now, Adobe has started to move forward again with interesting and effective filters. An increasing number of plug-ins are joining the Filter Gallery, which lets you preview and choose from among most of the filters that have their own sliders or other controls. Recent releases of Photoshop gave us new capabilities with filters like Fibers, Extract, Liquify, and Pattern Maker. Photoshop CS 2.0 has added six brand new filters discussed elsewhere in this book, including Box Blur, Shape Blur, and Surface Blur; Lens Correction; Reduce Noise; and Smart Sharpen. It's tough coming up with new visual effects that can be achieved only by pushing pixels around or changing their brightness. Some of them, like the Photo Filter effect, appear to be more of a shortcut for applying a change you can do manually than a true new filter. However, for those of us who like to tweak our photos to get new looks, any new filter or plug-in is a welcome addition.

After all, in the realm of conventional photography, filters have long been an important corrective and creative tool. The same is true in the digital domain. Filters created for Photoshop can fix bad images, add artistic flair, or transform a shoebox reject into a triumphant prize winner.

Anyone serious about photography comes to depend on his kit of filter attachments that fit in front of (or sometimes inside) his lens. Glass or gelatin filters can correct for improper lighting conditions, add a romantic fuzzy glow to an image, or provide incredible multi-image effects. Indeed, products like the versatile Cokin Filter System have become subgenres of photographic techniques on their own; there are entire books written on the use of Cokin filters, and a large number of unofficial websites dedicated to their use.

As you might guess, having ventured so deeply into this book, Photoshop can duplicate many of these effects through its built-in capabilities. For example, all the capabilities of color balancing filters can be mimicked using Photoshop's color correction features, as you learned in Chapter 6. Many of the special effects possible with Cokin and other filter sets can be achieved using the 100+ filters included with Photoshop, and will be addressed in this chapter. You'll also learn how to use the Photoshop CS Filter Gallery.

What Are Filters?

With traditional photography, filters are typically circles of glass that fit in front of a lens and change or attenuate the light passing through in some way. A few lenses with very large front diameters accept filters in a slot at the rear of the lens, to reduce the expense. My old 7.5mm fisheye and 16mm semi-fisheye lenses have a few filters built in which can be changed by rotating a wheel or dial. Filters also are available as inexpensive square sheets of gelatin that fit in holders that attach to the front of the lens.

Digital cameras, too, can use this kind of filter. Many digital camera lenses have threads on the front edge that accept conventional filters. Some cameras require a special adapter to let you mount filters.

They all work in much the same way. Some have a tint and partially or completely block the light of other colors, as when a red filter is used with black-and-white film to darken the blue of the sky and the green of foliage. Others may remove certain types of light to reduce glare, or break up an image into multiple fragments, as if your subject were viewed through an insect's eye. Filters can blur parts of your photo, or add star-like twinkles to bright highlights. Figure 8.1 shows a popular effect that can be achieved with a split filter, orange on top and blue on the bottom.

In Photoshop, filters can perform even more amazing magic tricks with your images. They can transform a dull image into an Old Masters painting with delicate brush strokes, or create stunning, garish color variations in a mundane photograph. Blast apart your images into a cascade of sparkling pixels, or simply add some

Figure 8.1 A split filter produces one color on top and another color on the bottom.

subtle sharpness or contrast to dull or blurred areas. Plug-in image processing accessories have the power to affect a complete makeover on all or parts of a scanned photo or bitmapped painting you created from scratch. You can also use these add-ons to produce undetectable changes that make a good image even better.

Figure 8.2 shows a variation on the flag picture used in Chapter 1. There, the intent was to show how Photoshop could duplicate traditional photographic effects. In this illustration, however, you can see what the same image looks like with six different filters applied in a deliberate attempt to create a more highly "processed" appearance. While Photoshop can duplicate many traditional camera effects, it can go far beyond them, too.

Photoshop-compatible plug-in filters are actually miniature programs in their own right, designed in such a way that they can be accessed from within an image-editing application, to manipulate the pixels of a file that is open in the parent application. Some plug-ins can load files on their own, too, without resorting to Photoshop at all.

They are called filters because in the most general sense they function much like filters you're familiar with in the real world. Like photographic filters, Photoshop's plug-ins can modify the bits of light/pixels that pass through.

For example, one of the simplest filters of all isn't even found in Photoshop's Filter menu. The Image > Adjustments > Invert feature of Photoshop is part of the program's basic capabilities and doesn't "plug-in" at all, but it acts in exactly the same manner as other filters.

Figure 8.2 Six different filters were applied to this image to create a combination of effects.

The Invert command looks at each pixel in your image in turn and simply "flips" it to the exact opposite value. That is, a pure white or light gray pixel will be changed to pure black or dark gray. The color value of the pixel will be changed to the color opposite on the "color wheel." A dark blue pixel will become light yellow; a light cyan pixel will become a dark red pixel, and so forth. Figure 8.3 shows some color chips representing an array of pixels. At top are two rows of pixels in their original colors; the set at the bottom shows the same two rows that have been flipped to their opposite color and brightness value by the Invert function.

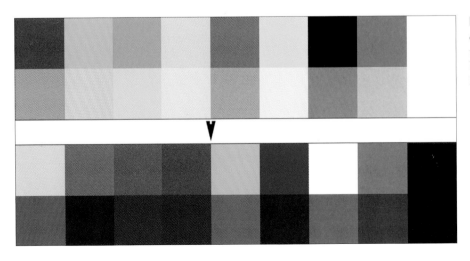

Figure 8.3 The top two rows of color patches are converted to the colors shown in the bottom two rows when inverted.

This is the simplest kind of filtering possible, because the values being modified are already stored as numbers, from 0 to 255 for each of the three color channels, plus gray. A single mathematical algorithm can be applied to each pixel to produce the filtered image. If you want an inside look at how filters work, check out Figure 8.4, Photoshop's "blank" filter, which goes by the name Custom, and is located in the Other submenu of the Filter menu.

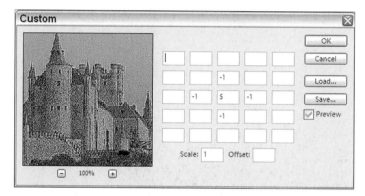

Figure 8.4 Photoshop's Custom filter shows how filters look at individual pixels in an image.

The center box represents the pixel being examined. When processing an image or selection, Photoshop will look at each pixel in turn, then adjust the values of the pixels that surround it, based on the numbers in the boxes that ring the target pixel. That part is simple. Knowing what numbers to plug in to achieve a particular effect is difficult. Fortunately, unless you're a filter fanatic, you'll rarely have to resort to that (although the Custom filter is fun to play with). Instead, you can put Photoshop's built-in filters to work to achieve the looks you want.

Some filters may remove pixels entirely, change their contrast (thus blurring or sharpening an image), or shift them around in an image in relation to others that remain in place, creating some degree of distortion. The programs that make up filters can be very simple and require no user input, or extremely complex and bristle with dialog boxes, slider controls, buttons, preview windows, and other features.

What makes Photoshop's filters so versatile is the fact that they don't have to be part of Photoshop's basic code. Photoshop includes a programming interface that lets it talk to external programs like filters, which need only to plug in at the appropriate places in the interface. Plug-ins are a brilliant concept, even if the idea was not original to Adobe, having been adapted from a facility in the Digital Darkroom program marketed by Silicon Beach. All Adobe had to do to provide the same capabilities was build certain "hooks" into Photoshop, bits of program code that allowed Photoshop itself to temporarily turn over control to an outside module, which could then work with and manipulate the pixels within currently open images.

Upgrading, adding, or removing a filter is as easy as deleting the old filter file and dragging a new one into the Plug-ins folder of your application. The next time you start Photoshop or another image editor, the application "builds" itself by looking for available modules, such as filters. Any suitable plug-ins automatically are added to the Filters or File > Import menus.

What Kinds of Filters Are Available?

The plug-ins available for Photoshop fall into several broad categories:

- **Image Enhancement filters.** I use this term for filters that improve the appearance of images without making basic changes in the content of the images. You have to apply the term "basic changes" loosely, since some of these can make dramatic modifications. Sharpen, Unsharp Mask, Dust and Scratches, and similar filters are all image enhancement plug-ins. Blur filters are also image enhancement filters: There are many images that can be improved through a little judicious blurring. This kind of filter can be applied to an entire image, or just a portion that you have selected.

- **Attenuating filters.** I borrowed this word from the photographic world to describe filters that act like a piece of glass or other substance placed between the image and your eye, superimposing the texture or surface of the object on your picture. Think of a piece of frosted glass, translucent scrap of canvas fabric, or a grainy sheet of photographic film. These, or any of dozens of other filters, including most Noise and Texturizing filters, can add a texture or distort your image in predictable ways. Attenuating filters may be applied to a whole image, or just a selection.

- **Distortion filters.** These filters actually move pixels from one place in an image to another, providing mild to severe distortion. Filters that map your image to a sphere, immerse it in a whirlpool, or pinch, ripple, twirl, or shear bits here and there can provide distortion to some or all of an image.

- **Pixelation filters.** Adobe's own terminology is good enough for me to use in referring to a group of filters that add texture or surface changes, much like attenuating filters, but take into account the size, color, contrast, or other characteristic of the pixels underneath. These include Photoshop's own Crystallize, Color Halftone, Fragment, and Mezzotint filters. The Pointillize or Facet filters, for example, don't simply overlay a particular texture—the appearance of each altered pixel incorporates the underlying image.

- **Rendering filters.** Again, Adobe's terminology is a good way to describe filters that create something out of nothing, in the way that a 3D rendering program "creates" a shaded model of an object from a wire-frame skeleton. These filters may or may not use part of the underlying image in working their magic: Photoshop's Clouds filter creates random puffy clouds in the selected area, while Difference Clouds inverts part of the image to produce a similar effect. Lens Flare and Lighting Effects generate lighting out of thin air, while the Chrome filter produces Terminator 2-like surfaces.

- **Contrast-enhancing filters.** Many filters operate on the differences in contrast that exist at the boundary of two colors in an image. Sharpening and blurring filters are types of filters that do this, but I've lumped them into the Image Enhancement category. Other contrast-enhancing filters are used to produce special effects. By increasing the brightness of the lighter color or tone, and decreasing the brightness of the darker color or tone, the contrast is increased. Since these boundaries mark some sort of edge in the image, contrast-enhancing filters tend to make edges sharper. The effect is different from pure sharpening filters, which also use contrast enhancement. Filters in this category include all varieties of filters with names like Find Edges, Glowing Edges, Accented Edges, Poster Edges, Ink Outlines, and even most Emboss and Bas Relief filters.

- **Other filters and plug-ins.** You'll find many more different add-ons that don't fit exactly into one of the categories above, or which overlap several of them, such as the color-correcting Photo Filter plug-in.

The About Plug-in option in the Help menu will show you what filters have been loaded by Photoshop. You don't have to wend your way through nested menus to view this list.

Using Filters

I'll explain how to use particular filters as we go along, but there are some general tips that apply to nearly all filters that we'll be working with. To apply a filter, follow these steps:

Choosing the Portion of an Image to Apply a Filter To

You don't have to apply a filter to an entire image or layer; many times you'll want to use the filter only with a portion of the image. Use any of the selection tools, including the Marquee, Lasso, Magic Wand, or one of Photoshop's advanced tools, such as Select > Color Range or Quick Mask mode.

It's often smart to copy the entire image to a duplicate layer (Layer > Duplicate) and make your selection on a copy. You can play around with different filter effects without modifying your original image. If you don't select a portion of an image, the filter will be applied to the entire image. Because it can take anywhere from a split second to a few seconds (or much longer), depending on the speed of your computer, the amount of RAM you have, and the size of your image/selection, you may want to work with a representative section of the image first before applying the filter to the whole thing.

Selecting the Filter

Some filters, such as Sharpen > Sharpen and Sharpen > Sharpen More, are known as single-step filters and operate immediately. They have no parameters to select, and thus offer less control over their effects. Other filters cause a dialog box to pop up with controls you'll need to adjust.

Most will also include a preview window you can use to get an idea of what your filter will do when applied to a selected portion of an image. You'll find this useful to make broad changes in parameters, but I think it's still a good idea to select a somewhat larger area of an image and apply the filter to that on a duplicate layer. A basic "old style" filter dialog box is shown in Figure 8.5. I'll show you Photoshop CS's "new style" Filter Gallery, with additional options, later in this chapter.

Figure 8.5 A typical filter dialog box looks like this.

Applying the Filter

Click on OK to apply the filter. If you have a very large image (say, 10MB or more), a slow computer, or a complex filter, find something to do. This might be a good time to set up your laptop on your desktop and get some work done. Even filter/image combinations that do magical things in less than a minute seem terribly slow when you're sitting there staring at the screen. If you've marked the Beep When Done box in the Preferences > General dialog box, Photoshop will chirp when it's finished with its calculations.

FADING FILTER EFFECTS

You can use the Fade command (Shift + Ctrl/Command + F) to reduce the amount of a filter's effects, moving a slider from 0 to 100 percent to adjust how much of a filter's modifications should be applied to your image, layer, or selection. However, I find that I have more options when I apply a filter to a duplicate layer. I can vary the amount of the filtration by changing the opacity of the filtered layer so it blends in with the unmodified layer underneath. I can selectively erase parts of the filtered layer so the filtration is applied only to portions of the image. I can use Photoshop's Mode controls to merge the filtered and unfiltered layers in creative ways. Fade is handy, but it's a fast and less versatile way of modifying a filter's effects.

When the filter is finished, be careful not to do anything else (for example, move the selection) until you've decided whether or not the effect is the one you want. Although Photoshop has multiple levels of Undo, you'll save effort any time you can avoid using the Edit > Step Backward (Alt/Option + Ctrl/Command + Z) command multiple times. That way, if you totally hate the result, you can quickly press Ctrl/Command + Z and try again.

Saving the Image or a Snapshot

When you're really, really certain that the effect is what you want, save the file under another name (use File > Save As and click the Save A Copy box if you want). Only flatten the layers to merge the effect with your main image when you're convinced you have the look you want. Some day, you'll be glad you saved a copy of the file when you change your mind about being really, really certain.

Photoshop CS's Filter Gallery

The last version of Photoshop CS introduced the Filter Gallery, which has been optimized in CS 2.0. Not all filters in the Photoshop repertoire are included in the Gallery. The roughly four dozen filters that are included have a new look that's compatible with the Filter Gallery interface. You'll find them in the Artistic, Brush Strokes, Distort, Sketch, Stylize, and Texture categories. Not all the filters in those general categories are included in the Filter Gallery. For example, the Stylize category, which includes 9 different filters, is represented in the Filter Gallery only by Glowing Edges. Other filters, found in the Pixelate, Render, Blur, Sharpen, and other categories are not included and use the familiar pre-Photoshop CS dialog box. With each new release of Photoshop, expect additional filters to join the gallery.

The only disadvantage to the Filter Gallery is that the first time you load it in a particular session, it can take a long time for the dialog box to appear. Subsequent appearances can be much quicker if you have lots of memory. I have 2GB of RAM in my computer and devote 60 percent of it to Photoshop (Edit > Preferences > Memory & Image Cache), so Photoshop is usually able to store the Filter Gallery in memory. (With Mac OS X, you'll find this setting at Photoshop > Preferences > Memory & Image Cache. Photoshop usually selects 50 percent as the memory allocation.)

There are several advantages to the Filter Gallery. These include:

- **Extra large preview area.** This is shown at left in Figure 8.6. This generous, zoomable preview lets you view the effects you've applied with the Filter Gallery before you commit to them.

Figure 8.6 The Filter Gallery has a new look and new features that plug-in users will love.

- **Multiple applications of the same filter.** You can apply the same filter several times and view the results in the preview window *before* committing to the special effect by clicking the OK button. Of course, you always could apply a filter repeatedly in Photoshop, but it was necessary to exit the filter dialog box and then repeat the action. If you decided you'd added too much of a good thing, you had to use the Undo option to cancel your last action (or two).

- **Apply multiple filters.** The Filter Gallery lets you apply several different filters in any order you want, using your choice of settings, before committing to a specific set of effects.

- **Change the order and settings of filters.** If you decide you want to apply a certain Texture filter *before* adding an Artistic filter into the mix (rather than vice-versa), you can do that.

Filter Gallery Basics

The best way to learn how to use this versatile tool is to jump right in and begin working with it. If you want to use the same image I'm going to play with, find the catbottle picture on the website (**www.courseptr.com/downloads**) for this book. The original picture is shown in Figure 8.7. Then follow the series of steps I'm going to outline in this section.

Prepping the Image

First, why not apply some of the techniques you've learned in this book to make the image even more suitable for some filter magic?

1. Choose Image > Adjustments > Shadow/Highlights to produce the dialog box shown in Figure 8.8. Click the Show More Options box so you'll see the full toolkit.

2. To lighten the shadows, the Shadows sliders should be set to Amount: 50 percent; Tonal Width: 50 percent; Radius: 30 pixels.

3. To darken the highlights, the Highlights sliders should be set to Amount: 25 percent; Tonal Width: 50 percent; Radius: 30 pixels.

4. Set the Color Corrections slider to 45 percent and watch the bottle become a deeper blue.

5. Click on OK to apply the change. The image will now look like Figure 8.9.

Figure 8.7 We're going to work with this photo.

Figure 8.8 Use the Shadow/Highlights command first to prep the image.

Figure 8.9 The modified image looks like this.

Accessing the Filter Gallery

The easiest way to access the Filter Gallery is to choose Filter > Filter Gallery. The Gallery dialog box shown in Figure 8.10 appears. (If you choose one of the filters included in the gallery from the Filter menu, the Filter Gallery also pops up.) If not all the filters in the gallery are visible, click the button to the left of the OK button. There are several components to work with. These include:

- **The Preview window.** At the bottom of the window are plus/minus buttons you can click to zoom in and out, an activity indicator that shows the progress of the filter as it is applied, and scroll bars (at both bottom and right side) you can use to view all of an image that won't fit in the preview window.

- **Categories/Thumbnails.** In the middle of the Filter Gallery is a list of filter categories that can display thumbnails of each filter available. The triangle next to each category name points toward the category when that folder is closed, and points downward when you open the category to display the filters it contains. You can show or hide all the filters in a category folder, and scroll through them.

- **Controls.** Each filter's controls, including sliders and buttons, appear to the right of the filter category list when a particular filter is selected. There is also a drop-down list you can use to scroll through an alphabetized listing of every filter in the Gallery.

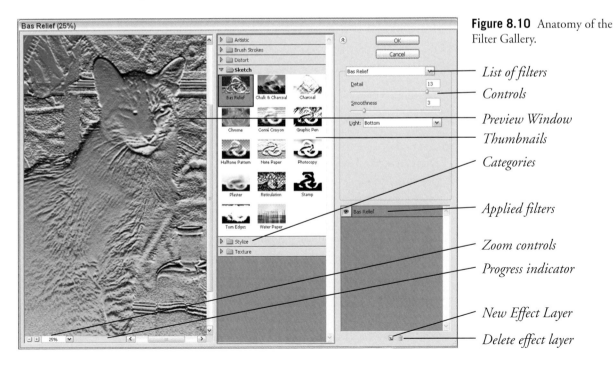

Figure 8.10 Anatomy of the Filter Gallery.

List of filters
Controls
Preview Window
Thumbnails
Categories
Applied filters
Zoom controls
Progress indicator
New Effect Layer
Delete effect layer

- **Applied Filters.** At the lower-right corner of the Filter Gallery is a list of the filters that have been applied in this Gallery session.

- **Sizing Controls.** As with many PC and Mac dialog boxes, you can enlarge the box to provide more room for previews, lists, and other features without scrolling.

Applying the First Filter

Let's jump right in and apply a filter to see how the Gallery works. Just follow these steps:

1. With the Filter Gallery visible, click the Zoom buttons until the catbottle image fills the preview area.

2. Open the Artistic folder in the categories/thumbnails area.

3. Select the Poster Edges filter, with the default settings. Photoshop applies the filter, and Poster Edges appears in the list of applied filters in the lower-right corner of the Filter Gallery.

4. Notice the Eyeball icon in the right-hand column of the applied filters area. Click the Eyeball to make the Poster Edges effect you've applied invisible. That will return the image to its original appearance.

5. If you decide you don't want to use Poster Edges, just click on a different filter. The original filter's effects will be removed and replaced by those of the new filter.

6. Note that you can show or hide the Poster Edges effect with the Eyeball, and change the settings of the effect at any time, up until you click the OK button to apply the modifications. The image will look like Figure 8.11.

Applying Another Filter

This is where the Filter Gallery gets very cool. You can add a second or third filter effect, view each of the effects separately or in any combination you choose, and modify any of their settings independently. Follow these steps to see for yourself:

1. To add an effect layer, click the New Effect Layer icon at the bottom left of the applied filters area. A new effect layer appears, listed above the Poster Edges effect (because the new effect will be applied "on top" of the original filter).

2. Open the Brush Strokes category and click the Sprayed Strokes thumbnail. Photoshop will add the Brush Strokes effect to the effect achieved by the Poster Edges filter. The image will look like Figure 8.12.

3. Repeat Steps 1 and 2 to add another filter effect of your choice.

Figure 8.11 With one filter applied, the image looks like this.

Figure 8.12 You can change the layer order of effects and turn them on or off.

Now you have two or three filter effects applied using the Filter Gallery. Here are some of the things you can do before clicking OK to apply the effects you've chosen:

- To view any of the filter layers individually or in combination, click the Eyeball icons to show or hide a particular filter effect.

- When you click in an effect's layer, you can change the settings for that effect.

- Drag a layer from one position in the stack to place it "above" another effect, so that it will be applied after the effects below it have been applied.

- If you decide you don't want to use an effect, select that layer and click the Trash icon at the lower right of the dialog box.

That's about all there is to using the Filter Gallery. With any luck, Adobe will add more filters to the Gallery in the next release of Photoshop.

Reproducing Photographic Filters in Photoshop

I'm going to divide the rest of this chapter into two parts. This next section will show you how to reproduce some of the most common photographic filters in Photoshop, whether the technique uses Photoshop's own filters or not. The section that follows this one will deal exclusively with using Photoshop's built-in filters.

Polarizing Filters

Polarizing filters can provide richer and more vibrant colors while reducing some of the glare that infects many photos taken in bright daylight. Polarizing filters work in much the same way as polarized sunglasses. Figure 8.13 is a simplified illustration that may help you understand how polarizing filters work.

In this figure, sunlight strikes all the shiny parts of the convertible (glass windows, the shiny plastic wheelcovers and trim, and so forth), although for simplicity I'm showing only the glare off the rear wheelcover. The light bounces off in many different directions. As you probably know, light moves in waves, and in this case the waves vibrate at many different angles; some side to side, some up-and-down, others at diagonal angles. It's difficult to illustrate this, but I think you know what I'm saying. Some of this hodgepodge of light strikes the lens of your camera, producing glare and reduced contrast.

A polarizing filter contains what you can think of as a tiny set of parallel louvers which filter out all the light waves except for those vibrating in a direction parallel to the louvers. Again, this is difficult to demonstrate in two dimensions, but you can see the net result in Figure 8.14. All the light waves are blocked except

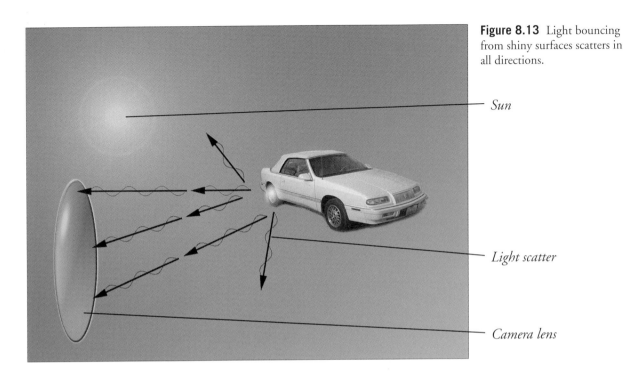

Figure 8.13 Light bouncing from shiny surfaces scatters in all directions.

Sun

Light scatter

Camera lens

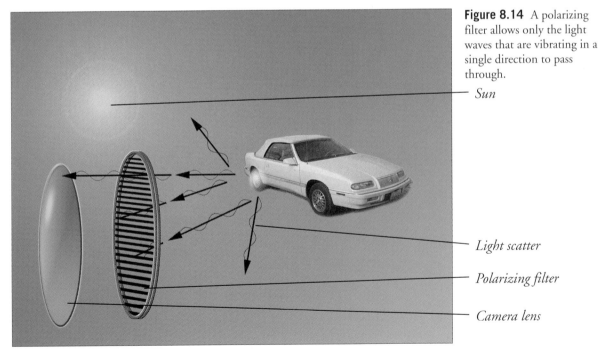

Figure 8.14 A polarizing filter allows only the light waves that are vibrating in a single direction to pass through.

Sun

Light scatter

Polarizing filter

Camera lens

for those vibrating from side to side (imagine them moving from side to side in the illustration) so they can pass through the horizontal louvers. The polarizer blocks all the scattered light.

A polarizing filter consists of two rings; one is attached to the lens, while the outer ring rotates the polarizing glass. This lets you change the angle of the louvers and selectively filter out different light waves. With a single lens reflex (SLR) camera (which lets you view through the same lens that takes the picture), you can rotate the ring until the effect you want is visible. Blue sky and water, which can contain high amounts of scattered light, can be made darker and more vibrant. You can also reduce or eliminate reflections from windows and other nonmetallic surfaces. The most dramatic changes can be produced when the sun is low in the sky and located off to your left or right shoulder.

As you might expect, polarizers work best with SLR cameras that let you preview the effect. If you're using a non-SLR digital camera, you may want to use the LCD viewfinder instead of the optical finder when making your adjustments.

Simulating a polarizer in Photoshop is tricky, because there is no easy way to replace information that is obscured by glare. Figure 8.15 shows a photo (at top) that's marred by unwanted reflections off the car windows. In this case, I was able

Figure 8.15 The unwanted reflections shown in the top image can be removed in Photoshop even without resorting to a polarizing filter.

to select the area of the glass that had the most glare, and reduce the brightness and contrast to bring that area back to the same level as the rest of the window. In other cases, you may have to use the Clone Stamp or Healing Brush tools to copy parts of the image that are glare-free over parts that have reflections. Then, you can adjust the overall brightness and contrast of the image to resemble what the image would look like if you had been able to use a polarizer filter.

Cross-Screen

Cross-screen filters are simple add-ons that let you make the specular highlights of an object sparkle, while providing a little bit of diffusion. My first cross-screen was a piece of tight-mesh window screen inside a set of empty Series 7 filter adapter rings. Later, filter manufacturers came out with glass versions of these with cross-hatch lines etched in the glass. Cross-screen filters work great with jewelry and other naturally sparkly items. Photoshop can easily duplicate this effect while giving you much greater control over the size and placement of your starbursts. Just follow these steps, using the Watch photo included on the website, or your own picture.

1. First create a cross-shaped star to add to your image. You can simply draw a star shape on a transparent layer, or do as I did by following the next couple steps.

2. Click the Brush tool in the Tool Palette, or press B to activate it.

3. In the Options bar, click the Fly-out menu and select Calligraphic Brushes from the drop-down list, as shown in Figure 8.16. A dialog box will appear asking if you want to replace your current brushes or append these new brushes to your current set. Choose Append.

4. Select the 28-pixel calligraphic vertical stroke, and use it to draw one ray of the star on a transparent layer in black. Draw another vertical ray directly underneath it.

5. Use the Lasso selection tool to select the two rays and then choose Edit > Transform > Rotate 90 Degrees Clockwise. The rays will now be horizontal.

6. Use the same brush to create another pair of vertical rays at right angles to the first two.

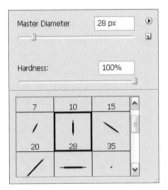

Figure 8.16 Add Calligraphic Brushes to your Brushes Palette.

7. Choose Filter > Stylize > Emboss to give the star a 3D texture, as shown in Figure 8.17.

Figure 8.17 The Emboss filter gives the star a 3D texture.

8. Although you can use the star shape as-is, you may want to rotate it 45 degrees (Edit > Transform > Rotate), and reduce it to a size more appropriate to the object you'll be adding cross-stars to. (Use Edit > Transform > Resize.)

CREATE A STAR-SHAPED BRUSH

You can also create a brush shaped like the star you just created. Select it with the Lasso tool, choose Edit > Define Brush, and give the new brush a name. Henceforth, anytime you want to add this star to an image, use the brush you just made.

9. Copy the star and apply it to several places on your image in a separate transparent layer.

10. Choose the Color Dodge mode for this transparent layer from the Layer Palette, as you can see in Figure 8.18.

11. Use Image > Adjustments > Brightness/Contrast to make the star as bright or as dark as you want for your particular image.

12. With the star layer still active, choose Filter > Blur More. This enhances the blurry star effect. Your finished image should look like Figure 8.19.

Figure 8.18 Use Color Dodge mode to merge the star layer with the rest of the image.

Figure 8.19 The finished image with artificial "stars" looks like this.

Split Filter

Split filters are nothing more than glass filters divided into two halves, each a different color. You see these used a lot in still photography to give the sky and ground an eerie look, and cinematographers use them extensively to create a moody atmosphere. Creating your own split filter in Photoshop is easy. Just follow these steps.

1. In a new, empty document create two transparent layers.

2. Choose the Gradient tool from the Tool Palette.

3. Select Linear Gradient from the Option bar, and choose the Foreground to Transparent gradient from the drop-down list, as shown in Figure 8.20.

4. Select your two colors as the foreground and background colors, using your favorite method (the Eyedropper tool in the Swatches Palette works for me).

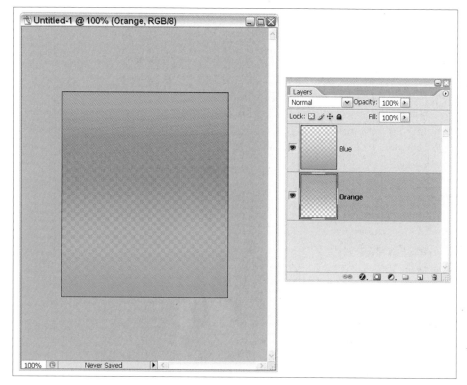

Figure 8.20 Use two gradients to create a split-filter effect in Photoshop.

5. Drag from the top to the bottom of one of the transparent layers, holding down the Shift key to make sure you drag in a straight line. This applies the foreground color as a gradient in that layer.

6. Press X to swap the foreground and background colors.

7. Drag from the bottom to the top in the other transparent layer to create the lower half of your split filter.

8. Choose Layer > Merge Visible to combine these two layers.

9. Save your split-filter document so you can use it as you want.

10. To use the "filter," copy the filter layer and paste it into the image you want to use it with, resizing so the filter covers the entire image. Use the Darken or Multiply layer modes to merge the filter layer with the underlying image without completely obscuring it. Figure 8.21 shows one typical result.

Figure 8.21 The split-filter effect can add a moody look like this.

Modifying Images with Photoshop's Filters

Photoshop's own filters offer a wealth of special effects you can apply to your photographs. Other than the Photo Filters, they may not resemble the filter effects you can get with conventional glass or gelatin filters, but that's the whole point. Photoshop lets you go beyond the limits of both film and digital cameras to create entirely new looks. This section will explore some of the things you can do with Photoshop's own filters.

The section will not cover every one of the 100+ Photoshop filters. Many of the filters, such as the Sharpen, Blur, Grain, and Lens Flare filters were covered in other chapters. Quite a few other filters, such as the Offset filter, do things that aren't particularly useful from a photographic standpoint, but which are consummately handy for other applications, such as creating seamless backgrounds for web pages. Instead, in this section we'll look at the best of the rest. I won't stick rigidly to Photoshop's filter menu hierarchy, either. Filters that provide painterly effects will be grouped together, while those that add textures or drawing effects will be bundled among their own.

I've found that the easiest way to compare filter effects is to compare the same image as it is transmogrified by a variety of different filters, so the examples in this section will use the same basic image, shown in Figure 8.22, in our examples. I have to warn you that not all filters look good with human subjects.

Figure 8.22 This picture is our starting point for the filters that follow.

Painting Filters

If you want to create pictures that look like they were painted, Photoshop offers some great filters. You can get brush strokes without ever touching a brush. You'll find these filters in Photoshop's Artistic, Brush Strokes, and Sketch submenus in particular. Digital effects applied with these filters can produce results in seconds that can't easily be achieved by an artist equipped with brush, paints, and traditional tools. It's also fairly easy to generate effects that are strongly reminiscent of the styles of "real" artists, using a group of filters found in the Pixelate and Stylize menus of Photoshop.

These kinds of filters all have one thing in common: They reduce the amount of information in an image by combining or moving pixels. Some overlay an image with a texture or pattern, while other plug-ins group similar colors together or transform groups of hues into new tones. The result is an image that has been softened, broken up, selectively increased in contrast, or otherwise "pixelated."

At first glance, these filters seem to have turned a photograph into a painting. Instead of the harsh reality of the original image, we have a softer, more organic picture that appears to have been created, rather than captured.

Just as the crystal clarity of video productions adds realism to documentaries and intimacy to videotaped stage plays or situation comedies, original photographs look real to us. For romantic stories and fantasy images, motion picture film provides a softer look with a feeling of distance, much like digital processing of still images. Would *Star Wars* or *Forrest Gump* have been as effective if originated on video, even though both contain digital effects? Do your hyper-realistic original photos qualify as portraits?

Of course, both kinds of images have their place. Painting-oriented filters are excellent for portraits, figure studies, or landscapes in which fine detail is not as important as general form, colors, or groups of shapes. Indeed, brushstrokes or other textures can mask defects, disguise or diminish distracting portions of an image, and create artful images from so-so photographs. That's especially true when the original image was too sharp, or, paradoxically, not sharp enough. Filters can tone down excessive detail while masking the lack of it.

You'll want to select your subjects for painting filters carefully. Pictures of older men and women may not look right when you blur all those hard-won wrinkles and character lines. Teenagers of both sexes, on the other hand, may prize the improvement to their complexions. Judicious application of a painting filter can add some softness to a glamour portrait, too.

Keep in mind that painting filters mimic, but do not duplicate the efforts of an artist. In real paintings, each brush stroke is carefully applied with exactly the right size, shape, and direction needed to provide a particular bit of detail. Years of experience and a good dose of artistic vision tell the artist where and how to put down those strokes.

A filter, in contrast, can base its operation only on algorithms built into it by the programmer. A skilled software designer can take advantage of variables such as lightness, darkness, contrast, and so forth to produce the illusion that an organic human, and not a silicon simulacrum, is behind the effect. You can further enhance the image by using your own judgment in applying parameters and choosing which sections of the picture are to be processed by a filter. However, you won't exactly duplicate the efforts of an artist with one of these plug-ins.

Craquelure

Professional photographers pay big bucks to have their photo labs give portraits an "old masters" look by cracking the surface as if it were a painting that had started to age. Paints used in ancient times weren't stable, as they were egg whites, clay, and plants used as pigment and used a protective varnish layer that tended to crack. Pro photographers sometimes have this texture applied to their photographs to give them an Old Masters patina. You can achieve a similar effect, which adds a nice 3D look, using the Craquelure filter.

Your controls can specify the crack spacing, depth, and brightness. You can adjust the spacing to produce a mixture of cracks and image area, and modify the depth and brightness settings to create deeper or shallower cracks.

Dark Strokes

The Dark Strokes filter reduces the number of tones in the image through a posterization-like effect that combines similar tones in an unusual way. Instead of grouping similar colors together, Dark Strokes makes dark tones darker and light tones lighter, increasing contrast, while rendering the image with diagonal brush strokes. Short strokes are used for dark tones and longer strokes for light tones. Figure 8.23 shows the Craquelure and Dark Strokes filters applied to the portrait image.

Figure 8.23 Craquelure (left) and Dark Strokes (right).

Dry Brush

The Dry Brush filter mimics a natural-media effect, that of stroking a canvas with a brush that's almost devoid of paint. It doesn't obscure as much detail as other painting-style filters, but retains a distinct painting look. As it posterizes your image, Dry Brush produces more distinct banding than Dry Strokes, combining all similar colors in a particular area. Adjust the size of the brush to produce different effects.

Paint Daubs

This Brush Strokes filter includes a selection of brush types and sizes, and sharpness controls. You can select from Simple, Light Rough, Dark Rough, Wide Sharp, Wide Blurry, or Sparkle Brush types. Figure 8.24 shows the Dry Brush and Paint Daubs filters in action.

Figure 8.24 Dry Brush (left) and Paint Daubs (right).

Fresco

Traditional fresco is a technique in which water colors are applied to wet plaster and allowed to dry, forming a permanent image on the wall or other structure containing the plaster. If you're an artist-type, and can work fast, fresco is a great way to produce murals using short, jabby strokes. If you're a photographer, you'll want to use the Fresco filter to create a smeary effect. This filter is otherwise quite similar to Dry Brush.

Poster Edges

This filter transforms your image into a poster by converting full-color or grayscale images into reduced color versions by combining similar colors into bands of a single hue, like the Photoshop Posterize command. However, Poster Edges outlines all the prominent edges with black, giving the photo a hand-drawn look.

Of course, the original non-electronic poster effect was created to allow simulating continuous tone images without actually using detailed halftones. The broad bands of color could each be printed on a separate run through a sheet-fed press at a relatively low cost. Posters were often created in this way for circuses, plays, and, later, motion pictures. Even when halftoning was a common and inexpensive process, poster printing techniques were an economical way to produce very large posters on thick stocks.

Poster Edges gives you three controls, allowing you to adjust the relative thickness of the black lines used to outline the edges, and specify their darkness or intensity. A third slider lets you specify the number of tones used to produce the effect. Figure 8.25 shows the Fresco and Poster Edges filter effects.

Figure 8.25 Fresco (left) and Poster Edges (right).

Spatter

The Spatter filter creates an airbrush-like painterly effect. You can use it to soften portrait or landscape subjects. Its controls include a Spray Radius slider, which adjusts the number of pixels covered by the spray of the airbrush, and a Smoothness control, which modifies the evenness of the effect.

Watercolor

Watercolors produce great pastel effects because their water-soluble pigments are not as opaque as oils or acrylics, and they tend to soak into the paper, producing a soft, diffused effect. It's a good plug-in for landscapes, female portrait subjects, or any image which can be improved with a soft look. While you can select the amount of brush detail, Watercolor doesn't work well with detailed strokes. Figure 8.26 shows the Spatter and Watercolor filters at work.

Figure 8.26 Spatter (left) and Watercolor (right).

Angled Strokes

Angled Strokes paints your image using diagonal strokes in one direction for the dark tones, and diagonal strokes going in the other direction to represent the light tones in an image.

With high resolution files, the effects may not be as noticeable unless you either reduce the size of the image to 25 to 50 percent of its original size before applying the filter (scale it back up when you're finished) or use a high sharpness setting. This filter can be applied to primary subjects, but also makes a good tool for creating artsy background textures.

Palette Knife

This filter applies irregular gobs of color to your image. The Stroke Size slider adjusts the size of the digital knife you're using. The Stroke Detail control can be used to specify how much of the detail in your original image is retained. The Softness control increases or decreases the roughness of the edges of the palette strokes.

While you can use this filter alone, it works well with other plug-ins, as a first step to reduce the amount of detail before you apply a second filter, such as Watercolor or Grain. Textures, particularly canvas, can add to the painterly effect of this filter. Figure 8.27 shows the Angled Strokes and Palette Knife filters.

Figure 8.27 Angled Strokes (left) and Palette Knife (right).

Pointillize

This filter provides a randomized image with lots of little dots on it, produced by cell sizes that range from 3 to 300 pixels. The tricky part about using this filter is choosing your background color, as all the spaces between the dots are filled in with your current background color. Instead of using white, try soft pastels that won't overpower the tones of your image. Figure 8.28 shows the kind of effects you can get with the Pointillize filter.

Sketching/Drawing Filters

You can also apply drawing-like effects, such as pen and ink, using Photoshop's filters. Here are the best of them.

Graphic Pen

The Graphic Pen filter applies monochrome strokes that can be applied diagonally, horizontally, or vertically, using the foreground color, while filling in the rest of the image with the background color. If you keep that in mind, you can create both positive (black on white) and negative (white on black) images. Controls include a Stroke Length slider that manages how much detail is preserved, and a Light/Dark Balance slider to select the areas of the image to which the strokes are applied. Lighter settings sketch in the highlights, while darker settings use the shadow areas for the strokes. Your choice of stroke direction should be determined by your subject matter: Horizontal strokes are great for vertically oriented subjects, such as buildings, while vertical strokes are best used on landscapes and other subjects with horizontal lines. Figure 8.28 shows the Graphic Pen filter's effects.

Ink Outlines

Ink Outlines produces an image with the outlines and edges enhanced, without losing the original colors. It creates an almost cartoon-like appearance.

Sponge

Sponge creates textured images with contrasting blobs of color. You can adjust brush size, definition, and smoothness, using the filter's slider controls. Figure 8.29 illustrates the Ink Outlines and Sponge filters.

Sumi-e

Sumi-e is a Japanese technique that involves using an ink-loaded wet brush to draw on highly absorbent rice paper, much like painting on a blotter. It works best with abstracts or landscapes, as it blurs portrait subjects a bit too much. The only controls are Stroke Width, Stroke Pressure, and Contrast.

Figure 8.28 Pointillize (left) and Graphic Pen (right).

Figure 8.29 Ink Outlines (left) and Sponge (right).

Edgy Filters

Some filters do their work by finding the edges in your image, then enhancing them in some way. These filters all produce somewhat abstract effects, but if you check out the photography magazines you'll see that they are quite popular with traditional and digital photographers.

Find Edges

The Find Edges filter produces some dramatic effects, similar to drawings created with colored pencils. There are no controls or dialog boxes. This filter makes a great springboard for combining several filters or using other controls to generate outrageous variations. Use the Image > Adjustments > Hue/Saturation dialog box's sliders to warp the colors in your edge-enhanced image, juice up the saturation, or lighten/darken the effect. Pixelate your image, or merge it with a copy of the original image, adjusting the Opacity slider in the Layers Palette to combine varying percentages of the unaltered and edge-enhanced versions. Figure 8.30 shows the Sumi-e and Find Edges filters applied to our portrait.

Glowing Edges

Glowing Edges adds incredible colors to the edges of your image. None of the images it produces will look realistic—but I guarantee they'll all be interesting! The controls are the same as with Accented Edges, but this filter does not reverse the tones of your image. The Edge Width control adjusts the relative width of the edges; Edge Brightness controls whether the edges are stroked in a dark or light tone, while Smoothness determines how closely the edges follow the actual edges in the image.

Accented Edges

The Accented Edges filter works a little like Find Edges, but with additional control over the width, smoothness, and brightness of the edges in the image. Edge Width adjusts the relative width of the edges. Edge Brightness controls whether the edges are stroked in a dark or light tone, while Smoothness determines how closely the edges follow the actual edges in the image. Higher settings produce more gradual transitions from one angle to the next. Figure 8.31 shows the Glowing Edges and Accented Edges performing their edgy magic.

Trace Contours

The Trace Contours filter is similar in concept to the Find Edges filter, but they produce very different looks. You can adjust the brightness level Trace Contours uses as the threshold to outline edges in your image. Trace Contours creates different outlines for each color channel. Experiment with this filter. This is another filter that can be used as a jumping-off point. Try different level settings, merge a contoured image with the original, or invert your contour to create new effects.

Figure 8.30 Sumi-e (left) and Find Edges (right).

Figure 8.31 Glowing Edges (left) and Accented Edges (right).

Emboss

Emboss finds the edges in your image and raises them, discarding most of the colors in your image in the process, and producing a stamped metal effect. You can specify the angle for the imaginary light source that casts the shadow of the raised surface. Values from 0 degrees (right side of the image) to 90 degrees (directly overhead) and on to 180 degrees (left side of the image) produce a raised effect. From −1 (right) to −90 degrees (directly underneath) to −179 degrees (left) make the image seem to be pressed into the surface.

You can also specify the height of the embossing, from one to 10 pixels. The larger the number is, the greater the 3D effect. Use this control with the Amount slider, described below. You can get some lovely, grainy effects even with only a one-pixel-high emboss if you ramp up the contrast by specifying 500 percent with the Amount slider. Also adjust the amount of embossing, from 1 to 500 percent. I've gotten some great results from using a very small height with a large Amount setting, and vice versa.

On its own, Emboss often isn't particularly useful with some images, since the 3D effect, while interesting, has bland coloration and featureless backgrounds. You'll want to combine this filter with other effects—pixelation, distortion, or even sharpening—to create a really outrageous image. Figure 8.32 shows the Trace Contours and Emboss filters applied.

Figure 8.32 Trace Contours (left) and Emboss (right).

Distortion Filters

Distortion filters are all "pixel movers." They operate by shifting pixels from one location to another. Because distortion filters cause such dramatic changes, you'll want to select the images you use them with carefully. Here are descriptions of some of the more useful filters that distort.

Pinch

The Pinch filter squeezes the contents of an image towards the center, or pushes it out toward its outer edges. The only control available is an Amount slider, which can be varied from 0 to 100 percent (to pinch inward) or from 0 to −100 percent (to push outward).

Figure 8.33 shows an entire image that has been pinched by 50 percent. However, if you're pinching a rectangularly shaped selection, the filter automatically blends the affected area into the surrounding image. That's because Photoshop applies the filter to the largest ellipse that will fit inside the square or rectangle. The effect is feathered into the rest of the selection, providing a smooth transition.

Ripple

The Ripple filter gives you a wavy effect, supposedly something like the ripples on a pond, except when we think of those we usually expect them to be concentric.

Figure 8.33 Pinch (left) and Ripple (right).

If that's what you want, investigate the Zigzag filter instead. Personally, I think Adobe has the names of these two filters reversed.

The Ripple dialog box allows you to specify an Amount from 0 (little ripples) to 999 (big ripples) or 0 to –999 (the ripples go the other direction). You can also choose Small, Medium, and Large from a drop-down list, which controls not the size of the ripples (as you might expect), but how closely spaced together they are. Go figure. This ripple frequency is calculated in proportion to the selection: Choosing Small will produce differently sized ripples in small selections than in large selections.

This is one filter that produces a stark transition with the rest of your image, unless you remember to feather the selection before you apply the effect. You can also produce some wonderful textures by applying the Ripple filter to the same selection multiple times, alternating negative and positive values, or mixing Small, Medium, or Large frequencies. Figure 8.33 shows the Pinch and Ripple filters.

Spherize

This filter wraps your image or selection onto a sphere. The dialog box shows a wireframe representation. You can specify outward and inward bulges from 0 to plus or minus 100 percent. The effect is quite similar to that of the Pinch filter. However, the Sphere filter also lets you distort your image around a vertical or horizontal cylinder, by choosing Horizontal Only or Vertical Only from a drop-down list. If your selection area is not round, Spherize will carve out a circular area in the middle of the selection, and distort that.

Spherize is great for creating spheres from scratch. If you want a plain sphere, try this trick: Select a circle and fill with a radial gradient. Position the center of the gradient up and to one side of the circle. Use Filter > Render > Lens Flare to make the surface even more realistic. Then apply the Spherize filter. Presto! One ball-shaped object, ready to roll.

Twirl

The Twirl filter swirls your image around like wet paint. The center pixels move more drastically than those on the periphery. The only control available is the slider that specifies degrees of twisting from –999 to +999 degrees (more than two full rotations) so you can create a whirlpool-like effect. Positive numbers give you a clockwise spin effect; negative numbers reverse the spin to counterclockwise. Figure 8.34 shows the Spherize and Twirl filters.

Figure 8.34 Spherize (left) and Twirl (right).

Wave

The Wave filter offers more than a dozen controls you can use to specify how your image is roiled up. There are three kinds of waves, and you can choose the number, size, and frequency of the ripples. The key controls include:

- **Number of Generators.** Or the number of points where waves are created, up to 999 (but that's far too many for most images). The effect is so muddled that each wave may be only a pixel or two wide. In my tests, high numbers ended up producing areas with plain tone, and no waves at all! You'll want to use from 5 to 20, tops.

- **Wavelength Minimum/Maximum.** Sets the distance from one wave crest to the next. What's the frequency, Kenneth? In this case, wavelength minimum and maximum (from 1 to 999) refer to the number of individual waves produced by each generator.

- **Amplitude Minimum/Maximum.** Controls the height of the waves, from 1 to 999.

- **Horizontal/Vertical Scale.** Adjusts the amount of distortion provided by each wave, from 1 to 100 percent.

- **How Undefined Areas Are Filled In.** Pixels can wrap around from one side to another, or stretch from the edge to fill the empty spaces.

- **Type of Wave.** Smooth sine waves, sharp triangle waves, or blocky square waves.

- **Randomize.** Applies random values to your wave's parameters.

Zigzag

The Zigzag filter is excellent for producing ripples in an image. You don't actually get zigzags at all with most settings. Choose the amount of distortion from –100 to +100 and the number of ridges from 1 to 20. You may also select pond-type ripples, ripples that emanate from the center of your selection, and whirlpool-like ripples that revolve around the center of the selection in alternating directions. The Zigzag filter is a good choice for creating any type of water effect, assorted liquids, and special textures. Figure 8.35 shows the Wave and ZigZag filters at work.

Figure 8.35 Wave (left) and ZigZag (right).

Pixelation and Stylizing Filters

These filters range from the mildly interesting to the wildly useful, and all of them provide distinct effects. You may have no parameters to enter, or just a few simple controls. Here's a quick rundown on the best of them.

Color Halftone

Don't confuse the Color Halftone filter with actual halftoning. Instead, it simply looks at the color layers of your image and changes them into a pattern of dots. As with real halftones, the highlight areas are represented by small dots, and shadow areas are represented by larger dots. The filter is a good way to add an interesting texture to your image.

Halftone Pattern

This is a versatile effect, changing your image into a black-and-white halftone screen, replacing all the original colors with shades of gray, or another set of colors, since Halftone Screen uses your application's current foreground and background colors. Only three controls are required, including a Size slider that controls the size of the fake halftone dots used. The others include the type of screen, from dot, line, and circle, and adjustment of the contrast of your image as the filter is applied. Figure 8.36 shows the Color Halftone and Halftone Screen filters.

Figure 8.36 Color Halftone (left) and Halftone Screen (right).

Crystallize

Crystallize converts an image to a series of random polygons, using a cell size you specify using a slider. As with the Color Halftone filter, the smaller the cell size, the more detail retained from your original image. Larger cells simplify your picture and mask defects.

Facet

Facet converts blocks of pixels of similar colors to a single tone, producing a faceted, posterized effect. This filter masks details, so it makes a good cover-up for subjects with defects in complexion or texture. This is one of those single-step filters that has no dialog box. Just apply it once or several times until you get the effect you want. Figure 8.37 shows the Crystallize and Facet filters at work.

Figure 8.37 Crystallize (left) and Facet (right).

Diffuse

If you know a bit about photography, don't confuse this digital diffuser with the kind you're used to. If you're a true photo nut, you'll know that diffusion can be produced by a conventional filter with a texture—something as simple as women's hosiery stretched over a frame is sometimes used in the darkroom to provide a diffusing effect when a print is exposed. A glass filter placed in front of the camera lens with petroleum jelly applied also can be used to create diffusion.

The Diffuse filter carves up your picture into four-pixel elements, then moves pixels towards the higher-contrast areas of your image, producing a smudgy effect. In photography, diffusing a positive image "spreads" lighter areas into darker areas, so an on-camera filter smudges highlights into the shadows. Diffusing a negative image during printing also spreads lighter areas into the darker areas, but in that case, those are the more transparent shadows of an image, smudged into the denser highlights. The final image diffused under the enlarger has a much different look than one diffused in the camera.

Photoshop's diffusion does not work in this way, so don't bother inversing a picture or selection before applying the Diffusion filter, and then converting it back. Even with multiple applications, the effect is virtually identical whether you diffuse a positive or negative image. Your only controls are options to perform this diffusion on all pixels, only darker pixels, or lighter pixels, and a new option, anisotropic (which is a type of surface in which long, thin features are aligned in one direction, such as brushed metal objects). You have to try this one out to see the interesting texture it produces.

Wind

Wind can create dozens of windy and streak effects. Although it works in a left to right or right to left direction, you can achieve vertical "wind" by rotating your image before applying the filter, then rotating it back to its original orientation. You'll get the best results if you work with images that have empty areas the wind can streak into. You can apply the filter several times from different directions to get some unique looks. It also works well with sports images. Wind looks especially good on silhouetted images. Figure 8.38 shows the Diffuse and Wind filters.

Chalk & Charcoal

This filter gives you the effects of a mixed-media drawing using rough chalk to express the midtones and highlights, and charcoal for the shadows. The diagonal lines used obliterate image detail, so this filter works best with photos that have strong areas. Choose background and foreground colors carefully to achieve different types of chalk/charcoal effects.

Crosshatch

Crosshatch adds a cross-pattern of pencil-like strokes to your image, adding texture without destroying all the original colors and detail of the original. It's a good arty effect with an unusual degree of control. Not only can you specify the stroke length and sharpness, but the number of times in succession the filter is applied. The more repetitions, the stronger the effect. Figure 8.39 shows the Chalk & Charcoal and Crosshatch filters.

Figure 8.38 Diffuse (left) and Wind (right).

Figure 8.39 Chalk & Charcoal (left) and Crosshatch (right).

Glass

The Glass filter provides effects you might get if you placed a glass block in front of your lens. You can specify the amount of distortion and the smoothness of the glass. A separate Surface Controls dialog box allows you to choose from glass blocks, frosted glass, tiny glass lenses, and even canvas. For images with individual features you can select a scaling to control the relative size of the image and the underlying texture, or invert the texture. Figure 8.40 shows two variations of the Glass filter.

Figure 8.40 Glass filter variations.

Next Up

The final chapter in this book is going to explain a little about how printers work with Photoshop, and includes an update of some special features that the very newest printers have.

9

Hardcopies Made Easy

In the 1970s, futurists were predicting the paperless office, with all documents created and managed using computers and electronics. We were all going to read books on our computers or (more recently) laptops or PDAs. That hasn't happened. In these days of e-mail and electronic funds transfer we may send fewer letters and never see our cancelled checks (if we even write checks in the first place), but paper documents continue to be used in growing numbers. After all, paper is the one form of information exchange that doesn't require some sort of special gadget to read it.

In the 1980s, it was prognosticated that images would suffer a similar demise. New electronic cameras that were emerging a quarter-century ago, like the Sony Mavica, and electronic viewing systems would displace hard-copy prints of pictures at lower cost and with greater convenience. That hasn't happened, either. Certainly, film is on its way out, but prints live on. Only the origination medium has changed.

The photographic print has a long and glorious history in photography. The earliest daguerreotypes and tintypes were very print-like, even though they were made of thin sheets of metal: They were positive images viewed by reflective light that could be displayed in frames or passed around for viewing. Later, paper prints grew beyond the original fuzzy efforts of William Fox Talbot to fully detailed copies made from film or glass plate negative originals, becoming the standard destination for photographic images.

Prints are what we think of when our mind's eye pictures a "photograph." Even photos originally captured and viewed as transparencies on a light box or with a slide projector frequently end up as reflective hard copies. Conventional photographers creating images with 120-format and larger transparency film or 35mm color slides make prints of their work. Digital photographers may capture, view, and store their images on a computer, but they still prize hardcopies for display or distribution. Despite entirely new channels for viewing photographic images, such as web pages or electronic presentations, prints remain an important destination for a significant number of pictures. This chapter will explore some of the print options available with Photoshop, as always, from the photographer's viewpoint.

Why Prints?

Back in 1990, I worked on the PR team that created publicity materials for an exciting new product: the Kodak Photo CD. The scientists who developed the technology showed me dozens of exciting applications for this high-resolution digital format. Many of these have come to pass, and today, more than 15 years later, you can drop your pictures off at many retail photofinishing outlets and receive an inexpensive Picture CD along with your prints. Professional Photo CDs are an important option for photographers who want to distribute their portfolios electronically in a format that allows both previewing of low-resolution prints and sale of "locked" high-resolution versions.

However, one of the most hyped capabilities of Photo CD technology never caught on. The prototype Photo CD players I looked at were cool enough. You could flip through your Photo CD albums at high speed on your own television screen, zooming in to view interesting details, moving back and forth in slideshow fashion. Plans were to have inexpensive printmakers attached to the Photo CD player to make hardcopies. By the 21st century, families would view their snapshots clustered around their television or home entertainment center. Certainly, prints would still be made, but viewing pictures on the TV would soon be the most popular mode.

What happened? What saved us from endless hours of viewing the neighbor's vacation pictures on television? The answer is a simple one: Even in this digital age, humans are in love with prints. We fight to get the first look at handfuls of snapshots fresh from the photofinisher. This is still true now that most pictures are taken with digital cameras: We love prints so much that dropping off memory cards (rather than film) at a digital lab for quick prints has become a whole *new* tradition.

We select our favorites for sharing, and like to hide or destroy the ones that make us look ugly. It's fun to pass a stack of photos around, letting each person view them at his own speed, hurrying through the boring ones and stopping to linger over the compelling images. Most of the time you don't want to call everyone into the family room to look at photos on the TV. You want to look at them where and when you want to.

Moreover, you can't stick a Photo CD on the refrigerator with a magnet or tack one on the wall of a cubicle at work. Photo CDs don't look good framed on the mantel, and can't be shown off in a gallery. Despite the encroachments of technology, we still like *prints*.

As a result, you can expect that prints will remain the favored end result of photography, in both digital and conventional realms. Those amateur photographers who still use film cameras work with negative films and make hardcopy prints. Even color transparencies, favored by professional photographers for their superior quality when reproduced, usually end up as paper prints or published in magazines.

Recently, digital photography has made some dramatic changes in the way we work with our images. Unlike photos captured on film, every digital picture you take isn't routinely converted into a print by a photofinisher. In that respect, digital pictures are like the color slides favored by amateurs and pros alike in the 1950s. Color slides and digital pictures are typically viewed on a screen and only the very best end up as prints.

Digital technology has further refined photographic Darwinism. Thanks to the "quick erase" buttons on many digital image grabbers, some pictures are deleted from your solid-state "film" before they even make it out of the camera. Only the most photographically fit images survive. Anyone who has shot an entire roll of film just to get a shot or two that was worth printing will appreciate the film-saving economy of a digital camera.

A significant number of electronic images are never intended for hard copies that you can pass around and show to friends. You might take a picture for a web page, such as the one shown in Figure 9.1, drop a shot into your PowerPoint presentation, or place an image in a desktop publication without the slightest need for a print.

Even so, we'll always need prints, and, if anything, the availability of inexpensive photo-quality printers encourages digital photographers to make bigger and better prints of their efforts. Photoshop and rampant computer technology not only lets you limit your hard copies to the prints you really want, but also makes the prints you do create better looking, with better colors, in larger sizes, and available faster than ever before.

Figure 9.1 Many photos are displayed only on websites, and are never made into hard copies at all.

Color Prints as Proofs

Most of the time, your color prints will be your finished product, whether your intent is to display the print in a frame or pass it around among friends and colleagues. A print is a typical end product for most amateur and professional photographers. If the print looks good to you, that's usually enough. You may need to work with Photoshop's color correction tools or your computer's color management system (as outlined in Chapter 6) so that producing pleasing color prints is fast and easy.

PROOFS VS. PROOFS

The word "proofs" has a dual meaning in photography. Portrait and wedding photographers create proof prints that are used by clients to select their final images. Today, it's more common to display proofs using a projection system or digital viewing system in the actual finished size of the print, but hard copy proofs are still used for this purpose by some photographers. A second kind of proof, discussed in this section, is a print used to judge the color balance and quality of an image as it will appear when printed.

However, professional photographers and serious photographic artists may have additional hardcopy concerns related to print permanence and image accuracy that aren't addressed fully by any of the output options outlined in the rest of this chapter. One of the most common pro applications for color prints is *proofs*, which are high-accuracy color prints designed to reflect how an image will appear when printed. While pre-press operations are beyond the scope of this book (and covered in depth by classics like Dan Margulis' *Professional Photoshop*), you should know some of what is involved.

In the printing industry, proofs are made of images that have been separated into their component colors (cyan, magenta, yellow, and black in the case of full-color images). Chromalin proofs are a standard, albeit expensive way of producing accurate color proofs of these color images. Chromalins are film proofs made using a patented DuPont system of mixing colored cyan, magenta, yellow, and black dye powders to approximate the printed colors, in the case of full-color images. (Chromalins can also be produced to proof spot color images using other colors of ink.) They provide a way of previewing a printed image without actually making plates and printing it on a press.

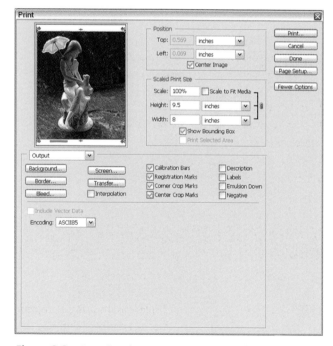

For digital prints, it's becoming more common to use Scitex Iris digital proofing devices, a kind of superexpensive inkjet printer on steroids that can produce hyperaccurate, hyperdetailed photos, for both proofing and making art prints intended for display. The quality is truly gorgeous, but the equipment is expensive (justifiable only by a service bureau or a high-volume internal department), and you should be prepared to pay $50 and up per print. Affordable desktop proofing devices, priced at less than a thousand dollars but capable of printing 11 × 14 and 11 × 17-inch photos or larger are available from companies like Hewlett-Packard and Epson.

Once you reach this print output stratosphere, you'll find that Photoshop has all the tools you need to create professional output. For example, Photoshop lets you print CMYK hard proofs from files that have been saved in CMYK format (not RGB) and include color calibration bars, registration marks, and other information. The File > Print with Preview dialog box, shown in Figure 9.2, lets you select any of these aids.

Figure 9.2 Photoshop lets you print hard proofs of CMYK images with registration marks and color calibration bars.

Your Output Options

If you want to examine digital printers using the darkroom analogy, they roughly correspond to an automated print processing system. You feed the paper into the processor, and the finished print comes out the other end. As with a darkroom print processor, you have relatively little control over the print once processing begins. The job of the printer/processor is to control variables and produce similar results every time when fed similar photos. A printer provides the repeatability and ease of use that a print processor offers. Photoshop and the printing controls included in your printer's driver software are the "enlarger" component in our digital darkroom.

If you still have doubts that paper prints will continue to thrive in the digital age, check out the ads in your local newspaper. You'll find sales on dozens of different color printers, including many capable of photo-quality reproduction from $49 to $149. You'll also see blurbs for photofinishers eager to make prints from your digital images sent to them over the Internet, on CD-ROM, or the most popular memory card formats. You'll also see promotions for those stand-alone photo kiosks that make it easy to capture an image of a print through a built-in scanner, or view your digital pictures from CD, floppy disk, or memory card, then crop, rotate, enlarge, and print them while you wait. There are many options for creating hardcopies, and you'll find all of them useful from time to time.

Laser Printers

If you work with text documents, create desktop publications, output lots of overhead transparencies, or are involved in other business printing, you already may have a black-and-white or color laser printer (or, alternatively, one that uses light emitting diodes (LEDs) to create an image instead of a laser). For business printing and making copies of documents, laser printers are great.

They're fast, especially when multiple copies are made, use ordinary paper, and subsist on a diet of powdered toner that is, page for page, much less expensive than the pigments or dyes used for other printing systems. These printers are best suited for text and line art. If you have business documents with black text spiced with spot color charts and graphs or colored headlines added for emphasis, a laser printer is ideal.

Photographers will find many applications for both black-and-white and color laser printers. For example, even a monochrome laser can produce an acceptable grayscale image that can be pasted into a layout on a "for position only" (FPO) basis. You can run off 20 or 30 copies quickly and inexpensively and route them for approval of pose or content, saving color hard copies for final approval. A color laser printer can be used for the same purposes at a slightly higher per-page cost, but with the added dimension of color. You might not want to use your laser printer for proofing, but it can have many other uses. When my daughter's cat ran astray, we printed up 100 "Have You Seen Our Kitten" miniposters on my black-and-white laser printer at a cost of a few cents per page. I've also used color laser printers for low-cost print-on-demand publications, like the one shown in Figure 9.3.

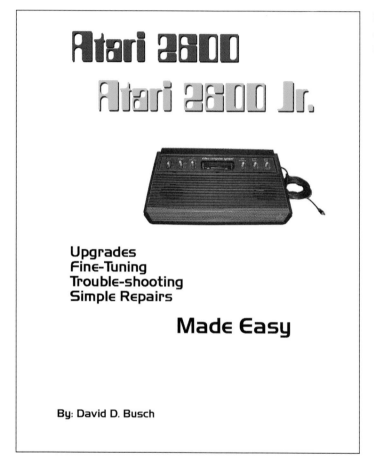

Figure 9.3 Color lasers are excellent for low-run print-on-demand publications.

Laser page printers are particularly fast when making multiple copies of the same original. The image is downloaded to the printer once, charging an electrically sensitive drum, which revolves at high speed, picking up toner and applying it to a sheet of paper. Once a page has been imaged on the drum, you can print multiple copies as quickly as the printer can feed sheets of paper. Inkjet printers, in contrast, must print each and every page dot by dot, line by line, whether you're printing one copy or 100 of the same image.

Color page printers work in much the same way as their black-and-white cousins. However, each image is run through the exposure, image writing, and toning steps four times, once each for cyan, magenta, yellow, and black portions of the image.

Obviously, separate toning stations must be provided inside the printer for each color, making for a larger, bulkier device. Once all four colors of toner are transferred to the electrically charged drum or belt, they are transferred to the paper and permanently heat-fused to the paper.

Because of their complexity, color page printers are often considerably more expensive, with the least expensive models starting at around $600 and moving swiftly to the $3,000 and up price range. Laser-type color printers typically don't provide quality that is as good as other types of printers for photographic output, but do much better on fine lines and text. These printers are best suited for spot color—images with specific elements that must be represented in cyan, magenta, yellow, red, green, or blue or some other shade. The consumables cost for ordinary paper and the color toners is likely to be less than for an inkjet printer, so if you have many images to print, a color laser can reduce your incremental per-print costs.

Inkjet Printers

Inkjet printers have become ubiquitous. You can buy them in your supermarket for $50, trot down to your electronics or computer store and purchase a photo-quality model for around $100, or spend as little as $300 to $400 for an inkjet specifically designed to print eye-popping color photos on glossy or matte paper. These printers are cheap enough to buy that virtually any amateur photographer can afford one, and serious amateurs and pros can easily justify the best models available.

Whether you can afford to *operate* an inkjet printer is something else again. One of the reasons inkjets are priced so low is that the vendors tend to make lots of money on the consumables. One inkjet printer I purchased last year cost $75 on sale. One month and two ink cartridges later, I'd spent more than my original investment on ink alone. I ended up giving the printer away and purchasing a more economical model.

Why do inkjet printers cost so much to operate? Start with the paper. Most inkjet printers can make acceptable prints on ordinary copier paper that costs a cent or two per sheet. However, the paper is thin and flimsy, has a dull paper-like finish, and neither looks nor feels like a real photograph. Plain paper inkjet prints have a look and quality that resembles a picture you might clip out of the newspaper rather than an actual photo.

For best results, you must use special "photo" papers that cost 50 cents to $1 a sheet or more. These sheets have a water-resistant plastic substrate that doesn't absorb ink, coated with glossy and matte surfaces (on alternate sides, so you can print on whichever side of the sheet you need). Because the ink doesn't spread, the printer is able to apply smaller, more distinct dots of color, producing sharper photographic-quality prints. While the improved quality is important, a buck per print isn't cheap, especially if you like to experiment or if you make many mistakes.

Special paper is only part of the cost. Color ink cartridges can cost $25–$35 each, and generally must be used in conjunction with a black-and-white ink cartridge at $20 and up. Some printers use two color cartridges (a "strong" color cart for cyan, magenta, and yellow; and a "weak" color cart for cyan and magenta) to provide additional tones. A single cartridge may output hundreds of pages if you're outputting text that covers roughly 5 to 15 percent of the page. A full-color image, on the other hand, typically covers 100 percent of the area printed (whether it's a 4 × 6 print or a full 8 × 10), so you may get as few as 20 to 30 full-page prints per ink cartridge. Plan on allocating another $1 per page just for ink.

It gets worse. If your particular printer's ink cartridge includes all three colors in a single module, you may find that one color runs out even more quickly (because, say, you're printing images that contain lots of yellow) and you must throw away a cartridge even when there are plenty of the other hues in the remaining tanks.

Of course, you may want to try out one of those inkjet refill kits, which come with bottles of ink and one or more syringes. They can provide two or three fillings at less than the cost of a single new tricolor cartridge. Some people swear by them, although I, personally, swear at them. The process takes a lot of time, which can be better spent taking pictures or working with Photoshop. If you have only one syringe, you must clean it with distilled water to remove all the ink before refilling another tank with a different color. If you use three syringes, you have to clean all three when you're done. The ink tends to spill and get all over your fingers and everything else in the vicinity. If you don't refill at exactly the right time, the innards of the cartridge may dry out, leaving you with a freshly refilled, non-working ink cartridge. Nor can cartridges be refilled indefinitely. If your printer uses nozzles built into the cartridge itself, these nozzles may wear out after a few refills. You'll have to buy a new one at full price and start over.

Many inkjet printers accept third-party ink cartridges that cost half or a third of what the vendor sells them for. Of course, you must take your chances that the cartridges are as good and that the ink is of the same quality and permanence as that in the vendor's own cartridges.

Saving Money with Inkjets

In the long run, of course, even an inkjet printer that is the most expensive to operate is still frequently cheaper to use than your photolab, as attractive as they are becoming today. For the Photoshop-adept, doing your own printing provides more control; it's the equivalent of working in a darkroom: You can tailor your output precisely to your own needs. Even so, you don't have to pay top dollar for your inkjet prints. Here are some tips for saving money.

Reducing Paper Costs

Paper costs are easy to trim. Try these cost-savers:

- **Buy photo paper in larger quantities**. You'll find that a 50-sheet or 100-sheet pack can be 50 percent cheaper per sheet than the 10-sheet or 25-sheet packages. Buy smaller quantities only to test the quality of a particular kind of paper. Once you're certain you like it, stock up on the larger packages.

- **Don't lock yourself into the vendor's product line**. Vendors guarantee that their papers will be compatible with their inks. In practice, there have been some combinations of paper stocks and inks that perform poorly, particularly when it comes to archival permanence. Use the wrong paper with the wrong ink and you may find yourself with faded photos in a few months. However, you should test a variety of papers, including generic store-brand stocks to see which provides the best combination of performance and longevity. For example, many of the color prints I make are submitted to newspapers. I don't care what they look like three months later; I never see them again.

- **Experiment with premium-quality plain paper**. I've used various brands with Bright White, Heavy Weight, or Premium Weight designations, including some that have a fairly glossy finish. I've even used old thermal printer paper stocks with inkjet printers. Paying $5.00 and up for a ream of "ordinary" paper can pay off if it gives you superior results when printing photos. You may have to test to see which of your printer's paper settings work best. For example, when I use glossy plain paper with my inkjet, I must use a High Resolution Paper setting (but not any of the glossy photo paper settings) to get the best results.

- **Choose appropriate print sizes**. If a 5 × 7 will do the job (which is the case with the prints I submit for publication), don't make an 8 × 10. You can fit two 5 × 7s on a single 8.5 × 11-inch sheet, which cuts your cost for paper in half.

- **Use plain paper instead of photo paper where plain paper will do the job**. You don't always need a glossy or matte photo-quality print. You'd be surprised at how good a picture can look on $2-a-ream paper that costs less than half a cent a sheet.

Reducing Ink Costs

The cost of ink is the consumable expense that offers the most options for control. Try these:

- **Choose an ink-frugal printer**. When I chucked my old ink-hog inkjet, I invested a whopping $149 in a Canon model that uses individual ink tanks for each color, plus black. I no longer worry about what mix of colors my prints have, or whether I'm about to deplete my yellow, cyan, or magenta inks.

When one color runs out, instead of dropping a new $35 cartridge in the printer, I replace only one color tank, for $10 or less. As a bonus, my new printer's larger tanks get many more prints per color than my old clunker.

- **Investigate less expensive ink sources**. Actually, I don't pay anywhere near $10 for an ink tank. I found a source that sells Canon-brand ink tanks, still factory sealed, for half the regular price. If you can't find discounted ink cartridges or tanks for your printer, check out third-party cartridges, which are available for the most common Epson and Hewlett-Packard models.

- **Give an ink refilling kit a try**. If you like to tinker and aren't as clumsy as I am, these could work for you. Shop carefully so you purchase kits with good quality ink. And don't forget to buy some extra syringes.

- **Watch those print sizes**. An 8 × 10 uses a lot of ink. Save the larger sizes for your portfolio, or for display on a mantel.

How Inkjets Work

Inkjet printers work exactly as you might think—by spraying a jet of ink onto a piece of paper, under precision computer control. Images are formed a dot at a time with a fine stream of ink, either water-based or solid (which is melted just before application) in disposable or (sometimes) refillable ink cartridges. With one common technology, piezoelectric crystals in the print head vibrate as electric current flows through them, issuing carefully timed streams of ink from a tiny nozzle, generating a precisely positioned dot.

Liquid inks tend to soak into regular paper, which enlarges the size of the dots in a process similar to the dot gain you see on printing presses. A low-end 720 dpi printer may produce output that looks no better than 300 dpi when the page dries. Liquid inks can also smear when wet. You may need to use a special paper stock for optimal results with this kind of printer.

The very first inkjet color printers used just three ink tanks—cyan, magenta, and yellow—and simulated black by combining equal quantities of all three colors. There may even be a few very low-end inkjet printers available that still use this method (I've seen no-name inkjet printers advertised as low as $19). However, there are several problems with the three-ink approach. So-called "composite blacks" tended to be brown and muddy rather than true black. In addition, black ink is a lot cheaper than colored ink, so it made little sense to use three times as much expensive ink to create black tones. Three-color printers are particularly wasteful when generating black-and-white-only pages, such as pages of text. So, the latest color inkjet printers from Canon, Epson, and Hewlett Packard today use at least four tanks, adding black. Some vendors have experimented with printers that use a total of six to eight color ink tanks, black, plus a "strong" cyan, "strong" magenta, and yellow ink plus a diluted "weak" cyan, and magenta (yellow only comes in one color: weak), or additional variations, such as two black tanks, with one dedicated to printing text.

The results with inkjet printers can be amazing. Figure 9.4 shows a digital camera image of about 2000 × 1500 pixels. The yellow box around the little girl's face marks a 240 × 200-pixel area. Figure 9.5 shows the original digital camera image of that area at left, with a high-resolution (6400 dpi) scan of that area from an actual 5 × 7 digital print. While you can clearly see the ink dots in the close-up

Figure 9.4 The original image looks like this. The enlarged portion in the figure below is highlighted in yellow.

Figure 9.5 Even a tiny portion of the original image looks sharp when enlarged, both in the original (left) and the inkjet print (right).

scan, the original print looks, for all intents and purposes, as if it were made on photographic paper from a photographic negative.

Inkjet printers are fairly low-maintenance devices. You'll have to clean the nozzles from time to time (the printer's driver software will offer an option for that chore). If the printer's nozzles are built into the printer itself rather than the ink cartridges, you may have to replace the nozzles after making many prints. I've personally found this to be a non-issue. My first "photo" printer, an ancient Epson Stylus Color from 1995 (which didn't produce true photo quality at all) is still plugging away with its original built-in print head after thousands of prints. Inkjet printers are now so inexpensive that you're likely to replace any model you own with a built-in print head within a year or two in favor of a newer, cheaper device that provides better quality, long before the original print head expires.

The chief danger to built-in heads is frequent changing of ink cartridges, especially those that have been refilled, because each change can introduce some dirt that can clog the head. I've had some luck cleaning my old Epson's print heads with a cotton swab dipped in alcohol. You can buy special cleaning tanks for most printers that will dissolve old, dried ink when you run them.

It's also important to keep the paper path and advance mechanism clean, because any "stutter" in the movement of your paper can cause a pattern of white lines in the finished output. You can wipe down the paper path and rollers with alcohol, too.

Dye Sublimation Printers

A third type of color printer uses a thermal process to transfer dye to the printed page. These are very popular devices in the "photo printer" arena, as low cost (roughly $150) printers that make only 4 × 6-inch photos. Larger dye-sub printers that produce up to 8 × 10-inch pictures are popular with event photographers, who set up shop at a prom, or sports contests, or other events and crank out prints on the spot.

The advantage of thermal dye sublimation is that the heat used to transfer the dye can be varied continuously over a range of 0 to 255, so, many, many different shades of a given color can be printed; the hotter the printing element, the more dye that is melted and applied. Other printers, in contrast, can provide only a single color of each pigment per dot (or, both strong and weak colors of each pigment), providing many fewer colors. Indeed, inkjet and laser printers use a dithering process to vary the amount of color by producing digital dots that are larger than the minimum size the printer can reproduce. That's why inkjet printers need high resolutions, on the order of 1440 to 2400 dots per inch or more, to achieve photo-quality dithering results in much lower effective resolution.

Dye-sub printers don't need dithering to produce many different colors. With 256 variations on each color available, such a printer can reproduce $256 \times 256 \times 256$ individual colors (16.8 million hues) at its maximum resolution. That's also why dye-sub printers don't need the super-high resolution that inkjets require to achieve true photographic quality. If you want the absolute best quality reproduction of your images, a dye sublimation printer is your best choice.

Unfortunately, most affordable and most common dye-sub photo printers today produce only snapshot-size prints, chiefly because of the complexity of the printing system and the fact that dye-sub consumables make inkjet materials look cheap by comparison. So, you can't use a low-cost dye-sub printer for enlargements, and their relatively low resolution means you can't use them to print documents. They are strictly photo printers. However, if you want to make lots of snapshots, a low-cost printer in this category can be a good choice. Larger dye-sub printers are priced in the $500 range.

Unlike inkjet devices, the typical dye-sub printer doesn't complete each line in all four colors before moving on to the next. Instead, each page is printed three or four times, once in each color, depending on whether a three-color or four-color process is being used. These printers must maintain rigid registration between colors to ensure that the dots of each color are positioned properly in relation to those of other colors. The need for precise registration makes larger format dye-sub printers (8×10 and larger) commensurately more expensive to design and produce. In most cases, only a professional photographer can justify a large format dye sublimation printer, or be able to justify the $2 per print cost of consumables.

How Dye Sublimation Printers Work

The dye sublimation device's print head includes tiny heating elements, which are switched on and off to melt dots of dye coated on a wide roll of plastic film. The roll contains alternating panels of cyan, magenta, and yellow (and, often, black), each the size of the full page. An additional panel that provides a clear protective overcoating is often used as well. The print head applies all the dots for one color at a time as the page moves past. Then the roll advances to the next color (each panel is used only once) and those dots are printed. After three or four passes, the full-color page is finished.

The dye-sub printer's image quality comes from its print head. However, these heaters aren't just switched on and off: Their temperature can be precisely controlled to transfer as much or as little dye as required to produce a particular color. The dye sublimates—turns from a solid into a gas, without becoming liquid—and then is absorbed by the polyester substrate of the receiver sheet. However, a special receiver paper with a substrate and coating that accepts the dye transfer is required for this type of printer. Media costs can run to several dollars per page when making 8 × 10 prints.

Because a dye-sub printer always uses all three or four panels in a set, some capacity is wasted if your image only requires one or two of those colors, or applies color only in a small area of a page. On the other hand, it costs no more to produce pages that have heavy color demands (such as overhead transparencies), so you may come out ahead of inkjet printers in cost (as well as image quality) if you do much work of that type. In addition, the capacity of each roll is precisely predictable: A roll capable of 100 images will produce 100 images, no more, no less. You'll never wonder about when your dye-sub printer's colors are about to poop out.

Because they don't need dithering to reproduce colors, dye sublimation printers can offer photographic quality without needing as high a linear resolution as other printers. The dots diffuse smoothly into the receiver sheet, producing smooth blending of colors. However, while you'd never notice that a dye-sub printer uses many fewer dots per inch to generate vivid full-color images, text printed in small sizes and finely detailed line art at that resolution definitely suffer from this diffusion. These printers are great for 24-bit images, but are less stunning when your bitmaps are combined with text or lines. You might find such output useful for preparing special reports and other photo-intensive material in small quantities. Thermal sublimation printers are expensive (both to buy and to operate) and slow. Since these printers are entirely practical for use as color-proofing devices, make sure you get and use a color matching system to calibrate your printer to the final output device.

Other Printer Types

There are other types of color printers still in use, but they are fading fast. Each has its own roster of advantages and disadvantages. For example, there are a few thermal wax printers, which use wax instead of ink or dye. While not as cheap as inkjet models, they are capable of producing great quality at high speeds. These printers no longer necessarily require special ultrasmooth paper, and many can now use ordinary cut-sheet paper.

Solid-ink printers use a block of wax or resin ink, which is melted and sprayed directly onto a page, or applied to a drum that rolls against a piece of paper like an offset printing press. These so-called phase change printers are less finicky about paper quality, since the ink is not readily absorbed by the substrate. On the flip side, solid inks can produce washed-out overheads when you print on transparency material, so your choice between these two technologies should include that factor, as well as the extra ink costs of phase change printers.

Using Professional Services

Serious photographers can be loathe to let their pictures out of their control. After all, making a print can be as important a part of the creative process as taking a photo. Even so, your best choice for getting the hard copies may be letting a professional service handle it. There are hundreds of eager picture services ready to create prints for you. They'll output your images directly from your camera's film card or allow you to upload them over the Internet for printing at a remote site.

The easiest way is to stop in at your local department store and look for one of those stand-alone kiosks, like the Kodak Picture Maker. I've used these when I was on the run, going directly from a photo opportunity to a nearby discount store, making a print, and dropping it off at a newspaper with handwritten cutline. Total elapsed time, 30 minutes, and at a cost of $5.99 for two 5 × 7 prints made from my camera's memory card.

Photo kiosks accept images in many formats, including CompactFlash, Secure Digital, xD, or Memory Stick cards, plus CDs and Photo CDs, floppy diskettes, or original prints, slides, or negatives. The latter are captured with a built-in scanner. It's worthwhile to check out your local kiosk *before* you need pictures in a crunch. The one located nearest to me doesn't accept memory cards and works only with original prints, floppy disks, and Photo CDs (not conventional CD-Rs with photos you've burned yourself). Determine whether the kiosk will accept the file types you want to work with, such as PCX or TIF. You may have to present the device with a JPG file when using a memory card, for example. (Save your JPG in its highest resolution, and you may not notice any loss of quality.)

This option is quick and dirty, but you don't lose all control. The kiosk's software has tools for fixing bad color, removing red eye, and adding borders or text. You can crop, enlarge, or reduce your photos, but not with complete freedom. You may have to crop using the aspect ratio of your selected picture size (for example, 5 × 7 or 8 × 10) and you may be unable to produce an odd-size image (say, a 3 × 7) using the kiosk's controls alone. (You can add white space yourself using Photoshop's tools, then print a 5 × 7 with very, very wide borders along the long dimension, for example.)

The kiosk will let you print various combinations of pictures that will fill an 8.5 × 11-inch sheet, such as a single 8 × 10, two 5 × 7s, four 4 × 5s, and so forth, but only with duplicates of a single image. You can't print two different 5 × 7s on one sheet, for example, without creating a special image in Photoshop. I've done this on occasion, ganging several images in one file, and then printing it on the kiosk as an 8 × 10. The latest kiosks will let you input your images to a connected digital minilab and output prints on regular photo paper at very attractive prices. As the use of film continues to fade, most in-store minilabs are doing an increasing amount of their work from digital originals.

You can also find printing services online. Companies like Kodak Picture Center Online let you upload your images, display them on webpages, or order prints. There also are firms that accept unprocessed or processed film and convert them to both hard copies and digital images that you can share, download over the Internet, or choose to receive on Photo CD. These are a good choice for those using conventional film and prints, but who don't have a scanner to make digital copies.

Getting Set Up

If you're setting up your first photo-quality printer, there are a few things to consider beyond what we've already discussed. Here are some points to think about.

- If you're selecting a printer and have a choice between one that has only a parallel port connection (probably an older printer that's no longer being sold new) and one that has a universal serial bus (USB) connection (or both USB and parallel), choose the USB printer. Printers used with Photoshop have in the recent past traditionally had parallel port connections (under Windows) or conventional serial port links (under Mac OS). While those worked fine, the traditional ports had some serious drawbacks, including limitations on the number of printers you could attach to your computer, so most printers sold today have a USB connection (or sometimes an Ethernet connection) in addition to (or instead of) a parallel port connection.

  The universal serial bus can handle 127 different devices, eases installation (especially under Windows; Microsoft's operating system will automatically locate your new printer and install the right drivers under most conditions), and allows hot swapping. You could, for example, unplug one USB printer and replace it with another, or with another device, such as a scanner, without bothering to reboot. While you can buy parallel-to-USB adapters that let you plug a parallel printer into a USB port, a native USB printer is your best choice.

- Take the time to calibrate your CRT monitor, scanner, and printer, as described in the manuals that came with each, and use Photoshop's calibration/characterization tools (discussed in Chapter 6). Spend the time now so that what you see more or less resembles what you get.

- Use plain paper rather than the expensive photo paper to do all your test prints and calibrations. As the long-distance commercial says, you can save a buck or two.

- Take some time to compare the results you get with different paper stocks and using different paper settings in your printer's driver. Don't automatically assume that choosing Plain Paper, Pro Paper, or Glossy Paper in the driver will give you the best results with any particular type of printing media.

■ Don't go overboard when you first get your printer set up. Resist the urge to print everything on your hard disk just to see how it looks. Instead, use Photoshop's Contact Sheet and Picture Package features to create multiple images on a single page to save time, paper, and ink.

A Typical Print Session

Each color printer you use will have its own options and features. I'm going to follow the typical workflow you might use to print a particular photograph to illustrate the choices you may have to make. Unless you use the same Canon inkjet printer I used, you can't follow along exactly, but I hope you'll get the general idea nevertheless. Your printer probably uses a similar routine.

1. Choose File > Print and, if you have more than one printer attached to your computer, select the printer you'd like to use from the drop-down list. The printer you've selected as your default printer will appear in the dialog box automatically, as shown in Figure 9.6.

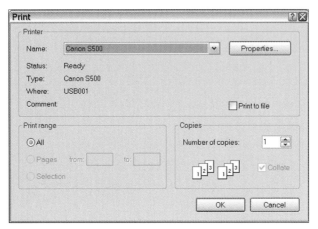

Figure 9.6 Your printer dialog box will show your default printer automatically.

2. Click Properties to produce your printer's particular options dialog box, shown in Figure 9.7. Your printer's dialog box will probably include several tabs to divide the choices by type of feature. This illustration shows the Canon printer's General properties.

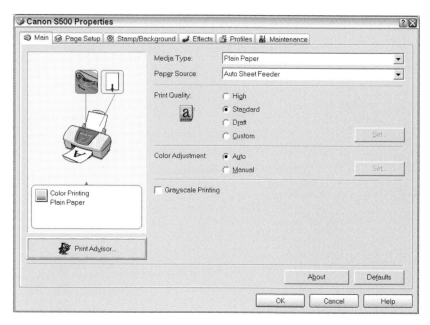

Figure 9.7 Set the default printer options in a dialog box like this one.

3. Choose the general properties you want to apply. In this case, I can choose from among:

- Paper type, including plain paper, various types of photo paper, photo film, transparencies, and other specialized stocks.

- Paper source, including the autofeed paper tray and individual sheet feeder. Your printer may have additional paper trays to choose from.

- Image quality, from among High (slow), Standard, and Draft (fast) choices.

- Automatic or manual color adjustment, letting you use the printer's built-in color tools or settings that you manipulate yourself, like those shown in Figure 9.8.

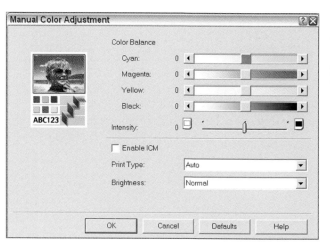

Figure 9.8 Many printers have automatic and manual color adjustment, a tool of last resort or a way of bypassing Photoshop if you're in a hurry.

- Whether you want grayscale printing of a color image.

- This particular Canon printer also has a Print Advisor wizard that leads you through the various options for printing.

4. Click the Page Setup tab (or your printer's equivalent) and choose from options like those shown in Figure 9.9.

   - **Page size**. Different from paper size. Some printers let you print pages that are larger than the paper size by automatically scaling the image down to fit the paper size you choose.

   - **Paper size.** Choose any paper size supported by your printer.

   - **Printing type.** Choices may include normal size printing, printing a page scaled to fit your particular page, poster printing (an image will be divided and printed in segments on several sheets which can be butted together to form a larger, poster image), and banner printing (which divides an image to create a long, banner-type print made up of several sheets).

   - **Orientation.** Either tall (portrait) or wide (landscape).

   - **Number of copies.**

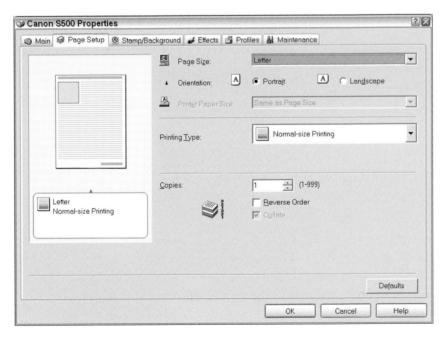

Figure 9.9 Set the orientation, paper size, and other page parameters in a dialog box like this one.

5. Click the tab for your printer's stamp/background or overprinting tab (or the equivalent). This option, shown in Figure 9.10, lets you create proof prints by putting watermarks or other messages on top of the image, as well as a background image of your choice. Portrait and wedding photographers like this feature because it lets them mark their proof prints in such a way that a client can't easily take their proofs to another photographer or their local photo kiosk and make their own copies.

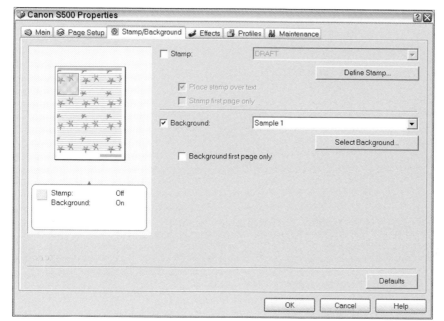

Figure 9.10 Some printers let you overlay an image with a watermark of some sort.

6. If your printer has an Effects tab, or something similar, you can use this dialog box to apply some Photoshop-like effects at the last minute, such as image smoothing, monochrome toning, and so forth. This option, shown in Figure 9.11, can be handy if you're in a hurry and don't have time to apply these effects in Photoshop.

7. Profiles are an option provided by some printers to let you set up categories of print jobs that can be selected with a few clicks. Parameters include the type of paper, paper source, quality level, orientation, and most of the other choices offered on the previous pages. With Profiles, shown in Figure 9.12, you can reuse a set of parameters with later jobs of the same type.

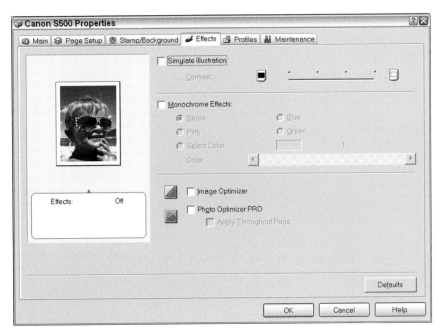

Figure 9.11 Some Photoshop-like effects may be available with your printer driver.

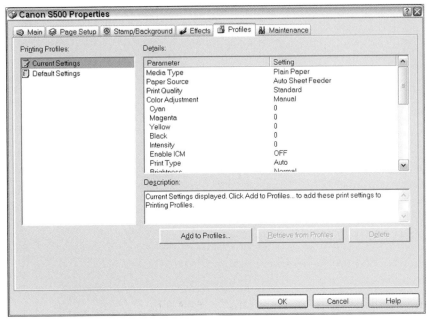

Figure 9.12 Profiles let you set printing parameters for reuse later.

8. Click the Maintenance tab, shown in Figure 9.13, and found in virtually every inkjet printer's driver, to perform important tasks like nozzle cleaning and print head alignment. Nozzles should be cleaned when your printer has sat idle for a few days or any time enough ink has dried in the nozzles to partially or completely block some of the head's orifices. You'll want to realign your print heads when you change ink cartridges. Realignment doesn't actually change the alignment of the print heads themselves; it informs your printer's driver software of their precise position so the actual location can be taken into account when printing. The printer generates a test sheet with horizontal and vertical lines arranged in a pattern. You choose the pattern that shows the lines aligned properly.

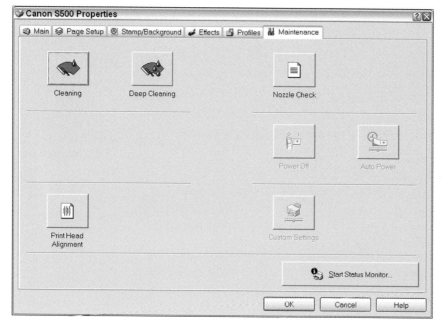

Figure 9.13 Printer maintenance tasks include nozzle cleaning and print head alignment.

Tips for Getting the Best Digital Prints

If you make prints from your digital images yourself, you'll want to keep these tips in mind to get the best quality and best economy.

■ Use Photoshop's provision for calibrating your monitor, using the Adobe Gamma Control Panel (Windows and Mac OS 9.x and earlier) or the Apple Calibration Utility (Mac OS). You'll find instructions for using the Adobe tool in Chapter 6. Your scanner also may have calibration procedures to help match your scanner's output to your printer. This will help ensure that what you see (on your monitor) is what you get (in your prints). If you're an advanced worker, learn to use the color matching software provided with your particular printer. Every device comes with different software, so we can't cover them here, but most have wizards and other tools to let you calibrate or characterize your equipment quickly.

- As mentioned earlier, if image quality is important to you, get the best glossy photographic paper for printing out your images. Experiment with several different stocks to see which you like best. You'll probably find that the paper offered by your printer manufacturer will be fine-tuned for your particular printer, but you needn't limit yourself to those products.

- Don't ruin one of those expensive sheets to a paper jam. If you're making prints one at a time, load your printer with one sheet of photo paper each time. Load multiple sheets only if you want to print many pages unattended, and even then make sure that only photo paper is loaded.

- Remember to clean your inkjet's print heads periodically and keep the printer's rollers and paper path clean. You'll avoid blurry or spotted prints and unwanted artifacts like visible lines.

- Don't touch your prints after they've emerged from the printer. Give them a chance to dry before you handle them. If you can't spread them out individually and must place them in stacks, put a sheet of plain paper between your prints so that any ink won't transfer to the print above.

- Experiment with special paper stocks that let you get even more use from your digital prints. You'll find paper designed especially for making t-shirt transfers, fabric printing, making greeting cards, or creating overhead transparencies.

- Don't enlarge digital camera images more than the resolution of your camera allows. Use these guidelines as a rule of thumb. The sensor dimensions in pixels are approximate, as different digital cameras offer different sized sensors in the same megapixel range:

Camera Resolution	Recommended Maximum Print Size
640 × 480 pixels (.3 megapixels)	4 × 5 inches
1024 × 768 pixels (.75 megapixels)	5 × 7 inches
1280 × 960 pixels (1.2 megapixels)	8 × 10 inches
1600 × 1280 pixels (2 megapixels)	11 × 14 inches
2400 × 1600 pixels (3.3 megapixels)	16 × 20 inches
3008 × 2000 pixels (6 megapixels)	20 × 30 inches
3600 × 2400 pixels (8 megapixels)	24 × 36 inches

Printers and Digital Cameras

In recent months, printers and digital cameras began working in tandem even more closely, with features found in both types of components that, sometimes, eliminate the need for Photoshop or even a computer altogether. Yes, it's now become easier to print your digital camera images directly, especially if your images don't require the manipulations Photoshop can provide.

For example, many digital cameras support the DPOF (Digital Print Order Format) so that the camera owner can select images for printing right in the camera. The DPOF file is written to the camera's removable media and is read and executed by photofinishers and other printing services as well as applications that are compatible with DPOF. You can use this format just as if you were filling out a film order envelope at your retailer's photofinishing counter. You can choose photos, quantities, specify index prints of thumbnail information, rotate your images, and include along with your print order a title and description for each print as well as your name, address, and other personal information.

PictBridge is another format that allows transferring pictures from a digital camera directly to a printer using a USB cable. However, unlike some proprietary camera-to-printer technologies available from a few manufacturers, PictBridge is an industry standard, so you can interconnect equipment from different vendors. Your Pentax digital camera can link with your Canon color printer, for example, because both support PictBridge.

PictBridge devices let you print multiple copies, specify print size, view images to be printed on an LCD screen, and choose options from a series of menus. Depending on the equipment models, you may be able to add date and time stamps. It's all very cool.

You may not even need to connect your digital camera to the printer. Some printers include built-in memory card readers like the one shown in Figure 9.14. Just slip the memory card out of your camera, plug it into the printer's card slot, and then view the pictures on the printer's LCD screen and choose your prints using the printer's function keys, similar to those shown in Figure 9.15.

Next Up

The next step is up to you. Neither photography in its last 160+ years nor Photoshop in its briefer dozen years of life has been fully explored by the millions of devotees. I hope this book has been an idea starter that showed you some of the exciting things you can do with the combined power of Photoshop and photography.

Figure 9.14 Some printers have multiple slots that accept digital camera memory cards.

Figure 9.15 View and choose your prints from the printer's control panel.

Appendix

Illustrated Glossary

You, too, can be Photoshop-literate! Here is a list of the most common words you're likely to encounter when working with photographs with your digital or film camera or within Photoshop. It includes most of the jargon included in this book, and some that is not within these pages, but which you'll frequently come across as you work. Although every Photoshop feature is not listed here, some of the most important new features are included to help you get your bearings.

16-bit images So-called "48-bit" image files that contain 16 bits of information (65,535 different tones) per channel, rather than the 8 bits per channel found in ordinary, 24-bit 16.8 million color images. Photoshop CS 2.0 has extended capabilities for working with 16-bit channels to provide more accurate colors in the final image. Photoshop's High Dynamic Range feature lets you work with these 16-bit channels.

additive primary colors The red, green, and blue hues which are used alone or in combinations to create all other colors you capture with a digital camera, view on a computer monitor, or work with in an image-editing program like Photoshop. See also *CMYK.*

airbrush Originally developed as an artist's tool that sprays a fine mist of paint, the computer version of an airbrush is used both for illustration and retouching in most image-editing programs, including Photoshop.

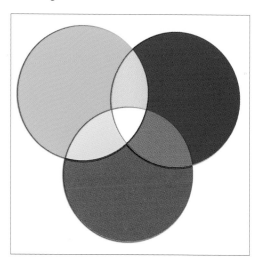

Figure A.1 The additive primary colors, red, green, and blue combine to make other colors, plus white.

ambient lighting Diffuse nondirectional lighting that doesn't appear to come from a specific source but, rather, bounces off walls, ceilings, and other objects in the scene when a picture is taken.

analog/digital converter In digital imaging, the electronics built into a camera or scanner that convert the analog information captured by the sensor into digital bits that can be stored as an image bitmap. See also *bitmap*.

angle-of-view The area of a scene that a lens can capture, determined by the focal length of the lens. Lenses with a shorter focal length have a wider angle-of-view than lenses with a longer focal length.

anti-alias A process in image editing that smoothes the rough edges in images (called jaggies or staircasing) by creating partially transparent pixels along the boundaries that are merged into a smoother line by our eyes.

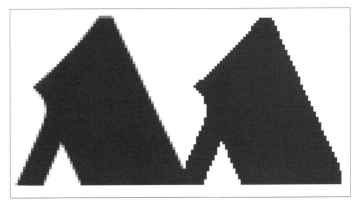

Figure A.2 A diagonal line that has been anti-aliased (left) and a "jaggy" line that displays the staircasing effect (right).

artifact A type of noise in an image, or an unintentional image component produced in error by a digital camera or scanner during processing.

aspect ratio The proportions of an image as printed, displayed on a monitor, or captured by a digital camera. An 8 × 10-inch or 16 × 20-inch photo each have a 4:5 aspect ratio. Your monitor set to 800 × 600, 1024 × 768, or 1600 × 1200 pixels has a 4:3 aspect ratio. When you change the aspect ratio of an image, you must crop out part of the image area, or create some blank space at top or sides.

background In photography, the background is the area behind your main subject of interest. In Photoshop, the background is the bottom-most layer in the Layers Palette.

back-lighting A lighting effect produced when the main light source is located behind the subject. Back-lighting can be used to create a silhouette effect, or to illuminate translucent objects. See also *front-lighting, fill lighting,* and *ambient lighting.* Back-lighting is also a technology for illuminating an LCD display from the rear, making it easier to view under high ambient lighting conditions.

balance An image that has equal elements on all sides.

Figure A.3 Backlighting produces a slight silhouette effect, and also serves to illuminate the translucent petals of this flower.

barrel distortion A lens defect that causes straight lines at the top or side edges of an image to bow outward into a barrel shape. See also *pincushion distortion*.

beam splitter A partially silvered mirror or prism that divides incoming light into two portions, usually to send most of the illumination to the viewfinder and part of it to an exposure meter or focusing mechanism.

bilevel image An image that stores only black-and-white information, with no gray tones.

bit A binary digit, either a 1 or a 0, used to measure the color depth (number of different colors) in an image. For example, a grayscale 8-bit scan may contain up to 256 different tones (2^8), while a 24-bit scan can contain 16.8 million different colors (2^{24}).

bitmap A way of representing an image as rows and columns of values, with each picture element stored as one or more numbers that represent its brightness and color. In Photoshop parlance, a bitmap is a bilevel black/white-only image.

black The color formed by the absence of reflected or transmitted light.

black point The tonal level of an image where blacks begin to provide important image information, usually measured by using a histogram. When correcting an image with a digital camera that has an on-screen histogram, or within an image editor, you'll usually want to set the histogram's black point at the place where these tones exist.

blend To create a more realistic transition between image areas, as when retouching or compositing in image editing.

blowup An enlargement, usually a print, made from a negative, transparency, or digital file.

blur In photography, to soften an image or part of an image by throwing it out of focus, or by allowing it to become soft due to subject or camera motion. In image editing, blurring is the softening of an area by reducing the contrast between pixels that form the edges.

bounce lighting Light bounced off a reflector, including ceiling and walls, to provide a soft, natural-looking light.

bracketing Taking a series of photographs of the same subject at different settings to help ensure that one setting will be the correct one. Many digital cameras will automatically snap off a series of bracketed exposures for you. Other settings, such as color and white balance, can also be

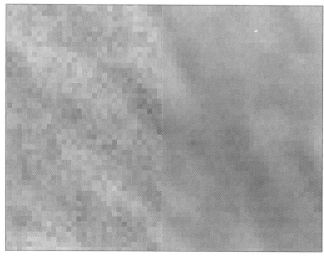

Figure A.4 Blurring reduces the contrast between pixels.

"bracketed" with some models. Digital SLRs may even allow you to choose the order in which bracketed settings are applied.

brightness   The amount of light and dark shades in an image, usually represented as a percentage from 0 percent (black) to 100 percent (white).

broad lighting   A portrait lighting arrangement in which the main light source illuminates the side of the face closest to the camera.

Bridge   A new stand-alone image browser provided with all Adobe Creative Suite applications, including Photoshop, to offer a common "bridge" to image access among these programs.

buffer   A digital camera's internal memory which stores an image immediately after it is taken until the image can be written to the camera's non-volatile (semi-permanent) memory or a memory card.

burn   A darkroom technique, mimicked in image editing, which involves exposing part of a print for a longer period, making it darker than it would be with a straight exposure.

burst mode   The digital camera's equivalent of the film camera's "motor drive," used to take multiple shots within a short period of time.

calibration   A process used to correct for the differences in the output of a printer or monitor when compared to the original image. Once you've calibrated your scanner, monitor, and/or your image editor, the images you see on the screen more closely represent what you'll get from your printer, even though calibration is never perfect.

Camera RAW   A plug-in included with Photoshop CS and Photoshop Elements 3.0 that can manipulate the unprocessed images captured by digital cameras.

Figure A.5 Use the Camera RAW plug-in to correct the color, sharpness, or other attributes of your original digital images.

candid pictures Unposed photographs, often taken at a wedding or other event at which (often) formal, posed images are also taken.

cast An undesirable tinge of color in an image.

CCD Charge-Coupled Device. A type of solid-state sensor that captures the image, used in scanners and digital cameras.

center-weighted meter A light-measuring device that emphasizes the area in the middle of the frame when calculating the correct exposure for an image. See also *averaging meter* and *spot meter.*

chroma Color or hue.

chromatic aberration An image defect, often seen as green or purple fringing around the edges of an object, caused by a lens failing to focus all colors of a light source at the same point. See also *fringing.*

chromatic color A color with at least one hue and a visible level of color saturation.

chrome An informal photographic term used as a generic for any kind of color transparency, including Kodachrome, Ektachrome, or Fujichrome.

CIE (Commission Internationale de l'Eclairage) An international organization of scientists who work with matters relating to color and lighting. The organization is also called the International Commission on Illumination.

circle of confusion A term applied to the fuzzy discs produced when a point of light is out of focus. The circle of confusion is not a fixed size. The viewing distance and amount of enlargement of the image determine whether we see a particular spot on the image as a point or as a disc.

close-up lens A lens add-on that allows you to take pictures at a distance that is less than the closest-focusing distance of the lens alone.

CMY(K) color model A way of defining all possible colors in percentages of cyan, magenta, yellow, and frequently, black. Black is added to improve rendition of shadow detail. CMYK is commonly used for printing (both on press and with your inkjet or laser color printer). Photoshop can work with images using the CMYK model, but converts any images in that mode back to RGB for display on your computer monitor.

color correction Changing the relative amounts of color in an image to produce a desired effect, typically a more accurate representation of those colors. Color correction can fix faulty color balance in the original image, or compensate for the deficiencies of the inks used to reproduce the image.

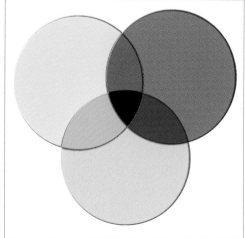

Figure A.6 The subtractive colors yellow, magenta, and cyan combine to produce all the other colors, including black.

Color Replacement A tool in Photoshop and Photoshop Elements that simplifies changing all of a selected color to another hue.

comp A preview that combines type, graphics, and photographic material in a layout.

composite In photography, an image composed of two or more parts of an image, taken either from a single photo or multiple photos. Usually composites are created so that the elements blend smoothly together.

composition The arrangement of things in an image, including the main subject, other objects in a scene, and/or the foreground and background.

compression Reducing the size of a file by encoding using fewer bits of information to represent the original. Some compression schemes, such as JPEG, operate by discarding some image information, while others, such as TIF, preserve all the detail in the original, discarding only redundant data. See also *GIF, JPEG,* and *TIF.*

continuous tone Images that contain tones from the darkest to the lightest, with a theoretically infinite range of variations in between.

contrast The range between the lightest and darkest tones in an image. A high-contrast image is one in which the shades fall at the extremes of the range between white and black. In a low-contrast image, the tones are closer together.

contrasty Having higher than optimal contrast.

crop To trim an image or page by adjusting its boundaries.

dedicated flash An electronic flash unit designed to work with the automatic exposure features of a specific camera.

depth-of-focus The distance range over which the film could be shifted at the film plane inside the camera and still have the subject appear in sharp focus; often misused to mean depth-of-field. See also *depth-of-field.*

densitometer An electronic device used to measure the amount of light reflected by or transmitted through a piece of artwork, used to determine accurate exposure when making copies or color separations.

density The ability of an object to stop or absorb light. The less light reflected or transmitted by an object, the higher its density.

depth-of-field A distance range in a photograph in which all included portions of an image are at least acceptably sharp. With a dSLR, you can see the available depth-of-field at the taking aperture by pressing the depth-of-field preview button, or estimate the range by viewing the depth-of-field scale found on many lenses.

depth-of-focus The range that the image-capturing surface (such as a sensor or film) could be moved while maintaining acceptable focus.

desaturate To reduce the purity or vividness of a color, making a color appear to be washed out or diluted.

diffuse lighting Soft, low-contrast lighting.

diffusion Softening of detail in an image by randomly distributing gray tones in an area of an image to produce a fuzzy effect. Diffusion can be added when the picture is taken, often through the use of diffusion filters, or in post-processing with an image editor. Diffusion can be beneficial to disguise defects in an image and is particularly useful for portraits of women.

digital zoom A way of simulating actual or optical zoom by magnifying the pixels captured by the sensor. This technique generally produces inferior results to optical zoom.

diopter A value used to represent the magnification power of a lens, calculated as the reciprocal of a lens' focal length (in meters). Diopters are most often used to represent the optical correction used in a viewfinder to adjust for limitations of the photographer's eyesight, and to describe the magnification of a close-up lens attachment.

Figure A.7 Diffusion can hide defects and produce a soft, romantic glow in a female subject.

dither A method of distributing pixels to extend the number of colors or tones that can be represented. For example, two pixels of different colors can be arranged in such a way that the eye visually merges them into a third color.

dodging A darkroom term for blocking part of an image as it is exposed, lightening its tones. Image editors can mimic this effect by lightening portions of an image using a brush-like tool.

dot A unit used to represent a portion of an image, often groups of pixels collected to produce larger printer dots of varying sizes to represent gray or a specific color.

dot gain The tendency of a printing dot to grow from the original size to its final printed size on paper. This effect is most pronounced on offset presses using poor-quality papers, which allow ink to absorb and spread, reducing the quality of the printed output, particularly in the case of photos that use halftone dots.

dots per inch (dpi) The resolution of a printed image, expressed in the number of printer dots in an inch. You'll often see dpi used to refer to monitor screen resolution, or the resolution of scanners. However, neither of these uses dots; the correct term for a monitor is pixels per inch (ppi), whereas a scanner captures a particular number of samples per inch (spi).

dummy A rough approximation of a publication, used to evaluate the layout.

dye sublimation A printing technique in which solid inks are heated and transferred to a polyester substrate to form an image. Because the amount of color applied can be varied by the degree of heat (and up to 256 different hues for each color), dye sublimation devices can print as many as 16.8 million different colors.

emulsion The light-sensitive coating on a piece of film, paper, or printing plate. When making prints or copies, it's important to know which side is the emulsion side so the image can be exposed in the correct orientation (not reversed). Image editors such as Photoshop include "emulsion side up" and "emulsion side down" options in their print preview feature.

equivalent focal length A digital camera's focal length translated into the corresponding values for a 35mm film camera, if that digital camera uses a sensor that is less than the size of a full 35mm film frame. For example, a 5.8mm to 17.4mm lens on a digital camera might provide the same view as a 38mm to 114mm zoom with a film camera. Equivalents are needed for non-full-frame digital cameras because sensor size and lens focal lengths are not standardized, and translating the values provides a basis for comparison.

Exif Exchangeable Image File Format. Developed to standardize the exchange of image data between hardware devices and software. A variation on JPEG, Exif is used by most digital cameras, and includes information such as the date and time a photo was taken, the camera settings, resolution, amount of compression, and other data.

existing light In photography, the illumination that is already present in a scene. Existing light can include daylight or the artificial lighting currently being used, but is not considered to be electronic flash or additional lamps set up by the photographer.

export To transfer text or images from a document to another format.

exposure The amount of light allowed to reach the film or sensor, determined by the intensity of the light, the amount admitted by the iris of the lens, and the length of time determined by the shutter speed.

exposure program An automatic setting in a digital camera that provides the optimum combination of shutter speed and f-stop at a given level of illumination. For example a "sports" exposure program would use a faster, action-stopping shutter speed and larger lens opening instead of the smaller, depth-of-field-enhancing lens opening and slower shutter speed that might be favored by a "close-up" program at exactly the same light level.

exposure values (EV) EV settings are a way of adding or decreasing exposure without the need to reference f-stops or shutter speeds. For example, if you tell your camera to add +1EV, it will provide twice as much exposure, either by using a larger f-stop, slower shutter speed, or both.

eyedropper An image-editing tool used to sample color from one part of an image so it can be used to paint, draw, or fill elsewhere in the image. Within some features, the eyedropper can be used to define the actual black points and white points in an image.

feather To fade out the borders of an image element, so it will blend in more smoothly with another layer.

fill lighting In photography, lighting used to illuminate shadows. Reflectors or additional incandescent lighting or electronic flash can be used to brighten shadows. One common technique outdoors is to use the camera's flash as a fill. Or, you can use Photoshop to lighten dark areas to produce the same effect.

Figure A.8 Photoshop can brighten the shadows on this mascot's jersey, producing a fill flash type effect.

filter In photography, a device that fits over the lens, changing the light in some way. In image editing, a feature that changes the pixels in an image to produce blurring, sharpening, and other special effects. Photoshop CS includes several new filter effects, including Lens Blur and Photo Filters.

FireWire (IEEE-1394) A fast serial interface used by scanners, digital cameras, printers, and other devices.

flat An image with low contrast.

flatbed scanner A type of scanner that reads one line of an image at a time, recording it as a series of samples, or pixels.

focal length The distance between the film and the optical center of the lens when the lens is focused on infinity, usually measured in millimeters.

focal plane An imaginary line, perpendicular to the optical access, which passes through the focal point forming a plane of sharp focus when the lens is set at infinity.

focus To adjust the lens to produce a sharp image.

focus range The minimum and maximum distances within which a camera is able to produce a sharp image, such as 2 inches to infinity.

four-color printing Another term for process color, in which cyan, magenta, yellow, and black inks are used to reproduce all the colors in the original image.

framing In photography, composing your image in the viewfinder. In composition, using elements of an image to form a sort of picture frame around an important subject.

frequency The number of lines per inch in a halftone screen.

fringing A chromatic aberration that produces fringes of color around the edges of subjects, caused by a lens' inability to focus the various wavelengths of light onto the same spot. *Purple fringing* is especially troublesome with backlit images.

front-lighting Illumination that comes from the direction of the camera. See also *back-lighting* and *sidelighting*.

Figure A.9 Extreme magnification reveals fringing, a chromatic aberration caused by the lens' inability to focus all the colors of light on the same spot.

f-stop The relative size of the lens aperture, which helps determine both exposure and depth-of-field. The larger the f-stop number, the smaller the f-stop itself. It helps to think of f-stops as denominators of fractions, so that f2 is larger than f4, which is larger than f8, just as 1/2, 1/4, and 1/8 represent ever smaller fractions. In photography, a given f-stop number is multiplied by 1.4 to arrive at the next number that admits exactly half as much light. So, f1.4 is twice as large as f2.0 (1.4 × 1.4), which is twice as large as f2.8 (2 × 1.4), which is twice as large as f4 (2.8 × 1.4). The f-stops which follow are f5.6, f8, f11, f16, f22, f32, and so on.

full-color image An image that uses 24-bit color, 16.8 million possible hues. Images are sometimes captured in a scanner with more colors, but the colors are reduced to the best 16.8 million shades for manipulation in image editing.

gamma A numerical way of representing the contrast of an image. Devices such as monitors typically don't reproduce the tones in an image in straight-line fashion (all colors represented in exactly the same way as they appear in the original). Instead, some tones may be favored over others, and gamma provides a method of tonal correction that takes the human eye's perception of neighboring values into account. Gamma values range from 1.0 to about 2.5. The Macintosh has traditionally used a gamma of 1.8, which is relatively flat compared to television. Windows PCs use a 2.2 gamma value, which has more contrast and is more saturated.

gamma correction A method for changing the brightness, contrast, or color balance of an image by assigning new values to the gray or color tones of an image to more closely represent the original shades. Gamma correction can be either linear or nonlinear. Linear correction applies the same amount of change to all the tones. Nonlinear correction varies the changes tone-by-tone, or in highlight, midtone, and shadow areas separately to produce a more accurate or improved appearance.

gamut The range of viewable and printable colors for a particular color model, such as RGB (used for monitors) or CMYK (used for printing).

Gaussian blur A method of diffusing an image using a bell-shaped curve to calculate the pixels which will be blurred, rather than blurring all pixels, producing a more random, less "processed" look.

GIF An image file format limited to 256 different colors that compresses the information by combining similar colors and discarding the rest. Condensing a 16.8-million-color photographic image to only 256 different hues often produces a poor-quality image, but GIF is useful for images that don't have a great many colors, such as charts or graphs. The GIF format also includes transparency options, and can include multiple images to produce animations that may be viewed on a webpage or other application. See also *JPEG* and *TIF.*

graduated filter A lens attachment with variable density or color from one edge to another. A graduated neutral density filter, for example, can be oriented so the neutral density portion is concentrated at the top of the lens' view with the less dense or clear portion at the bottom, thus reducing the amount of light from a very bright sky while not interfering with the exposure of the landscape in the foreground. Graduated filters can also be split into several color sections to provide a color gradient between portions of the image. Photoshop can easily duplicate many graduated filter effects.

grain The metallic silver in film which forms the photographic image. The term is often applied to the seemingly random noise in an image (both conventional and digital) that provides an overall texture.

gray card A piece of cardboard or other material with a standardized 18 percent reflectance. Gray cards can be used as a reference for determining correct exposure.

grayscale image An image represented using 256 shades of gray. Scanners often capture grayscale images with 1024 or more tones, but reduce them to 256 grays for manipulation by Photoshop.

halftone A method used to reproduce continuous-tone images, representing the image as a series of dots.

Healing Brush The Healing Brush and Spot Healing Brush tools are Photoshop tools that copy pixels from one portion of an image (or images) to another, adjusting the brightness and color of the copied to take into account the values of the pixels they are being copied over.

high contrast A wide range of density in a print, negative, or other image.

High Dynamic Range (HDR) Photoshop's new facility for working with images that have 16 bits or more of information per color channel. Photoshop uses *floating point* numbers that can be 32 bits long, allowing for a much larger range of tones in a scene. Photoshop can also combine two images taken at different exposures, merging them to create an image that includes the dynamic ranges of both.

highlights The brightest parts of an image containing detail.

histogram A kind of chart showing the relationship of tones in an image using a series of 256 vertical "bars," one

Figure A.10 The dots of a halftone simulate continuous tones in a printed image.

for each brightness level. A histogram chart typically looks like a curve with one or more slopes and peaks, depending on how many highlight, midtone, and shadow tones are present in the image.

Histogram Palette A new palette in Photoshop that allows making changes in tonal values using controls that adjust the white, middle gray, and black points of an image. Unlike the histogram included with Photoshop's Levels command, this palette is available for use even when you're using other tools.

hue The color of light that is reflected from an opaque object or transmitted through a transparent one.

image rotation A feature found in some digital cameras, which senses whether a picture was taken in horizontal or vertical orientation. That information is embedded in the picture file so that the camera and compatible software applications automatically can display the image in the correct orientation.

incident light Light falling on a surface.

indexed color image An image with 256 different colors, as opposed to a grayscale image, which has 256 different shades of the tones between black and white.

infinity A distance so great that any object at that distance will be reproduced sharply if the lens is focused at the infinity position.

interchangeable lens Lens designed to be readily attached to and detached from a camera; a feature found in more sophisticated digital cameras.

International Standards Organization (ISO) A governing body that provides standards used to represent film speed, or the equivalent sensitivity of a digital camera's sensor. Digital camera sensitivity is expressed in ISO settings.

interpolation A technique digital cameras, scanners, and image editors use to create new pixels required whenever you resize or change the resolution of an image based on the values of surrounding pixels. Devices such as scanners and digital cameras can also use interpolation to create pixels in addition to those actually captured, thereby increasing the apparent resolution or color information in an image.

invert In Photoshop, to change an image into its negative; black becomes white, white becomes black, dark gray becomes light gray, and so forth. Colors are also changed to the complementary color; green becomes magenta, blue turns to yellow, and red is changed to cyan.

iris A set of thin overlapping metal leaves in a camera lens that pivot outwards to form a circular opening of variable size to control the amount of light that can pass through a lens.

jaggies Staircasing effect of lines that are not perfectly horizontal or vertical, caused by pixels that are too large to represent the line accurately. See also *anti-alias.*

JPEG (Joint Photographic Experts Group) A file format that supports 24-bit color and reduces file sizes by selectively discarding image data. Digital cameras generally use JPEG compression to pack more images onto memory cards. You can select how much compression is used (and therefore how much information is thrown away) by selecting from among the Standard, Fine, Super Fine, or other quality settings offered by your camera. See also *GIF* and *TIF.*

Figure A.11 Jaggies result when the pixels in an image are too large to represent a non-horizontal/vertical line smoothly.

Kelvin (K) A unit of measurement based on the absolute temperature scale in which absolute zero is zero; used to describe the color of continuous spectrum light sources. For example, an incandescent light might have a color temperature of 3400K, while daylight measures 5500-6000K. The color differences of these light sources to our eyes can be corrected by filtration, by a digital camera's white balance controls, or in Photoshop.

landscape The orientation of a page in which the longest dimension is horizontal, also called wide orientation.

latitude The range of camera exposures that produces acceptable images with a particular digital sensor or film.

layer A way of managing elements of an image in stackable overlays that can be manipulated separately, moved to a different stacking order, or made partially or fully transparent. Photoshop allows collecting layers into layer sets.

lens One or more elements of optical glass or similar material designed to collect and focus rays of light to form a sharp image on the film, paper, sensor, or a screen.

lens aperture The lens opening, or iris, that admits light to the film or sensor. The size of the lens aperture is usually measured in f-stops. See also *f-stop* and *iris.*

lens flare A feature of conventional photography that is both a bane and creative outlet. It is an effect produced by the reflection of light internally among elements of an optical lens. Bright light sources within or just outside the field of view cause lens flare. Flare can be reduced by the use of coatings on the lens elements or with the use of lens hoods. Photographers sometimes use the effect as a creative technique, and Photoshop includes a filter that lets you add lens flare at your whim.

lens hood A device that shades the lens, protecting it from extraneous light outside the actual picture area which can reduce the contrast of the image, or allow lens flare.

lens shade A hood at the front of a lens that keeps stray light from striking the lens and causing image flare.

lens speed The largest lens opening (smallest f-number) at which a lens can be set. A fast lens transmits more light and has a larger opening than a slow lens. Determined by the maximum aperture of the lens in relation to its focal length; the "speed" of a lens is relative: A 400 mm lens with a maximum aperture of f/3.5 is considered extremely fast, while a 28mm f/3.5 lens is thought to be relatively slow.

Figure A.12 Even when the sun or another bright object is not actually within the picture area it can cause reduced contrast and bright areas in an image.

lighten A Photoshop function that is the equivalent to the photographic darkroom technique of dodging. Tones in a given area of an image are gradually changed to lighter values.

lighting ratio The proportional relationship between the amount of light falling on the subject from the main light and other lights, expressed in a ratio, such as 3:1.

line art Usually, images that consist only of white pixels and one color, represented in Photoshop as a bitmap.

line screen The resolution or frequency of a halftone screen, expressed in lines per inch.

lithography Another name for offset printing.

lossless compression An image-compression scheme, such as TIFF, that preserves all image detail. When the image is decompressed, it is identical to the original version.

lossy compression An image-compression scheme, such as JPEG, that creates smaller files by discarding image information, which can affect image quality.

luminance The brightness or intensity of an image, determined by the amount of gray in a hue.

LZW compression A method of compacting TIFF files using the Lempel-Ziv Welch compression algorithm, an optional compression scheme offered by some digital cameras, and available in Photoshop.

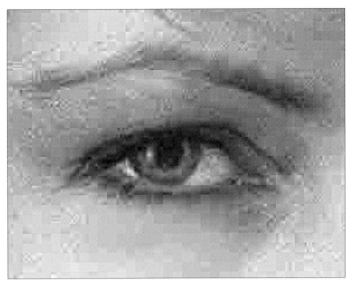

Figure A.13 When carried to the extreme, lossy compression methods can have a serious impact on image quality.

macro lens A lens that provides continuous focusing from infinity to extreme close-ups, often to a reproduction ratio of 1:2 (half life-size) or 1:1 (life-size).

macro photography The process of taking photographs of small objects at magnifications of 1X or more.

magnification ratio A relationship that represents the amount of enlargement provided by the macro setting of the zoom lenses, macro lens, or with other close-up devices.

Match Color A feature of Photoshop that allows synchronizing color palettes between images to provide consistent hues.

maximum aperture The largest lens opening or f-stop available with a particular lens, or with a zoom lens at a particular magnification.

mechanical Camera-ready copy with text and art already in position for photographing.

midtones Parts of an image with tones of an intermediate value, usually in the 25 to 75 percent range. Many image-editing features allow you to manipulate midtones independently from the highlights and shadows.

moiré An objectionable pattern caused by the interference of halftone screens, frequently generated by rescanning an image that has already been halftoned. An image editor can frequently minimize these effects by blurring the patterns.

monochrome Having a single color, plus white. Grayscale images are monochrome (shades of gray and white only).

negative A representation of an image in which the tones are reversed: blacks as white, and vice versa.

neutral color In image-editing's RGB mode, a color in which red, green, and blue are present in equal amounts, producing a gray.

neutral density filter A gray camera filter reduces the amount of light entering the camera without affecting the colors.

noise In an image, pixels with randomly distributed color values. Noise in digital photographs tends to be the product of low-light conditions and long exposures, particularly when you have set your camera to a higher ISO rating than normal.

noise reduction A technology used to cut down on the amount of random information in a digital picture, usually caused by long exposures at increased sensitivity ratings. Noise reduction involves the camera automatically taking a second blank/dark exposure at the same settings that contains only noise, and then using the blank photo's information to cancel out the noise in the original picture. With most cameras, the process is very quick, but does double the amount of time required to take the photo. Noise reduction can also be applied by software, including Photoshop, which has a new Noise Reduction filter.

normal lens A lens that makes the image in a photograph appear in a perspective that is like that of the original scene, typically with a field of view of roughly 45°. A quick way to calculate the focal length of a normal lens is to measure the diagonal of the sensor or film frame used to capture the image, usually ranging from around 7mm to 45mm.

optical zoom Magnification produced by the elements of a digital camera's lens, as opposed to *digital zoom* which merely magnifies the captured pixels to simulate additional magnification. Optical zoom is always to be preferred over the digital variety.

Figure A.14 Higher ISO settings lead to the random grain patterns known as noise.

orthochromatic Sensitive primarily to blue and green light.

overexposure A condition in which too much light reaches the film or sensor, producing a dense negative or a very bright/light print, slide, or digital image.

panning Moving the camera so that the image of a moving object remains in the same relative position in the viewfinder as you take a picture. The eventual effect creates a strong sense of movement, because the main subject will be in relatively sharp focus, while the surrounding area will appear blurred.

panorama A broad view, usually scenic. Photoshop's new Photomerge feature helps you create panoramas from several photos. Many digital cameras have a panorama assist mode that makes it easier to shoot several photos that can be stitched together later.

parallax compensation An adjustment made by the camera or photographer to account for the difference in views between the taking lens and the viewfinder.

perspective The rendition of apparent space in a photograph, such as how far the foreground and background appear to be separated from each other. Perspective is determined by the distance of the camera to the subject. Objects that are close appear large, while distant objects appear to be far away.

Photo CD A special type of CD-ROM developed by Eastman Kodak Company that can store high-quality photographic images in a special space-saving format as multiple picture "packs", along with music and other data.

pincushion distortion A type of lens distortion in which lines at the top and side edges of an image are bent inward, producing an effect that looks like a pincushion. Photoshop's Lens Correction filter can compensate for this kind of distortion.

pixel The smallest element of a screen display that can be assigned a color. The term is a contraction of "picture element."

Figure A.15 This exaggerated example shows pincushion distortion (top) and barrel distortion (bottom).

pixels per inch (ppi) The number of pixels that can be displayed per inch, usually used to refer to pixel resolution from a scanned image or on a monitor.

plug-in A module such as a filter that can be accessed from within an image editor to provide special functions.

point Approximately 1/72 of an inch outside the Macintosh world, exactly 1/72 of an inch within it.

polarizing filter A filter that forces light, which normally vibrates in all directions, to vibrate only in a single plane, reducing or removing the specular reflections from the surface of objects.

portrait The orientation of a page in which the longest dimension is vertical, also called tall orientation. In photography, a formal picture of an individual or, sometimes, a group.

positive The opposite of a negative, an image with the same tonal relationships as those in the original scenes—for example, a finished print or a slide.

prepress The stages of the reproduction process that precede printing, when halftones, color separations, and printing plates are created.

process color The four color pigments used in color printing: cyan, magenta, yellow, and black (CMYK).

RAW An image file format offered by many digital cameras that includes all the unprocessed information captured by the camera. RAW files are very large, and must be processed by a special program after being downloaded from the camera.

red eye An effect from flash photography that appears to make a person's eyes glow red, or an animal's yellow or green. It's caused by light bouncing from the retina of the eye, and is most pronounced in dim illumination (when the irises are wide open) and when the electronic flash is close to the lens and therefore prone to reflect directly back. Image editors can fix red eye through cloning other pixels over the offending red or orange ones. Photoshop's Red Eye Tool can quickly remove such color casts.

red-eye reduction A way of reducing or eliminating the red-eye phenomenon. Some cameras offer a red-eye reduction mode that uses a preflash that causes the irises of the subjects' eyes to close down just prior to a second, stronger flash used to take the picture. Photoshop CS 2.0 has a new red-eye correction tool.

reflection copy Original artwork that is viewed by light reflected from its surface, rather than transmitted through it.

Figure A.16 Digital cameras usually have several features for avoiding the demon red-eye look, but you'll still get the effect when you least want it.

reflector Any device used to reflect light onto a subject to improve balance of exposure (contrast). Another way is to use fill in flash.

register To align images.

registration mark A mark that appears on a printed image, generally for color separations, to help in aligning the printing plates. Photoshop can add registration marks to your images when they are printed.

reproduction ratio Used in macrophotography to indicate the magnification of a subject.

resample To change the size or resolution of an image. Resampling down discards pixel information in an image; resampling up adds pixel information through interpolation.

resolution In image editing, the number of pixels per inch used to determine the size of the image when printed. That is, an 8 × 10-inch image that is saved with 300 pixels per inch resolution will print in an 8 × 10-inch size on a 300 dpi printer, or 4 × 5 inches on a 600 dpi printer. In digital photography, resolution is the number of pixels a camera or scanner can capture.

retouch To edit an image, most often to remove flaws or to create a new effect.

RGB color mode A color mode that represents the three colors—red, green, and blue—used by devices such as scanners or monitors to reproduce color. Photoshop works in RGB mode by default, and even displays CMYK images by converting them to RGB.

saturation The purity of color; the amount by which a pure color is diluted with white or gray.

Figure A.17 Fully saturated (left) and desaturated (right).

scale To change the size of all or part of an image.

scanner A device that captures an image of a piece of artwork and converts it to a digitized image or bitmap that the computer can handle.

selection In image editing, an area of an image chosen for manipulation, usually surrounded by a moving series of dots called a selection border.

selective focus Choosing a lens opening that produces a shallow depth-of-field. Usually this is used to isolate a subject by causing most other elements in the scene to be blurred.

sensitivity A measure of the degree of response of a film or sensor to light.

sensor array The grid-like arrangement of the red, green, and blue-sensitive elements of a digital camera's solid-state capture device. Sony offers a sensor array that captures a fourth color, termed *emerald*.

shadow The darkest part of an image, represented on a digital image by pixels with low numeric values or on a halftone by the smallest or absence of dots.

Shadow/Highlight Adjustment A new Photoshop feature used to correct over-exposed or underexposed digital camera images.

sharpening Increasing the apparent sharpness of an image by boosting the contrast between adjacent pixels that form an edge.

shutter In a conventional film camera, the shutter is a mechanism consisting of blades, a curtain, plate, or some other movable cover that controls the time during which light reaches the film. Digital cameras can use actual shutters, or simulate the action of a shutter electronically. Many include a reassuring shutter "sound" that mimics the noise a mechanical camera makes.

Figure A.18 Increasing the contrast between pixels (right) makes an image appear to be sharper than the unprocessed version (left).

sidelighting Light striking the subject from the side relative to the position of the camera; produces shadows and highlights to create modeling on the subject.

single lens reflex (SLR) camera A type of camera that allows you to see through the camera's lens as you look in the camera's viewfinder. Other camera functions, such as light metering and flash control, also operate through the camera's lens.

slave unit   An accessory flash unit that supplements the main flash, usually triggered electronically when the slave senses the light output by the main unit, or through radio waves.

slide   A photographic transparency mounted for projection.

slow sync   An electronic flash synchronizing method that uses a slow shutter speed so that ambient light is recorded by the camera in addition to the electronic flash illumination, so that the background receives more exposure for a more realistic effect.

SLR (single lens reflex)   A camera in which the viewfinder sees the same image as the film or sensor.

smoothing   To blur the boundaries between edges of an image, often to reduce a rough or jagged appearance.

soft lighting   Lighting that is low or moderate in contrast, such as on an overcast day.

solarization   In photography, an effect produced by exposing film to light partially through the developing process. Some of the tones are reversed, generating an interesting effect. In image editing, the same effect is produced by combining some positive areas of the image with some negative areas. Also called the Sabattier effect, to distinguish it from a different phenomenon called overexposure solarization, which is produced by exposing film to many, many times more light than is required to produce the image. With overexposure solarization, some of the very brightest tones, such as the sun, are reversed.

Figure A.19   Digital photographers can manipulate the color curves of an image to simulate one kind of solarization.

specular highlight   Bright spots in an image caused by reflection of light sources.

spot color   Ink used in a print job in addition to black or process colors.

spot meter   An exposure system that concentrates on a small area in the image. See also *averaging meter*.

subtractive primary colors Cyan, magenta, and yellow, which are the printing inks that theoretically absorb all color and produce black. In practice, however, they generate a muddy brown, so black is added to preserve detail (especially in shadows). The combination of the three colors and black is referred to as CMYK. (K represents black, to differentiate it from blue in the RGB model.)

T (time) A shutter setting in which the shutter opens when the shutter button is pressed, and remains open until the button is pressed a second time. See also *B (bulb)*.

telephoto A lens or lens setting that magnifies an image.

thermal wax transfer A printing technology in which dots of wax from a ribbon are applied to paper when heated by thousands of tiny elements in a printhead.

threshold A predefined level used by a device to determine whether a pixel will be represented as black or white.

thumbnail A miniature copy of a page or image that provides a preview of the original. Photoshop uses thumbnails in its Layer and Channels palettes, for example.

TIFF (Tagged Image File Format) A standard graphics file format that can be used to store grayscale and color images plus selection masks.

time exposure A picture taken by leaving the shutter open for a long period, usually more than one second. The camera is generally locked down with a tripod to prevent blur during the long exposure.

time lapse A process by which a tripod-mounted camera takes sequential pictures at intervals, allowing the viewing of events that take place over a long period of time, such as a sunrise or flower opening. Many digital cameras have time-lapse capability built in. Others require you to attach the camera to your computer through a USB cable, and let software in the computer trigger the individual photos.

tint A color with white added to it. In graphic arts, often refers to the percentage of one color added to another.

tolerance The range of color or tonal values that will be selected with a tool like the Photoshop's Magic Wand, or filled with paint when using a tool like the Paint Bucket.

transparency A positive photographic image on film, viewed or projected by light shining through film.

transparency scanner A type of scanner that captures color slides or negatives.

tripod A three-legged supporting stand used to hold the camera steady. Especially useful when using slow shutter speeds and/or telephoto lenses.

tungsten light Light from ordinary room lamps and ceiling fixtures, as opposed to fluorescent illumination.

underexposure A condition in which too little light reaches the film or sensor, producing a thin negative, a dark slide, a muddy-looking print, or a dark digital image.

unipod A one-legged support, or monopod, used to steady the camera. See also *tripod.*

unsharp masking The process for increasing the contrast between adjacent pixels in an image, increasing sharpness, especially around edges.

USB A high-speed serial communication method commonly used to connect digital cameras and other devices to a computer.

viewfinder The device in a camera used to frame the image. With an SLR camera, the viewfinder is also used to focus the image if focusing manually. You can also focus an image with the LCD display of a digital camera, which is a type of viewfinder.

vignetting Dark corners of an image, often produced by using a lens hood that is too small for the field of view, or generated artificially using image-editing techniques, often to highlight an image such as a portrait.

white The color formed by combining all the colors of light (in the additive color model) or by removing all colors (in the subtractive model).

white balance The adjustment of a digital camera to the color temperature of the light source. Interior illumination is relatively red; outdoors light is relatively blue. Digital cameras often set correct white balance automatically, or let you do it through menus. Image editors can often do some color correction of images that were exposed using the wrong white balance setting.

white point In image editing, the lightest pixel in the highlight area of an image.

wide-angle lens A lens that has a shorter focal length and a wider field of view than a normal lens for a particular film or digital image format.

zoom In image editing, to enlarge or reduce the size of an image on your monitor. In photography, to enlarge or reduce the size of an image using the magnification settings of a lens.

Index

M

N

O

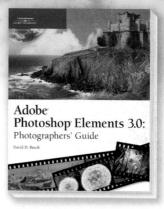
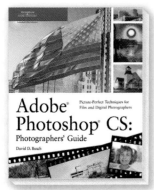
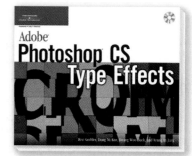

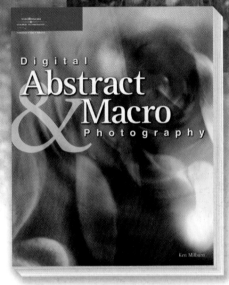
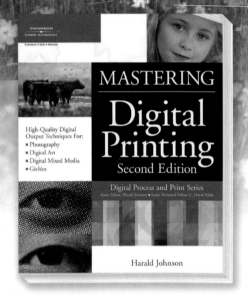

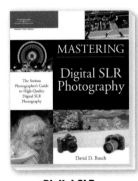
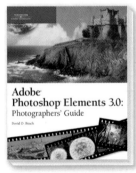
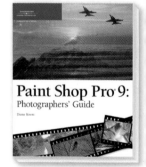